Heart of the Gorbals

THE AUTHOR

Rudolph Kenna was born in Glasgow of Scottish-American parentage. A graduate of the University of Strathclyde, he has written many best-selling books on his native city, including *Glasgow Then and Now* and the *Glasgow Pub Companion*. Kenna recently contributed a series of essays to the *Glasgow Story*, a website dedicated to the city's history which is run by a consortium made up of Glasgow City Council and the city's three universities.

Heart of the Gorbals

RUDOLPH KENNA

Fort Publishing Ltd

First published in 2004 by Fort Publishing Ltd, Old Belmont House,
12 Robsland Avenue, Ayr, KA7 2RW

Printed by Bell and Bain, Glasgow

Cover illustration of Gorbals Cross by Jon Berkeley

Graphic design by Mark Blackadder

Typeset by S. Fairgrieve (0131–658–1763)

ISBN 0-9544461-7-8

PREFACE

Though the legendary Glasgow Gorbals has had more publicity than most places in the British Isles, much of what has appeared in print has been unabashed nostalgia or lurid sensationalism. This book, an intimate survey of the newsworthy community over a considerable period of time, is an attempt to set the record straight. It begins in 1900, when the close-packed tenements of the Gorbals housed Scotland's most polyglot population, and ends in the opening years of the present century, with a vibrant new Gorbals taking shape.

A child of the 1950s, I grew up in Glasgow's industrial East End, and Bridgeton Cross, which happily escaped redevelopment, was the hub of my personal universe. I also had a nodding acquaintance with Gorbals Cross, because my great-aunt Kate lived in a tenement house in Laurieston. The flat had a plumbed-in bath, and my aunt owned a piano. She was, in fact, well off by Glasgow standards.

As a small boy, I was aware that the Gorbals was very different from my home patch. The streets were wider for a start. There were handsome public buildings. Some of the tenements had imposing classical porches, and many of the shops had exotic names.

By the time I started to write about my native city, much of Glasgow had been levelled by the planners. Gorbals Cross, with tenements designed by world-famous architect Alexander 'Greek' Thomson, no longer exists, and to capture the flavour of the vanished Gorbals, I have had recourse to a wide range of materials, not least newspapers. My thanks go to the staff of the Glasgow room at the Mitchell Library for entrusting me with sadly disintegrating early-twentieth-century newsprint. I am also indebted to my publisher James McCarroll for his infectious enthusiasm. Finally, warm thanks to my computer guru, Gwyneth, the resourceful answer to a Luddite's prayer.

Rudolph Kenna,
Glasgow 2004

INTRODUCTION

Like New York's Bronx and Bowery, Gorbals is colloquially preceded by the definite article. Nobody, however, is absolutely sure what 'the Gorbals' – known the world over for all the wrong reasons – actually means.

In the Middle Ages, 'the lands of Gorbals' belonged to the church, and it has been suggested that Gorbals originated in the ecclesiastical Latin *garbales* meaning tithes paid to the clergy in the form of sheaves of grain. Alternatively, the name could be derived from the Gaelic words *garbh* and *baile*, meaning rough village, for the original settlement was no more than a cluster of rudimentary huts, roofed with heather from the surrounding moor.

When leprosy ravaged Scotland in the fourteenth century, the local ecclesiastical authorities had to provide a hospital for afflicted members of their flock, and it had to be situated well away from the town. St Ninian's hospital, built at the southern end of Glasgow bridge, was the first habitation in the Gorbals.

By the early sixteenth century members of the influential Elphinstone family were tenants of 'the lands of Gorbals', and in 1579 merchant George Elphinstone converted the tenancy into a permanent possession by obtaining a charter from the Archbishop of Glasgow for £6 annual feu duty and eight bolls of meal (grain) a year. After his death the agricultural holdings passed to Robert Douglas, Viscount Belhaven, who settled them on his son-in-law, Sir Robert Douglas of Blakerton.

By the early seventeenth century, the village of Gorbals consisted of a number of cottage dwellings. There was also one important stone building, a baronial tower erected by the Elphinstones. In 1650 Glasgow town council, Hutcheson's hospital and the Trades' House jointly acquired the lands of Gorbals from Sir Robert Douglas of Blakerton. Owing to the Civil War, the English invasion and bad harvests, the investment wasn't immediately profitable. The patrons of Hutcheson's hospital had hoped to use the Gorbals rents to fund their charity school for boys, but instead they had to send the lads home to their parents and dismiss the schoolmaster!

While the sixteenth century village had been known for the production of swords, by the early eighteenth century it enjoyed a reputation for worsted plaids and quality firearms, but there was a lot of poverty even in those days: in 1741 cash-strapped inhabitants of the Gorbals asked for a handout from Glasgow's town council, pleading that there were 'very many poor among them'. In 1745 some of Charles Edward Stuart's troops were quartered in the village and supplied with forage for their horses. To the villagers' disgust, the soldiers left without paying for the provender.

Three years later a 'great fire' laid waste to the village, despite the use of three primitive fire engines. With so much trouble on their own doorstep, the distressed Gorbalites didn't take kindly to indigents from outside the area. In 1749 an Irish family of 'strolling beggars' were banished from the Gorbals. By 1778 the main street of the village stretched from Glasgow bridge as far as Shields Loan, roughly the line of modern Cumberland Street. Hand-loom weaving was the main local industry, with upwards of five hundred looms in use. There were also shoemakers, skinners, tailors, wrights and maltmen, the latter producing the malted barley sold for brewing purposes.

At the end of the eighteenth century, the Trades House and Hutcheson's hospital began to feu their Gorbals holdings for housing and industrial purposes. Tradeston and Hutchesontown were respectively developed to the east and west of present-day Eglinton Street. The Trustees of Hutcheson's hospital laid out their new district with broad, straight streets, and houses which, until decades of neglect took their toll, were very desirable residences. In Crown Street, they built their boys' grammar school (1841), which remained a feature of the area until 1959. The Trades' House initially feud their holding for residential purposes and the first house, in Centre Street, was completed in 1791. By the early 1800s, Tradeston – bounded on the east by Bridge Street and on the west by West Street – was a pleasant suburb of villa residences, but by the middle of the nineteenth century the area had become almost completely industrial.

With the development of Hutchesontown and Tradeston, the old Gorbals village passed to the town council of Glasgow, losing its administrative independence altogether in 1846 when it was annexed by the city. The city also retained Kingston, a piece of land lying between West Street on the east and the Kinninghouse Burn on the west.

As the population of the Gorbals grew in numbers – from three thousand in 1771 to over five thousand in 1811 – the villagers retained a strong local identity. There were regular Saturday night 'bickers' between Glaswegians and Gorbalites, both sides fighting for possession of an islet in the middle of the shallow river Clyde. Grown men as well as young boys took part in the bickers, which were fiercely contested and frequently won by the Gorbals contingents.

Laurieston (1802–30), bounded on the east by Buchan Street and Portugal Street and on the west by Bridge Street and Eglinton Street, was one of the most prestigious housing developments in early nineteenth century Glasgow. Originally a piece of land called Kirkcroft, which had been allocated to Hutcheson's hospital, it came into the possession of developer David Laurie, who set about creating a Regency new town of wide streets and palace-fronted tenements, with street names such as Oxford, Cumberland, Norfolk, Portland, Surrey, Warwick and Bedford to recall the dukes and earls of England and add to the snob value of a house in the swanky new transpontine suburb. Carlton Place, overlooking the river bank and consisting of two stately terraces, was named in honour of the Prince Regent, whose London home was Carlton House. A suitably grand place of worship, Gorbals parish church, designed by fashionable architect David Hamilton, was built at the east end of Carlton Place, and its 174-foot spire was for many years the principal landmark on the south side of the river.

David Laurie tried to make Carlton Place as exclusive as its name implied by putting up gates at either end. Sadly for the developer's aspirations, his posh estate began to lose caste after 1837 when industrialist William Dixon opened the Govan Iron Works – an iron-smelting operation – in Crown Street. The open-topped blast furnaces of the Iron Works bathed the greater Gorbals district in a lurid nocturnal glow and gave rise to the name Dixon's Blazes.

Laurieston was also downwind of the mephitic vapours of Tradeston, which was rapidly becoming a hive of industry. But Mr Laurie's dream suburb didn't go downhill overnight, and for many years it continued to provide quality middle-class housing, and rich pickings for petty criminals such as 'child-strippers', who removed clothing from well-dressed children and crossed the Clyde to sell or pawn the garments in the slum warrens of Briggait, Saltmarket and High Street.

By the 1820s, the greater Gorbals area was attracting increasing numbers of economic migrants from the Highlands and Islands of Scotland and from Ireland. Many of the incomers found work in cotton-spinning mills where conditions were harsh and workers struggled to have their combinations (trade unions) recognised.

At the time of the 1841 census, it was disclosed that seven out of ten inhabitants of the Gorbals had been born in Ireland. Most of the newcomers came from Mayo, Donegal, Sligo and Galway. With the arrival of the Irish, who represented both religious currents of John Bull's Other Island, names such as Lynch, Boyle, O'Donnell, McGinty and Lafferty became familiar in the Gorbals. The great famine following the disastrous Irish potato blight of 1846 brought eight thousand desperate Irish people a week to Glasgow. Passage across the Irish Sea cost only a few pence per head, though regrettably some of the emaciated passengers were dead on arrival.

With growing social problems, exacerbated by poverty and overcrowding, it is not surprising that the Gorbals had its share in public disturbances such as the notorious Bread Riots of March

1848, when provisions' shops in Main Street were looted by bands of starving demonstrators. Troops were mobilised from the cavalry barracks in Eglinton Street; the Riot Act was read, and the horsemen charged and cleared the streets.

As late as the 1870s, Laurieston and Hutchesontown still contained much middle-class housing, but many of the substantial tenements had been subdivided to accommodate mill and factory workers. Back lands – properties erected in tenement back-courts – had been hastily thrown up to accommodate the area's new inhabitants and the old Gorbals village, centred on Main Street, had become a notorious slum quarter.

Using powers obtained by an Act of Parliament, the city fathers began tearing down the most decrepit properties in the Gorbals. By the 1880s a new Gorbals of gridiron streets and handsome tenements of dressed stone – some designed by Alexander 'Greek' Thomson – was rising. But the Gorbals remained an explosive cocktail of Catholics and Protestants and the police had their work cut out to keep order, especially on Saturday nights or during the annual twelfth of July Orange celebrations to mark the anniversary of the Battle of the Boyne (1690).

Some parts of the district, notably Rutherglen Road, Crown Street and Thistle Street, already had a reputation for rowdyism. In 1887 a Main Street ratepayer complained that Gorbals Cross, planned in the Parisian manner as the *grande place* of the new Gorbals, was 'marred by the hordes of loafers who daily hang about the water fountain underneath the clock'.

Jews started to arrive in the Gorbals in the 1870s, at which time there were only a few hundred of their co-religionists living in Glasgow. In the early 1880s, the area's first synagogue was opened in Commerce Street, Tradeston. There were so many tailors among the Jewish settlers that the new synagogue, described as 'an ill-ventilated room in a squalid crowded neighbourhood', was known as the tailor's synagogue.

Gorbals Jewry grew slowly, and it wasn't until new waves of Czarist persecution in the last quarter of the nineteenth century that there was a considerable influx of Jewish immigrants from the Russian Empire, which included Lithuania, Estonia and much of Poland. By 1900, the Gorbals was firmly established as a place where the Yiddish-speaking newcomer could receive a welcome and perhaps even get in touch with a *lansmann* from his old home town in Eastern Europe. But immigration was becoming an emotive issue, and in 1905 the Aliens Act was introduced to limit the numbers of Jews seeking asylum in Britain.

Between 1900 and 1920 evangelical churchmen made strenuous efforts to convert the Jews of the Gorbals to Christianity, with little success. Jewish community leaders complained that the missionaries tried to bribe poor immigrants with gifts of food, clothing and medicine. When Jewish-Christian converts such as Jacob Sensen addressed crowds at Gorbals Cross, the police sometimes had to intervene to prevent a riot. Even before the outbreak of war in 1914, some Jews had already moved out of the area to pleasant southern suburbs such as Crosshill and Mount Florida. But as late as the 1940s, there were still shops in the Gorbals with Hebrew lettering on the fascias and barrels of herring in the doorways, reflecting the fast-receding lifestyle of *der heim*, the community left behind in Poland, Latvia or Lithuania.

By the Edwardian period many Italians had also made the Gorbals their home, though the city's Italian immigrants – mainly from the town of Barga in the north of the country – also settled elsewhere in the fast-growing city. One pioneer, Giovanni Oddio, arrived in Glasgow in 1890, took lodgings in Commercial Road and began in business by selling 'hokey pokey' (ice-cream) from a barrow. His wife joined him in 1890, and by 1929 the family owned shops in Rutherglen Road, Crown Street, Waddell Street and Main Street. The increasingly polyglot Gorbals soon got used to names such as Bonnaficolli, Catani, Fugaccia, Gizzi, Lombardi and Tognarelli.

By the end of the nineteenth century, the greater Gorbals had become one of the most cosmopolitan areas in the British Isles, and Scottish and Irish Gaelic, Italian, Russian, Polish, Lithuanian, and Yiddish could be heard in the district's shops, cafés and restaurants. Gorbals Cross was the area's speaker's corner, where religious zealots, socialists and temperance enthusiasts all had their say, in a bewildering variety of tongues. There was poverty in the district, but there was also considerable diversity.

The streets of the early twentieth century Gorbals teemed with life: itinerant hawkers, Salvation Army bands, Boys' Brigade and Jewish Lads' parades, Italian vendors of hot chestnuts and ice-cream, buskers, organ grinders and even dancing bears. The district also boasted an astonishing variety of self-help and mutual-aid organisations, many of which focused on a single issue, such as teetotalism, child poverty, evangelism, or domestic and foreign missionary work. Of course, large numbers of people had no safety net of any description, except the pawnshop. Pawnshops were ubiquitous in the old Gorbals, and just about anything – from a Bible to a piano – could be left in pledge.

Along with pubs, music halls – and, to a growing extent, cinemas – were the principal avenues of escapism. The Royal Princess's theatre, Palace theatre and Coliseum theatre reflected the area's ethnic composition by featuring Irish melodramas and Hebrew comedians. By the early 1900s, however, the Gorbals had already acquired a bad reputation for 'hooliganism' and the district was the stamping ground of two notorious gangs, the Village Boys and the Tim Malloys.

Strong beer and raw, fiery whisky kept the Southern Police Court in Oxford Street busy with 'drunk and disorderly' charges. By law, the pubs of early twentieth century Gorbals had to close at eleven p.m., but shebeens and shebeeners were on hand to ensure that drink flowed after hours. The typical shebeen (illegal drinking-den) was simply a tenement flat where booze could be obtained at unorthodox times. There were also peripatetic shebeeners who lurked up closes and lanes with jars of rotgut whisky and solicited passing trade.

Gorbals men fought in the 1914–18 war in all three services and as a result, the community lost many irreplaceable individuals. Of those who survived, many returned disabled by shells and poison gas. Children grew up during the years of conflict with the minimum of adult supervision. Fathers went off to war; mothers found employment in munitions factories; youth movements and church organisations were stripped of volunteers, and special constables – middle-aged civilians in uniform – took the place of hardbitten regular coppers. Gorbals hooligans who tried to take advantage of inexperienced 'specials' – some of them immigrants with a limited knowledge of the King's English – were warned that the authorities would lean heavily on offenders who resisted arrest.

The men of the district returned from vermin-infested trenches to rat-ridden tenements. It was in the inter-war period that the Gorbals became a byword for urban decay, helped by overcrowding, deep poverty, unemployment, gang strife and the publication of the sensational novel *No Mean City* (1935). With birth control virtually non-existent – and in any case opposed by the Catholic hierarchy – the area teemed with children: families of twelve or fifteen were by no means uncommon. Children's play was defined by religious territorialism, and boys would ask each other: 'Are ye a Billy, a Dan or an auld tin can?' (a Jewish lad had to admit to being an auld tin can).

The worst Gorbals back lands of the inter-war period were bug-infested, with gas lighting, and iron bars instead of glass in the stairhead windows. The typical single end (one-apartment flat) was living room, kitchen and bedroom all in one, with the bed located in a hole-in-the-wall recess. With large numbers of people sharing a poorly maintained stairhead water closet, dysentery was rife. Fire was also an ever-present hazard, not least because the greater Gorbals was full of factories, flour mills, bonded warehouses and small workshops packed with inflammable materials. Many of these tinderbox buildings were located in back-courts, adding to the difficulties of fire-fighters and the insecurity of residents.

Despite high levels of unemployment during the worst economic slump of the twentieth century, there was little serious crime in the modern sense of the term. Petty crime was rife, however, as was domestic violence. With off-course betting on horse races illegal, bookies and their runners were fair game for the police who resorted to bizarre disguises to secure convictions. As in the early twentieth century, Saturday night street-brawls were common in the Gorbals in the inter-war years, and police constables had to be physically big men to take charge of offenders, many of whom were out of their skulls on methylated spirits or red biddy (cheap red wine). Many of the worst offenders had little to fear from jail since they either slept rough or dossed down in common lodging-houses, great barracks of buildings in Portugal Street and Buchan Street.

Yet the inter-war Gorbals wasn't simply a collection of teeming slums. The district had its share of fine buildings. In Laurieston and Hutchesontown, uniformly four-storey tenements lined the wide streets, and as late as the 1950s, the spacious flats in South Portland Street and Apsley Place housed many business and professional people. But the Gorbals, and Bridgeton and Calton on the north side of the river Clyde, were particularly hard hit by the economic depression. Some of the unemployed youths, for want of anything better to do, formed gangs. In 1930 a Glasgow newspaper, the *Evening Citizen,* launched an investigation into local gangs and concluded that the 'gang menace' was exaggerated by sensational press reports: the purpose of the gangs was 'primarily to amuse themselves'.

The gangs were territorial: in the Gorbals, the Coburg Erin ruled the roost in Coburg Street while Cumberland Street was home to the Beehive gang, named after a local retail warehouse. Gang skirmishes – including incursions into 'enemy' territory – broke the monotony of life on the dole. Outsiders were seldom molested, though the *Evening Citizen* admitted that members of the public kept indoors 'to escape stray missiles' that were 'not aimed at them'.

To help alleviate the chronic boredom which all too frequently led to gang associations, Revd John Cameron Peddie, a Church of Scotland minister, set up unconventional social clubs in the Gorbals, with himself as honorary leader. The clubs, which by 1933 numbered thirty with a combined membership of around four thousand, were run by the members themselves. Drinking, betting and bad language were banned. Peddie found that the Gorbals gangsters had their own peculiar code of honour; they wouldn't give their worst enemy away to the police. The only preaching he permitted himself was to urge the youths to be true to their faith, whether they were Protestants, Catholics or Jews. Having won the respect of the district's young tearaways, Revd Peddie was called on to mediate between local gangs and reconcile sworn enemies. He was even presented with weapons as souvenirs!

Jewish community life flourished in the Gorbals of the inter-war years, when the Jewish population of the area reached its peak. On Sundays, all Jewish shops in the area were open and Gorbals Cross was a hive of activity. Comparatively well-off Jews lived in spacious (by Gorbals standards) flats in South Portland Street and Apsley Place, while their poorer co-religionists huddled in single ends and room-and-kitchen flats in Thistle Street or Crown Street. By the inter-war years, the Jews of the district had their own mutual aid societies, leisure and sporting clubs and Masonic associations. By the end of the 1930s the Hebrew Benevolent Loan Company, operating from premises in Thistle Street, had granted nearly £90,000 in loans to help Gorbals Jews set up their own businesses. There was also a more idealistic tradition, exemplified by the Workers' Circle with its well-thumbed copies of Marx, Engels, Lenin and Kropotkin and its sepia pictures of revolutionary heroes.

A feature of the old Gorbals was the *shabbos goy* or *shabbos shiksa* – the Gentile who agreed to light fires and lamps and perform other tasks forbidden in an orthodox Jewish household on the Sabbath, which lasted from dusk on Friday till sunset on Saturday. To mark the Passover, an eight-day spring festival, local pubs – more often than not owned by Gentiles – provided special facilities: wines from Palestine, and delicacies such as wurst, pickled herrings, saveloys, gherkins and matzos (biscuits of unleavened bread). Gorbals licensees, many of them of Highland or Irish stock, were able to profit from two New Years, Jewish and Gentile!

By the 1930s, the Gorbals had a small Asian community that consisted for the most part of self-employed itinerant peddlers. They were Muslims from the West Punjab, now in Pakistan, and Hindus and Sikhs from the East Punjab, now in India. Some of the first Asians to settle in the west of Scotland started their working lives as Lascar seamen employed in the British mercantile marine at a fraction of the wages paid to their white counterparts. Gorbals Asians spoke very little English and the all-male community kept very much to itself. In the Gorbals, Asian peddlers, whatever their real names, answered to the name of Johnnie, like Ahmed in Robert McLeish's play *The Gorbals Story* (1946). In 1940 the Muslim community converted a flat in Gorbals Street into Scotland's first mosque, and the following year the Sikh Association acquired a makeshift temple in South Portland Street.

With the outbreak of the Second World War, the district's Asian communities dwindled in numbers: some of the men joined the British forces, while a few returned to the subcontinent. The rest took work in factories, where they came into close contact with local people for the first time. The war put a stop to immigration, and it wasn't until the 1950s that Asians began to reappear in the Gorbals in significant numbers.

With immigration from the subcontinent at its peak between 1958 and 1962, when it was restricted by the Commonwealth Immigrants Act, the Gorbals was for a short time the main area of Asian settlement in Scotland. Draconian redevelopment in the 1970s prevented the district from developing an Asian culture as colourful as that of the old Jewish Gorbals, but by the 1980s the greater Gorbals area had Scotland's largest and most modern mosque, a thriving Islamic centre and a number of huge cash and carry warehouses that testified to Asian business acumen.

By the 1950s, the Gorbals had probably had more adverse publicity than almost anywhere else on earth. In the wake of *No Mean City*, Fleet Street dubbed the area Hell's Hundred Acres and Little Chicago on the Clyde. But in spite of the squalor, the district still boasted one of the highest population densities in the country, with a vibrant social life centred on cinemas, dance halls, pubs, cafés, churches, synagogues, mission halls and clubs.

Until the era of Comprehensive Development (1957–74), pockets of Laurieston and Hutchesontown still recalled the faded elegance of the early nineteenth century. With hindsight, it is evident that the district's architectural jewels could have been saved, but such was the evil reputation of the Gorbals that the planning authorities had no hesitation in making a clean sweep of the area. The planners were under tremendous pressure to rehouse huge numbers of people as quickly as possible; as late as 1965, 98,000 houses in Glasgow were officially described as 'unfit for human habitation'. There was another spur to redevelopment: in post-war Glasgow, the death-rate from tuberculosis was more than twice that of either Manchester or Birmingham.

Apart from being rat-infested and insanitary, some Gorbals tenements were literally falling down; the local MP quipped that they were held together by 'six or seven layers of wallpaper'. As a substitute for their disintegrating tenements, the people of the Gorbals were promised 'tower blocks like Babylon'. Sir Basil Spence, post-war Britain's most successful modern architect, assured the planners that the cantilevered balconies of his Queen Elizabeth Square slab blocks would, in no time at all, be a riot of flowers. In practice, the Gorbals slab blocks were as grey, monotonous and monolithic as their counterparts in other cities, and nothing was planted in Sir Basil's windswept 'gardens in the sky' but metal clothes poles set in concrete.

As the tower blocks went up, the drawbacks soon became apparent. Children had nowhere to play and the safe if dirty seclusion of tenement back-courts became a thing of the past. High-rise children were pitied as 'kids in the clouds' and 'tower-block toddlers'. Glasgow songwriter Adam McNaughtan lamented: 'Oh, ye cannae fling pieces oot a twenty-storey flat. Seven hundred hungry weans 'll testify tae that.'

By the late 1980s the greater Gorbals area, which in the 1940s had housed ninety thousand people of diverse cultural and religious backgrounds, had less than eleven thousand inhabitants, most of whom lived in vertical streets. Gorbals Cross – the focal point of the district for over a hundred years – had been swept away, as had most of the local landmarks, from Geneen's kosher hotel in Abbotsford Place to the 'coffin building' (Frazer's mattress-making establishment in Govan Street, formerly Ballater Street).

The controversial Gorbals had reached its nadir, and the road to recovery beckoned. The area was fortunately spared the final indignity of the south flank of the inner ring-road (M8). After a spirited campaign by local people, the authorities agreed that the stinking wet concrete Hutchesontown Area E deck-access flats had no future. The curse of Babylon struck when the media-acclaimed towers designed by Sir Basil Spence were 'blown down' with explosives. By the late 1990s, the Crown Street regeneration project of mixed social and private housing – all of it human in scale and some of it imaginative in design – had begun the long overdue process of renewal. But there is more to the historic Gorbals than luxury penthouses, currently selling for up to £300,000. Pockets of deep poverty exist in an area which has had more than its fair share of deprivation during the past hundred years, and it remains to be seen if a new, socially inclusive community can emerge in the twenty-first century.

1900 BLACK DEATH

The Gorbals had its first cases of plague – the infamous Black Death of the Middle Ages – for centuries. When four members of a Thistle Street family died of plague after attending a wake in Rose Street, the Roman Catholic authorities banned wakes for the duration of the emergency. The disease had first been diagnosed when a dock labourer living in Rose Street took ill. The plague had been brought to the city in a rat-infested Portuguese ship that had docked in Glasgow harbour. By the end of the year there had been thirty-six cases of plague and sixteen deaths, all south of the river.

Patriotic fever swept the Gorbals, and every other district of Glasgow, when the small town of Mafeking in Cape Province – besieged by the Boers for 217 days – was relieved by British forces on 16 May. The news reached London on the evening of Friday, 18 May, and on Saturday local drapers did a brisk trade in bunting. Working men paraded along the streets carrying unflattering effigies of the Boer leaders and played bagpipes, flutes and drums. Pubs were filled to overflowing, and everywhere the usual Scottish reserve broke down.

The Royal Princess's theatre in Main Street presented an Irish drama called *The Wearing o' the Green*. Gorbals public school in Oxford Street had 199 Jewish pupils, out of a total of 402. The Gorbals Jewish community opened the Jewish free-reading-rooms in Oxford Street to counteract Christian missionary activity among Jews of the district.

1901 MIDDEN-RAKING

Plainclothes policemen accompanied by sanitary inspectors and doctors went the rounds of the Gorbals and other areas of Glasgow that were infected with smallpox – introduced in 1900 by a seaman newly back from India – and urged people to be vaccinated or re-vaccinated free of charge. Landlords were told to have the walls and ceilings of tenement closes whitewashed and back-court middens lime-washed.

Speaking at the opening ceremony of the Great Synagogue in South Portland Street, the largest in Scotland, Julius Frankenburgh referred to 'the great growth of the Jewish colony in the Gorbals district within recent years'. Anthony Butler (13) received twelve strokes of the birch for stealing a bottle of beer from a lorry in Cumberland Street. For leaving his wife 'a mass of bruises from head to foot', Thomas Sloag of Portugal Street was banged up for nine months. It was stated that the accused 'had been given to drink and had sold the furniture eight times'.

At the annual 'conversazione' of the Laurieston parish church Young Men's Guild and Bible Class, dancing was 'kept up till early next morning'. For having accidentally smothered her illegitimate baby, Sarah McCue of South Coburg Street – described as a drunken mother – was sent to prison for two months. Peter Allegretti, one of the city's 449 ice-cream shop proprietors, was fined two guineas with the option of thirty days for slugging a man with a bottle in front of his Crown Street premises. Sixteen young Gorbals lads were fined sums varying from 5s. to 10s. 6d. for playing football in the streets. In Centre Street, Tradeston a little barefooted boy, son of a labourer, was injured by boiling tar.

Glasgow Corporation cleansing committee banned 'midden-raking', a common pursuit in the Gorbals and other deprived areas of the city. The Royal Princess's theatre presented 'The new Irish singing comedian, Myles McCarthy, in the play *Dear Hearts of Ireland.*' Catherine Laird, lessee of seventeen 'farmed-out' (sublet) houses in Spring Lane, was fined 10s. 6d. for failing to keep the water closets clean. Mr J. A. Cassels of Main Street advertised his availability as a 'standard Scotch comedian and vocalist'.

1902 IRISH TRASH

In the Gorbals, flags were unfurled and rejoicing was 'spontaneous' when peace was concluded in South Africa on 31 May after a war lasting two years and seven months. Andrew McLean of Thistle Street, Peter McLeish of Hospital Street and Patrick Monaghan of Caledonia Road were among the injured when a terrace collapsed at Ibrox Park during the Scotland versus England football international. Twenty-three men lost their lives and over five hundred were injured. The Onward Temperance Choir gave a concert in the Grand National Halls in Main Street. Gorbals licensed grocers sold Australian Boomerang burgundies.

At a meeting of Govan Parish Council – which had responsibility for the destitute poor of the Gorbals – an official described paupers as Irish trash. Samuel Stewart was fined 10s. 6d. for driving an electric tramcar 'in a reckless and culpable manner' in Warwick Street. Mrs Sophia Douglas donated the hand bell of the Barony of Gorbals, dated 1747, to the Gorbals Free Library in Main Street. Thieves used a charge of gunpowder to blow open a safe in a building contractor's office in Mathieson Street.

A Glasgow Jewish Workers' Co-operative Society, described as 'the cleanest and most attractive Jewish shop in the city', opened premises in Thistle Street. All the goods were obtained from the Scottish Co-operative Wholesale Society. Family Bibles were among items held in pledge by Gorbals pawnbrokers. In 'a lover's quarrel' in Crown Street, John 'Midget' Hart stabbed his sweetheart Kate Fisher. There was a large turnout of spectators for water polo at the Gorbals public baths in Main Street.

The Royal Princess's theatre was decked out with bunting and coloured electric lights for the coronation of Edward V11. Robert Harper, a chain-snatcher, was run to earth in Main Street after robbing a gent of his watch chain in Bedford Street. Constable Duncan Cameron found a 'carefully and warmly dressed' baby lying on a tenement stair in Greenside Street. The Cumberland House in Cumberland Street offered bargains in 'sailor hats' and 'feather boas'.

Mrs Neilson, owner of the Rob Roy bar in Main Street, announced that her premises had been 'newly fitted up with electric light'. Among the other popular watering holes in the district were the Curler's bar in Main Street, the Balmoral bar in Elgin Street and the Windsor bar in West Street.

Death duty of £63,687. 12s. 8d. was levied on the estate of boot-and-shoe manufacturer James Dick. James and his brother Robert first experimented with gutta-percha in 1846 in a wash-house behind a tenement in Crown Street, melting lumps of the substance in a frying pan and using the solution to sole and heel footwear.

1903 DANCING BEARS

Crowds gathered in Main Street to marvel at two dancing Russian bears. The people of the Gorbals were also intrigued by a lady organ-grinder dressed in 'a neat and fashionably-cut morning costume'. In a tenement in Cumberland Street, detective Rankin of the Southern police division arrested two housebreakers by knocking them cold, placing a knee on each of their necks and holding them secure till the arrival of two constables. One of the burglars had been armed with a jemmy (crowbar). When searched, Edward Kelly and John Quinn were found to be in possession of several skeleton keys.

In Tradeston, evangelist Paddy Black started a mission that soon played an important part in the life of the community, with its own Girls' Guildry, Boys' Brigade and silver band. Crown Street was one of the first streets in the Gorbals to be 'lit up with electric light'. A reporter visited Hendry's Glasgow Business College in Cumberland Street (established 1874) and saw 'dozens of young lady typists working nimbly and deftly at typewriting instruments'. The College awarded the Sir Samuel Chisholm medal for 150 words of shorthand per minute, and the Ross gold medal for the best typists.

As Glasgow welcomed King Edward V11 and Queen Alexandra, the streets of the Gorbals were 'rendered well nigh impassable by orderly, if rather hilarious, crowds'. John McPhie (10), found guilty of stealing 21s. 6d. from his father, was sent to an industrial school for six years. Helen Wallace of Crown Street offered the white jap-silk Parisian blouse for 9s. 11d.

In one week, in April, the Gorbals Free Library loaned seventy books on philosophy and religion, thirty-one books on sociology and fifty-nine books on science. The south-eastern branch of the British Women's Temperance Association held 'a very successful social meeting' in the South Side assembly rooms, Crown Street. Residents of Main Street complained about 'black smoke and cinders' from chimney stacks in the vicinity. Hutcheson's Educational Trust Foundationers announced that they were prepared to admit into their boys' and girls' grammar schools in Crown Street and Elgin Street a limited number of poor scholars, who would receive a free education.

After threatening his wife with a revolver in their Adelphi Street flat, Frank Gallacher was fined a guinea with the option of fourteen days' imprisonment. John Brodie, a wife-beater with a track record for the offence, went to prison for sixty days for assaulting his spouse in a house in Hospital Street. To mark the twelfth of July anniversary of the 1690 Battle of the Boyne, Orangemen, including Canadians and Americans, marched through the Gorbals with 'bands, brass, flute and pipe'. Members of the Gorbals United Free Church in South Portland Street held a grand *kinderspiel* (children's show) in aid of church funds. During the month of October, 5,505 males and 308 females patronised the swimming pool of the Gorbals baths. At the private hot baths there were 2,906 males and 783 females. Hugh Kelly, a 'whisky hawker' was fined £10 for plying his illegal trade in the Gorbals.

For assaulting no fewer than six policemen in South Wellington Street, Hutchesontown, Thomas McCuddan and James Phillips were remitted to the Sheriff Court. Hooligans reportedly disturbed the peace in Crown Street 'night after night'. Members of the Gorbals Burns Club went on a trip to Ayr and Mauchline. Two fifteen-year-old Gorbals boys, sent to a reformatory for five years for petty theft, had been 'sleeping on stairs for the past six weeks'. Robert Brand advertised his Devon Street dairy: 'Corporation telephone No. X. 197. Telegrams, Milkyway, Glasgow'. The Jews of the Gorbals were described as 'a thriving and busy colony of aliens'.

1904 RUFFIANS AT STREET CORNERS

On New Year's Day, local children were treated to lemonade, buns and fruit in the Christian Social Institute in Rutherglen Road. Revd Edward Balvaird Hewitt died aged fifty-eight. An Oxford graduate, he purchased a hall in South Coburg Street in 1886 and – with his wife Mary – launched the non-sectarian Guild of Aid to encourage thrift and self-help. The Guild's day nursery for the children of working mothers was one of the earliest such facilities in the city, while its thrift clubs for rent, clothing and emergencies helped many to stay out of debt. The Guild also pioneered sheltered homes for the aged. After Revd Hewitt's death, his widow continued the work with the help of friends and with the support of many influential citizens, including wealthy shipowner Sir William Raeburn.

For pinching six scones from a shop in Eglinton Street, James Drummond, a juvenile offender, was sent to a reformatory for five years. Revd John McNeil conducted evangelical services in a marquee at Gorbals Cross. One of the oldest landmarks in the Gorbals, a three-storey house in Main Street inscribed with the date 1782, was demolished to make way for a bank. The William O'Brien Branch of the United Irish League held a St Patrick's Day social in the Grand National Halls in Main Street. Matthew McCluskey, a Jew, was found guilty of robbing a foreigner of an Albert (a pocket watch chain) in a close in Thistle Street. The victim stated that he was attacked by several men but identified the accused by his crutch.

The Gorbals ward committee (established 1860) took up the issue of 'ruffians at street corners' and donated five guineas to the Consumptives' Fund. Hutchesontown Ancient Order of Foresters celebrated their thirtieth annual general meeting with a social function in Augustine United Free Church in Mathieson Street.

Unemployed Gorbals men were put to work breaking stones at the Corporation works in Copelawhill. Using heavy sledgehammers, they had to break quarry boulders into small pieces of stone suitable for road-making. The Bee-Hive warehouse in Cumberland Street offered bargains in bedding, bonnets and flannels.

There was jubilation in the Gorbals when Dan Flynn – born in Crown Street – became champion cyclist of Scotland, winning the quarter-mile, mile and twenty-five mile events at the Scottish Cyclists' Union national championships, held at Celtic Park. At London's Crystal Palace, Flynn made it to the semi-final round of the world amateur cycling championships. Richard Waldon and Thomas Barrasford opened the Palace Theatre of Varieties in Gorbals Main Street. The Indian-themed auditorium featured 'beautifully modelled Nautch girls and gorgeous Hindoo pagodas'.

Some lucky Gorbals youngsters got a summer holiday, thanks to the Poor Children's Fresh-Air Fortnight scheme. At a grand musical evening, organised by the David Livingstone Tent of Rechabites (a temperance friendly society), Mr Sheriff 'proved an adept at the mandolin'. The Wellington Palace music hall in Commercial Road featured Prince Bendon's Bioscope. Three hundred canaries were exhibited at a bird show in the Gorbals. A pawnshop in Eglinton Street had a 'store room for pianos'.

The pupils of Robertson's Business College in Carlton Place gained sixty-nine shorthand certificates. Young Gorbals men were reported to be sporting natty bow ties. The Palace Theatre of Varieties featured Gus Harris, Hebrew character actor and Tom Jenkins, the champion catch-as-catch-can wrestler of America, who offered £25 to any local wrestler who could avoid defeat for ten minutes.

1905   TIM MALLOY

The people of the Gorbals were plagued by the Tim Malloy band of hooligans, a mainly Catholic gang of youths. At 40 Cumberland Street, Mr D. H. Thomson taught dancing, callisthenics and deportment. The Glad Tidings Foreign Missionary Union operated from a hall in Main Street. The Hebrew Boot and Clothing Guild was established to provide footwear and wearing apparel for poor Jewish immigrants, who were arriving in the Gorbals in considerable numbers. Nine-year-old Moses Mirsky officiated as *chazan* (cantor) at a Sabbath service in the Great Synagogue in South Portland Street. The Beth Jacob (House of Jacob) synagogue was opened in Main Street.

Tears were shed in abundance when the Royal Princess's theatre presented a five-act melodrama entitled *An Abandoned Woman*. A Gorbals man was fined a tenner for 'shebeening in a farmed-out house in Hospital Street'. In McKinlay Street, two youngsters were run over by a cab while they were scrambling for pennies scattered in honour of a newly married couple. In a Saturday night brawl in the Gorbals, police officers were 'kicked, cuffed, and hit with stones and iron nuts'.

The Children's Mission and Newsvendors' Association, based in Gloucester Street, Tradeston announced plans for 'coffee booths on wheels where the lads can buy a cup of coffee or tea, with bread, for a halfpenny, without interfering with the sale of their papers'. Master James Reid's exhibition of Indian club swinging and McSherry's Band were highlights of the Adelphi Terrace gymnastic club's annual social. Cycling champ Dan Flynn became amateur middleweight boxing champion of Scotland.

The Coliseum theatre, designed by the country's leading theatre architect, Frank Matcham, for Moss Enterprises, opened in Eglinton Street. All the great stars of Edwardian variety – including Harry Lauder – trod the boards of the 2,893-seater Coliseum, which also became a leading venue for reviews and musical plays. The architect's magnificent auditorium with its marble-framed proscenium was destroyed in 1962 when the theatre was converted for Cinerama.

The employees of hosiery manufacturer John Grimmond, Mathieson Street, chartered the *Gypsy Queen* for an autumn cruise along the Forth and Clyde canal. Scott's of Cumberland Street announced the arrival of twenty thousand Irish eggs. In a factory in Govan Street (later Ballater Street) known as the coffin building because of its sinister shape, there was an outbreak of the deadly disease anthrax among workers preparing skins for furriers. Mr

Marshall Brisbon of South Portland Street, 'late of New York', offered his services as a tenor; 'speciality Irish gatherings'.

1906   VILLAGE BOYS

Eleven people were injured, one fatally, when several vats containing hot water and grain sediment burst in the Loch Katrine distillery in Muirhead Street (later Inverkip Street). Two of the injured were 'dashed so violently against the walls that their clothes were almost torn from their bodies, and in this semi-nude condition they were swept in the flood of warm water and draff out through the gateway into Muirhead Street'. James Ballantyne, a farm servant from Busby, was engulfed with his horse and cart and suffered such severe injuries that he died shortly after being admitted to the Royal Infirmary. When news of the accident reached the headquarters of the St Andrew's Ambulance Association, officials dispatched four ambulances, including a recently-acquired motor vehicle. The accident occurred when collapsing iron supports caused the uppermost vat to crash down onto the others below.

After a member of the Rangers football team 'got a very severe handling in Morrison Street', losing several teeth, hooliganism was reported to be 'still rampant' in the Gorbals. The Southern Police Court in Oxford Street had 'all the appearance of a public-house' when shebeener Mary Mulney's stocks of beer and whisky were arrayed before the bench. For selling whisky from a four-gallon jar in a close in Rose Street in the wee small hours of a Sabbath morning, Mary Grant had to fork out £10.

At the door of an Italian café in Bedford Street, John McAndrew of Bedford Row was shot dead by Joseph Ventura. McAndrew, described as a prominent member of a gang of hooligans called the Village Boys, had been released from prison after serving three months for breaking into Ventura's premises. It was said that the Italian lived in terror of the gang. The Gorbals Benevolent Society celebrated its centenary with a lavish dinner in the upmarket Grosvenor restaurant in central Glasgow. Hutchesontown Free

Library, a handsome building in the French Renaissance style, was opened in McNeil Street. The Waukeneeze Shoe Company opened a branch in Cumberland Street.

Sentenced to thirty days, a member of the Tim Malloy gang of hooligans shouted to his mates in the courtroom: 'Cheer up, boys, it's only a month.' In Rose Street United Free Church, Revd Alexander Macinnes delivered a lecture on 'The problem of the hooligan'. Councillor Primrose announced that he was 'in favour of the lash' for Gorbals tearaways. John Mason of Surrey Street, described as 'a good husband when sober', was fined twenty-one shillings for assaulting his wife.

In the Gorbals ward there were 92 pubs and 10 licensed grocers; one licence to every 350 inhabitants. At the Gorbals Cross Mission Sabbath school *soirée*, little Peggy Gemmell's solo was 'well received, especially by the juveniles, who encored vociferously'. The Royal Princess's theatre presented Go-Won-Go-Mohawk, the Indian actress. The Bonar Memorial Mission to the Jews held its annual general meeting in Gorbals United Free Church hall, South Portland Street. The Empire Music Warehouse in Crown Street offered to take worn, cracked or broken records in part exchange for new ones. In Caledonia Road United Free Church, Revd James Hutchison discoursed on 'Some anti-Christian theories of evolution'. Hackenschmidt, 'the world's strongest man', was a star turn at the Coliseum.

1907   AMERICAN TEETH

There was another outbreak of plague in the Gorbals. Suspected cases were removed to Belvidere hospital in the city's East End. Hooliganism was becoming something of an obsession with the great and the good of the district. In Rose Street United Free Church, Revd Alexander Macinnes told his flock: 'Christ loved the hooligan and wept over him.' In the Coliseum, 'De Graci's trained elephants' played a game of cricket, while Belle and Bijou appeared in a Suffragette sketch. In the Guild of Aid hall, South Coburg Street, 'the very poor' of the Gorbals were treated to a concert of conjuring and vocal and instrumental music. The Glasgow Hebrew Burial Society, based in Rutherglen Road, was set up to provide obsequies for Jewish paupers. The newly founded Hamilton's Annuity Fund offered pensions of £4 per annum to 'decayed natives' of the Gorbals.

The Grand National Halls in Main Street were the venue for a Gaelic League ceilidh of Irish music, song, dance and story. In St Francis's League of the Cross hall in Errol Street, Father Daniel administered the temperance pledge to forty new members. At the Glasgow Fair, the League disbursed over £300 to members, many of whom planned to holiday in the Emerald Isle. At a concert in the League's hall, the big attraction was Miss Daisy Postlethwaite, 'the champion cake walker of all England'. A. L. Marco of Cumberland Street offered 'best American teeth at hospital prices'.

1908 McGLYNN PUSH

Rabbi Hillman, from Russia, was appointed religious leader of Gorbals Jewry. Three men sustained stab wounds when two rival gangs, the Village Boys and the McGlynn Push, fought a pitched battle in Norfolk Street. Mrs Cross Lynch gave a lecture to the St Francis's Young Men's Society on the topic of China and western civilisation. For an unprovoked assault on a policeman in Main Street, Thomas Flannagan, a member of the Village Boys, went to jail for sixty days. At the British Empire cycling championships, held in Belfast, Dan Flynn won both the quarter-mile and ten-mile events. The Royal Princess's theatre presented a 'thrilling melo-drama' called *Convict 99*.

Abraham Goldberg arrived in Glasgow from Dublin and settled in a room-and-kitchen flat in Gorbals Main Street. He started up in business by buying bales of cloth and making them up into piece-goods for sale to wholesalers. By the 1970s, the firm of Goldberg's had stores throughout Britain.

Enrolment at Gorbals Talmud Torah school for the study of Hebrew literature, held in Gorbals public school, reached 376 pupils.

The congregation of the Beth Hamedrash Hagadol (great house of study) synagogue left rented accommodation in the Breadalbane halls in Oxford Street to relocate in a former United Presbyterian church at the corner of Cumberland Street and Mathieson Street.

St Mary's Clothing Society – a Catholic charitable organisation – distributed boots and stockings to needy Gorbals children and held their annual at home in St Mungo's halls in Govan Street, where upwards of 150 couples danced to the music of the Martin Marks orchestra. Courtesy of Glasgow Corporation, tenement dwellers in Tradeston were treated to a summer concert of songs, dances and pipe music in a Commerce Street back-court. On the twelfth of July Orange Walk, police made a record 153 arrests. At Glasgow Fair, it took five policemen and a hand barrow to lodge one young Gorbals lady in the lock-up. Drunken women, if persistent offenders, could be sectioned under an 1898 Act of Parliament and sent to Glasgow Corporation's Girgenti Home for Female Inebriates in Ayrshire. The Palace theatre starred Bijou Russell, 'coon singer and sand dancer'. The Coliseum featured the Ten Loonies.

For stealing 46 lbs. of lead from a tenement roof in Mathieson Street, Charles McGeachy went inside for fourteen days. John Halley and Co. of Eglinton Street offered gents' dress suits ('luxuriously silk lined, and rich silk facing') for £4. 10s. There was advertised Mac's Alhambra billiard rooms, Norfolk Street ('facing Gorbals Cross').

1909   MERRY DEVIL

Under the previous year's Old Age Pensions Act, Gorbals inhabitants aged over seventy qualified for non-contributory pensions: five shillings for a single person and 7s. 6d. for a married couple. Only people with an annual income of less than £21 were eligible. Crown Street post office started off with 230 pensioners on its roll. At Merryflatts poorhouse (now the Southern General hospital), which served the Gorbals and Govan, a new building was opened to accommodate 250 cases 'of the class commonly known as "Ins and Outs", the dissolute and undesirables'; the intention being to segregate them from 'the more decent poor'.

In the Coliseum theatre, medical students bombarded Dr Walford Bodie, billed as the Electric Wizard, with flour, peasemeal, eggs and tomatoes. An Aberdonian, Bodie claimed to be able to cure epileptics and paralytics by means of electro-hypnotism. One of the best-paid performers in show business, he festooned theatre foyers with crutches which had allegedly been thrown away by people he had 'cured' and he had been prosecuted for printing the letters MD after his name (he told a court that the letters stood for Merry Devil).

Forty-eight men – nearly all Jews – were arrested when police made a betting raid on a billiard hall in Main Street. While a fancy-dress-and-cycle parade passed along Eglinton Street, collections were taken to provide footwear for needy Gorbals children. For stealing gas pipes in Gorbals, James Thom and James Gilbert were sent down for sixty days. The Coliseum presented a sketch called Kleptomaniacs.

The Glasgow Jewish Evangelical Mission – operating from the Hebrew Christian House in Abbotsford Place, and headed by Revd Aaron Matthews – claimed 'several cases of genuine conversion'. Violinist Carl Volti of Abbotsford Place published a volume entitled *Reminiscences and Verses*. Gorbals Cross Mission workers held a musical *soirée* in the Grand National Halls, Main Street. Families residing in Oxford Street had to flee in the middle of the night because of an outbreak of sewer gas poisoning. At the Palace theatre, the legendary Harry Houdini escaped from a straitjacket and an airtight galvanised-iron tank. In a 'hooligan onslaught' on policemen in Commercial Road a constable had his skull fractured by a blow from a bottle.

1910   RUSSIAN ALIEN

Arthur Granville Elder MA (28), of Sunnyside, Johnstone, a son of the manse with a criminal record for fraud and 'a well-dressed young man of highly respectable appearance', was arrested in a pawnshop in Elgin Street (later Turriff Street) while trying to pawn a pair of brand-new binoculars. The pawnbroker, suspecting that the binoculars had been stolen, telephoned the police. Elder was taken to the Southern police office in Oxford Street and interviewed by detectives.

As he was about to be searched, he pulled a revolver from his belt and fired a shot into his own abdomen before discharging a further two shots at random. One of the bullets wounded police constable Adam Hastings. Elder then placed the revolver to his head and pulled the trigger, falling dead on the floor. When Elder's body was searched, it was discovered that he had another revolver, unloaded, in a pouch attached to his belt. Also in his possession was a pearl brooch and another pair of binoculars. The items had been obtained 'on approval' from various Glasgow shops. Dr Chalmers of Abbotsford Place was summoned to dress Hastings's wound – the bullet had passed through his left arm – and the injured officer was taken in a cab to his tenement home in Hospital Street. After a brief period of sick leave, he returned to duty.

The Tradeston Mills in Commerce Street were turned into a model lodging house with accommodation for seven hundred homeless men. At the Southern Police Court, a Crown Street woman was fined five shillings for having allowed fifteen adults to sleep in a single end – a tiny single-apartment flat 'ticketed' by the local authorities for the accommodation of three adults. The accused told the court that the people were potato gatherers and had no place to go. Gorbals resident Myer Stringer, a professional boxer, was said to be taking home around £50 per fight. The Oxford Star club, an amateur football team, was set up by Gorbals Jews.

At Glasgow Fair, the Mathieson Street Penny Savings Bank, conducted by members of Caledonia Road United Free Church, paid out 'upwards of £270'. The Charity Organisation Society, which listed 'the repression of mendacity and the exposure of imposture' among its aims, operated from the Gorbals United Free Church in South Portland Street. The Jewish Hospital Fund and Sick Visiting Association established a dispensary in the Gorbals, offering free medicines to the needy sick. In Tradeston, 1,884 women signed a petition in favour of women's suffrage. It was reported that 'many of the wealthier class of Jews' had moved from the Gorbals to Langside and Crosshill. In a typical Saturday night mêlée in Rutherglen Road, a police constable sustained injuries when a hostile crowd tried to release a prisoner. Ben Cohen, a Russian-born Gorbals baker, was deported for an infringement of the 1905 Aliens Act. At Exeter, Dan Flynn won the ten miles British Empire cycling championship event in twenty-six minutes and nineteen seconds.

1911 GORBALS GHETTO

After the Siege of Sydney Street – a shoot-out between three supposed East European anarchists and Scots Guards in London's East End – it was alleged that anarchists of foreign extraction were residing 'within the area of Gorbals Cross known as the Ghetto'. Eight people died in a devastating explosion in William Primrose and Sons' flour mill in Centre Street, Tradeston. The mill was in a heavily populated area and three of the victims were local children, killed by debris. William Cavanagh of Rose Street, an employee of the firm, suffered severe burns. A fatal-accident inquiry concluded that the explosion occurred when highly volatile flour dust was ignited by a gas burner.

Inmates of Merryflatts poorhouse reached a record number of over two thousand, due to 'a period of painful depression'. The Coliseum featured Lipinski's Forty Dog Comedians and Captain Jack Kelly, the Australian Stock-Whip King. A crowd of seven hundred watched an illegal bare-knuckle fight in the Gorbals. George Green, showman proprietor of the Old Barracks Carnival in Glasgow's East End, opened the Picturedrome, a 900-seat cinema, in Govan Street (now Ballater Street), near Gorbals Cross. The United

Free Church appointed Revd W. M. Christie, a Hebrew scholar, to head the Bonar Memorial Mission to the Jews of the Gorbals. Twenty betting slips were found in Max Riffkin's possession when he was arrested for 'loitering' in Main Street and Oxford Street. The Jewish Young Men's Institute opened clubrooms in Carlton Place.

The private hot baths at the Gorbals public baths were reported to be the most popular in Glasgow. Among the clubs attached to the baths was the Premier Ladies' swimming club, whose instructress was Miss Etta Mackay, 'the world's champion lady swimmer'. The building also housed a steamie (public wash-house) where, for tuppence per hour, up to fifty-four women were supplied with an unlimited quantity of hot water, steam (for drying purposes) and wringers.

At Glasgow High Court, Mrs Sarah McFarlane, 'a poorly dressed woman', was sentenced to three years' penal servitude for killing her husband Thomas by fracturing his skull with a beer bottle in the couple's single end in Wallace Street. Mrs McFarlane had eight previous convictions for assault, one by stabbing and two accompanied by robbery. A witness told the court that on a previous occasion, she had seen Thomas McFarlane beating his wife with a poker, and he had served a sixty-day sentence for assaulting his spouse. Lord Guthrie remarked that cases of a husband killing a wife in a fit of violence were by no means unusual, while cases of a wife killing a husband under such circumstances were rare. Mrs McFarlane had shown a disposition to reform and had gone to a home (Glasgow Corporation's Girgenti Institution for Female Inebriates) for five months.

John Ord, an Ayrshire man who had joined the City of Glasgow Police in 1885 and risen to the rank of superintendent of the criminal investigation department, was put in charge of the Southern division of police, a post he held until 1925.

At London's Crystal Palace, in the British Empire cycling championships, Dan Flynn won the mile event by inches. When one of the riders had a puncture, the others sportingly dismounted and waited until he fixed it! The 600-seat Eglinton Electreum picture house opened in Eglinton Street. Manager Grant Gilchrist advised mothers: 'Bring your babies and we will take care of the perambulators.'

1912 JEW VERSUS GENTILE

Competition in the Gorbals hairdressing trade was described as acute, with Italian, Jewish, Irish and Scottish barbers making a speciality of penny shaves and twopenny haircuts. The ever-versatile Dan Flynn became heavyweight boxing champion of Scotland. Dixon's Iron Works suspended five hundred employees as a result of the nationwide miners' strike. The men were given only one day's notice. With many Glaswegians making for the wide open plains of Canada, a Gorbals emigration agent promised: 'To deal with Cummings means travel with the worry left out.' The Eglinton Electreum picture house was described as 'one of the most comfortable in the city'. The Coliseum theatre presented *Son of a Jew.*

City sanitary authorities reacted swiftly to an outbreak of typhus fever in Commercial Road, site of a cheap lodging house where men dossed in large numbers. Over fifty people were removed to the city's fever hospital. In 1909 it had been discovered that body lice were the agents of infection. Ten boys were arrested and their fathers each fined a guinea after a fight between Jewish and Gentile boys in Adelphi Street. Aspiring sculptor Benno Schotz, born in Estonia, arrived in Glasgow from Germany via Rotterdam and Leith and moved into rented accommodation in the Gorbals. Members of the Jewish Young Men's Institute refused to have a bar in their new club rooms in Carlton Place, opting instead for 'social and sober intercourse'.

Police raided a coiner's den in South York Street and found a quantity of counterfeit florins (two-shilling pieces). The Coliseum featured illusionist Chung Ling Soo and also showed 'sensational pictures' illustrating the loss of the *Titanic.* Charles Cunningham (26), a labourer, attacked his wife Mary in a shop in Waddell Street with a razor and then committed suicide by cutting his own throat. The injured woman's wounds were dressed in South Wellington Street (later Lawmoor Street) police office, and she was then taken in an ambulance to the Royal Infirmary.

A Gorbals branch of the Workers' Circle commenced activities using the Grand National Halls in Main Street as a venue. In addition to providing the usual benefits of a friendly society, the Circle promoted further education in the working-class Jewish community through lectures, debates and discussions.

The Mathieson Street Penny Savings Bank was reported to have 'done a power of good in the district'. Hutcheson's girls' grammar school, opened in Elgin Street in 1876, moved out of the Gorbals to Kingarth Street in the more salubrious district of Queen's Park. A Gorbals bookie whose nickname was Wee Titch turned a former Free Church in Cumberland Street into the Paragon picture house. The Royal Princess's theatre featured a 'powerful and impressive' melodrama called *How Girls are Brought to Ruin*.

1913   BLOOD LIBEL

Gorbals boxing legend Benny Lynch was born at 17 Rose Street (later renamed Florence Street). The son of a Donegal man, he was taught to box by a Roman Catholic priest, Father James Fletcher, worked as a fairground boxer and turned professional in 1931. Seven cases of 'enteric fever' (typhus) were removed to Belvidere hospital from a room-and-kitchen flat in Crown Street. No fewer than thirteen adults and children lived in the tiny flat.

After Mendel Beilis, a middle class Jewish man went on trial at Kiev in the Russian Empire accused of the ritual murder of a Christian boy – the pernicious anti-Semitic blood libel which alleged that Jews slaughtered Christian children and used their blood to make unleavened Passover bread – Jewish delegates met in the Great Synagogue in South Portland Street to set up the Jewish Representative Council, with premises in Thistle Street. The case – which attracted worldwide publicity – took two years to reach court and, after hearing the evidence, the jury found the accused man not guilty.

Diamond's dance hall in South Portland Street was reported to be a popular venue for Jewish social functions. Alexander's Ragtime

Band was the big attraction at the Coliseum theatre. The Gorbals was selected as the venue for a conference of dancing masters. In a tenement near Gorbals Cross, jeweller Manuel Lipowsky threw acid in his stepmother's face then committed suicide by cutting his throat with a razor. On the advice of Dr David Chalmers, casualty surgeon for the Southern police division, the unfortunate woman was conveyed in a cab to the Royal Infirmary.

In Main Street, Herbert Johnstone (22), chased by two men, produced a revolver and fired at his pursuers. One of the bullets struck errand boy Hugh Sweeney. Constable William Martin saw Johnstone running towards Gorbals Cross, gave chase and wrested the revolver from him. The weapon on examination was found to be a five-chambered Young America double-action handgun containing four spent cartridges. The fifth chamber was empty. The boy Sweeney was examined by police surgeon Chalmers, who brusquely pronounced his leg wound to be superficial and allowed him to walk home to Sandyfaulds Street. In recognition of Martin's bravery, the chief constable presented him with a parchment citation and a pound note.

The Great Synagogue was redecorated 'in Moorish style with the ceiling painted deep blue with gold stars'. In the Grand National Halls in Main Street, junior members of the Gorbals Cross Mission were treated to 'a limelight lecture' on missionary work in the Congo. A Jewish home-for-the-aged was opened in a rented flat in Nicholson Street. Morris Gerskovitz appeared in court after police made a betting raid on his barber's shop in Main Street. Charles Douglas was charged with 'an unnatural offence' in a Gorbals stable.

1914 JEWISH YOUNG LADIES

Courtesy of Glasgow Corporation, over four hundred regular inmates of the Portugal Street model lodging-house sat down to a slap-up New Year dinner, followed by a concert. The Coliseum presented a revue called *Irish, and Proud of It*. Bonetini Felippi of Crown

Street was fined a guinea with the option of ten days in jail for having in his premises a penny-in-the-slot gambling machine. The Jewish Workers' Circle had ninety members. Officials at Merryflatts poorhouse agreed to the opening of a kosher kitchen. No fewer than 1,600 young Gorbals men applied to be registered as lodger voters.

Francis O'Rorke, described as 'a respectably dressed young man', pleaded not guilty to causing the death of Thomas Mullin by beating him with his fists, knocking him down and fracturing his skull. The assault took place in Caledonia Road after the two men had been drinking. The jury by a majority found O'Rorke guilty but strongly recommended him to the leniency of the court. Sheriff Craigie passed a sentence of two months' imprisonment. Police raided a tobacconist's shop in Main Street and discovered that it was a front for illegal betting. Bonfires blazed in the back-courts of the Gorbals to celebrate Victoria Day (25 May).

The Revd W. M. Christie, head of the Bonar Memorial Mission to the Jews of the Gorbals, opined: 'Many of the Jews dared not cross the threshold of a church, but they gather in their thousands round Gorbals Cross . . . and they listen intently.' John MacCabe was fined £50 for using his Main Street flat as a shebeen. Superintendent John Ord of the Southern division was awarded the King's Police Medal for 'effecting the arrest of numerous dangerous criminals'. The citation added: 'On several occasions he arrested criminals at great personal risk, sometimes sustaining serious injuries.'

The Eglinton Electreum popularised the newfangled tango with a silent movie showing the correct dance steps. Joseph Kaveney of Caledonia Road copped three months' hard labour for living on immoral earnings. Andrew Riddell recommended his Main Street pub 'for a glass of good ale, or a half of good whisky'. The Crown picture house opened in Crown Street.

After war was declared on 4 August many young Gorbals men 'joined the colours', falling in behind the local Territorials as they paraded along Eglinton Street. In imitation of the 'Terries', little boys marched through the Gorbals with toy drums. The area presented 'a striking appearance' as 'Jewish young ladies ardently and loyally canvassed' on behalf of War Relief charities. With the outbreak of war, all aliens in Glasgow had to register with the police. The Jewish Representative Council guaranteed the conduct of unnaturalised Jews and this arrangement proved acceptable to the authorities. A Gorbals hosier did good business selling patriotic ties. The Women's Unionist Association of Tradeston collected over six hundred garments for the men at the front, while Tradeston men too old for military service were enrolled in the Citizens' Training Force.

A Gorbals shopkeeper appealed: 'Be patriotic! Keep on purchasing, and let the hands be kept on full time.' In Eglinton Street, the National Union of Women's Suffrage Societies opened a 'cheer-up club' for wives and mothers of servicemen. Constable William Martin (28), hero of a firearms incident in the Gorbals in 1913, died of wounds while on active service. Model troops 'arranged in trenches of real earth' were a feature of a Christmas window display in a Gorbals toy shop.

1915   EXILE OF ERIN

Gorbals-born all-round athlete Dan Flynn enlisted in the Royal Flying Corps. The members of Gorbals ward committee agreed to subscribe £2 weekly to a fund for the relief of Belgian refugees. In France, Seaforth Highlanders private Peter Hamilton of Rose Street, who had joined up in September 1914, was killed by a sniper. Frank Green, employed in the galvanising works of Messrs Smith and MacLean, was found dead in one of the cubicles of the model lodging-house in Portugal Street. Local chemists stocked the Liverpool Virus for Rats at 2s. 6d. per tin. Mrs Fairlie of Dale Street, Tradeston, received word that her husband Thomas – who left Glasgow in 1913 to work in Canada – had been killed in action. When war broke out he had joined the Montreal Highlanders.

Mr and Mrs Craig of Cumberland Street were told that their son Robert had been gassed during the disastrous Battle of Loos (21 September–16 October) and sent home to a hospital in Blighty.

Upwards of three hundred wounded soldiers from Stobhill and other Glasgow hospitals were treated to tea and cakes in the Crown picture house. The exterior of the Eglinton Electreum was redecorated with a montage of Allied flags. Miss Emily Miller, Glasgow's first policewoman, made her official debut at the Southern Police Court in Oxford Street. Private John Devlin of Sandyfaulds Street and private Terence McCarthy of Mathieson Street were killed at Gallipoli, where the Allies suffered a quarter of a million casualties. The recruiting offices in Eglinton Street and Cumberland Street were reported to be doing brisk business.

Mrs Galt of Caledonia Road heard through the Red Cross that her husband Alan was a prisoner of war in Germany. Jewish special constable Hermon Sragowitz received a citation for his zeal while making an arrest in the Gorbals. Locals were warned to beware of 'German plotters in public houses'. Sculptor Benno Schotz began work in a makeshift studio in a flat in a Gorbals tenement. He soon found the environment too inhospitable and left it for a studio in the city centre. The Gorbals telephone exchange in Apsley Place had around one thousand subscribers.

A Catholic weekly newspaper called the *Glasgow Observer* began to serialise *An Exile of Erin, or an Irish Girl in Glasgow*. Although lacking in literary merit the story is vividly written and gives a flavour of Glasgow's sectarian divisions. The fictional heroine, Hannah Purcell, a native of County Cavan, finds a good job as a live-in maid in the West End but decides to give it up because there is no Catholic church close at hand. Hannah also discovers that religious differences are not always resolved peacefully: one day, curiosity takes her to a public meeting in the City Halls, where the star attraction was a nun, Sarah McGrath, who had supposedly escaped from an Irish convent. Fighting breaks out between Protestants and Catholics and Hannah suffers superficial injuries. She is nursed back to health by friends in Methven Street, Gorbals, described as the Irish quarter.

The pious and virtuous Irish colleen then finds a job in a city warehouse, where she is the only Catholic employee apart from the doorman. Soon her faith comes under attack from workmates, including the zealous Andrew Petrie: 'a religious crank who attended revivalist meetings, Bible classes etc and had the usual strong desire to show a Papist all the enormities of Roman Catholicism . . . he had voluminous quantities of "No Popery" literature which he vainly endeavoured to get Hannah to look at.' But Hannah is more than capable of debating with Petrie and strongly defends her faith.

There is a strong thread of melodrama in the story but interestingly it does not deal with Catholics and Protestants but rather with the often problematic relationship between Catholics and Jews. Hannah is warned by her friend and work colleague – Nelly Morrison, a Protestant – about their superior, the cashier: 'I don't like him. He is called Mr Pendleton, but I'm sure that is not his real name, for he is a kind of Polish Jew, one of those oily, sneaking kind of people you can never understand.' When Hannah resists the cashier's advances, Pendleton falsely accuses her of embezzlement and threatens her with prosecution in order to blackmail her into marrying him. But the long-running serial ends happily, with the villain – who turned out to be a convicted forger – unmasked and the pretty Irish girl married to her sweetheart Maurice Reilly and living in 'a neat little cottage in the suburbs'.

The story – which ran for six months – was avidly followed by the Irish community of the Gorbals and must have had strong resonances with their everyday lives. The anti-Semitic undertones are particularly striking. In one telling passage Maurice informs Hannah that Jews are only too happy to exploit 'the hated Gentile' and explains: 'They stick by each other at all costs. Let a man be ever so great an offender against the Gentiles, it does not count against him if he is a Jew; it is rather in his favour.' Although fictional, the serial was not out of step with the editorial policy of the *Glasgow Observer*. The paper was edited by Charles Diamond, a controversial figure who was jailed for six months in 1920 for an article he wrote supporting the armed struggle against British rule in Ireland. Under Diamond the *Observer* frequently attacked Jews in a highly intemperate way referring to them, for example, as odious and unscrupulous exploiters. It was only after Diamond's death in 1934 that this editorial line was modified; indeed by the late 1930s the paper was a staunch critic of Hitler's persecution of the Jews.

1916 BLOODHOUND FLYING CORPS

A tenement flat in Eglinton Street was reported to be a meeting place of Irish revolutionaries, some of whom took part in the Easter Rising in Dublin (24–29 April). Countess Constance Markievicz, lieutenant-commander in the Irish Citizen Army – a Republican workers' militia – had allegedly visited the house shortly before the insurrection, and one of the men residing in the flat was killed in the fighting. A Gorbals youth, Philip Dalton, was arrested for using seditious language by shouting 'three cheers for the Sinn Féiners of Ireland'. Mrs Middleton of Thistle Street heard that her husband Thomas had been killed when the battle-cruiser *Invincible* blew up during the Battle of Jutland on 31 May. Constable Adam Hastings, injured in a firearms incident in the Southern police office in 1910, was killed in action while serving with the Scots Guards in France.

For running 'houses of ill-fame' in the Gorbals, William McBrien and his sister Mary were sent to prison, while 'Madam Durant' of Eglinton Street was fined 10s. 6d. for telling fortunes. After a police raid on a Jewish gaming house in Hospital Street, the proprietor, Nathan Gordon, was fined £10 with the option of sixty days in prison. When police entered the flat, a dozen young men were 'playing with cards for money at a game called Jewish brag'. An entertainment for Jewish servicemen began with a service in the Great Synagogue. A policeman was overpowered while trying to arrest an absentee soldier in a Portugal Street back-court. The squaddie got away. Mrs Tait of Commerce Street received word that her eldest son, Highland Light Infantry (HLI) private Matthew Tait, had been killed on 1 July, the first day of the Battle of the Somme. He was one of nearly sixty thousand British casualties on what proved to be the blackest day of slaughter in the entire history of the British Army.

At the Coliseum theatre, three thousand wounded soldiers got free seats at a patriotic review featuring flag-waving 'joy-belles'. Revd Alex Hay of Chalmers United Free Church in Pollokshaws Road urged his flock to take the war more seriously: 'Perhaps it was desirable that the horrors of modern warfare should be brought home to us in Scotland. Some people did not yet recognise that we were at war; they regarded the war as something in the nature of a side-show.' After a sanitary inspector called at a single-apartment flat in Crown Street, the elderly tenant was fined three guineas for overcrowding her single end with two men, one woman and four children. For falsely describing her eggs as Best Irish, a Main Street shopkeeper was fined £3. The former Hutcheson's girls' grammar school in Elgin Street became the Jewish National Institute.

Alice McFadgen was sent to prison for sixty days for assaulting two policemen. Police superintendent John Ord explained that not only had the woman's allowance as a soldier's wife been stopped because of her fondness for drink, but also that her three children had been taken from her and put in a home. Charged at the same court with failing to report for military service, Owen Gallacher stated that he could neither read nor write and didn't know what the call-up papers were for. An East End gang called the Redskins caused a disturbance in a Gorbals music hall. Charged with sending his small daughter to the pub for a jug of beer, a Gorbals man said: 'I am not in the habit of standing at a public-house bar.'

In Govan Street, police broke up a fight involving members of the Gorbals-based Bloodhound Flying Corps and the Waverley gang from Bridgeton. For assaulting two special constables in Crown Street, father and son hell-raising duo Christopher and John Kelly were each fined six shillings, with the option of thirty days in jail. Referring to unruly young Gorbals girls, who had broken panes of glass in house and shop windows, police superintendent Ord said that it was a pity that the law didn't permit girls to be whipped. He 'personally saw no objection to girls being whipped for such conduct'.

Three local schools – Adelphi, Abbotsford and Gorbals – had a total of 1,000 Jewish pupils, out of a grand total of 1,600. Mr and

Mrs Reid of Hospital Street received notice that their sons, Joseph and Alexander, had been killed in action. Both young men had joined up in 1914. Jacob Sensen and two other 'missionaries to the Jews' were arrested for causing an obstruction while haranguing a crowd at Gorbals Cross. They were found guilty and admonished. With imported grain supplies menaced by German submarines, Gorbals pubs sold Munition Ale, weaker than pre-war brews.

1917 ABSENT FATHERS

The greater Gorbals area had 90,000 inhabitants. The irrepressible Jacob Sensen was fined 10s. 6d. for breach of the peace after police intervened to restore order when the Christian missionary was addressing a hostile Jewish crowd in the Gorbals. The death was reported of Emmanuel Isaacs. Known as the father of the Gorbals Jewish community, he had settled in the area in the 1870s and held positions on the Board of Guardians, the Great Synagogue and the Benevolent Loan Society. Royal Flying Corps lieutenant Julius Diamond MC, of Abbotsford Place, several times mentioned in dispatches, was officially reported as 'missing'.

Private George Simpson, King's Own Scottish Borderers, taken prisoner during the 1914 retreat from Mons, went home to Caledonia Road after being repatriated from a German prisoner of war camp. A thirteen-year-old Gorbals lad, 'found in a helpless state of intoxication', was sent to the industrial training-ship *Empress* which was anchored in the Gareloch. Commenting on the disturbing rise in juvenile crime in the Gorbals, police superintendent Ord said that it was 'traceable to the absence of the fathers on active service'. There were complaints that Gorbals women had to queue for hours in all weathers outside Crown Street post office 'for the money earned by their absent ones in the trenches'. A Gorbals youth called David Wiseman was sent to prison for trafficking in discharges, having sold a seaman's official certificate of discharge to a man trying to avoid military service.

George Fullerton was fined £5 for kicking constable Shearer in

Rutherglen Road and trying to free a youth who was being taken to the police office. Rabbi Solomon Seifer and his friend Barnet Cantor were on their way to the Great Synagogue when they saw the attack and came to the officer's assistance. At the instigation of superintendent Ord, both men were called before the magistrate and thanked for their public-spirited conduct. With conscription taking its toll, membership of the Jewish Workers' Circle was down to twenty-eight. For the theft of an Adelphi Street lamp-post, James McKenna and Adam Johnston were each fined £3.

Royal Flying Corps pilot Jack Shaw of Apsley Place was awarded the Military Cross for conspicuous bravery. Before joining the RFC, he had been discharged from the army suffering from shell shock. Rebuking a young Gorbals woman charged with a breach of the peace, the magistrate remarked: 'While your husband is in France you're having a high old time of it.' Private John Murray of Florence Street, injured at Loos in 1915, invalided home and sent back to the trenches, died of his wounds. A provision merchant in Bedford Street was handed a heavy fine for selling margarine as butter. At a packed meeting in the Palace theatre, Glasgow Jews hailed the Bolshevik coup in Russia and rejoiced 'in the abolition of repressive laws against the Jews, and the grant of equal rights to all nationalities'.

1918 GORBALS MACHINE GUN

The Coliseum put on a show called *Singing Wounded Tommy*. To mark War Weapons Week, a local minister of the Gospel chose as his topic, 'A Gorbals Machine Gun'. While trying to arrest a woman in Norfolk Street, two special constables were 'roughly handled' by an angry crowd. The prisoner made her escape. A Norfolk Street landlord was fined £20 after it was revealed that his female lodgers picked up soldiers in Argyle Street and brought them back to the house for 'immoral purposes'. There were eighty-five pensioners on the roll of the Gorbals Benevolent Society.

A Gorbals man wrote from Ruhleben prisoner of war camp

near Berlin, stating that he was 'making the most of his lot, but would rather be back in the Gorbals again'. Harris Cantor of Crown Street was fined the huge sum of £40 for selling methylated spirits to two alcoholic women in his cabinet-making shop in Muirhead Street. Mrs Blaney of Naburn Street learned that her son Samuel had died of wounds in a German hospital.

Two Gorbals girls aged eight and ten were sent to Dalbeth RC industrial school for picking the pocket of a woman munitions worker in a dairy in Cumberland Street. Private Harry Fowler made a celebrity appearance at the Coliseum. In 1916, during the Battle of the Somme, he had been buried alive by a shell and deprived of his sight for eight days. Margaret Regan of Surrey Street was fined the substantial sum of £5 for taking matches into a munitions factory.

An HLI private – Andrew Bower of Waddell Street – won the Military Medal for carrying a wounded officer to a place of safety under heavy shellfire. A deadly new strain of influenza, first officially reported in Spain, reached Glasgow and in the week ending 19 October, 336 Glaswegians died of Spanish flu. Mr and Mrs Fraser of Main Street lost two sons in the last months of the Great War. Both men, regular soldiers, held the Mons Star and had been at the front since 1914.

Private James Quinn of Apsley Street was killed by a bullet twelve hours before the guns fell silent on 11 November. Constable William Tait Brown of the Southern division was awarded the King's police medal for rescuing two attempted suicides from the river Clyde. The Talmud Torah Hebrew school, with 700 pupils, moved to the Jewish National Institute – the former Hutcheson's girls' grammar school – in Elgin Street.

In the general election, John Maclean – who had been adopted by the Gorbals Labour Party by an overwhelming majority, while serving a five-year sentence for sedition – was beaten by George Barnes, a cabinet minister in Lloyd George's coalition government. On an uncompromising revolutionary programme, Maclean polled 7,436 votes as against 14,247 for Barnes. William Gallacher, a prominent Red Clydesider, contended that two out of every three soldiers who recorded their votes in the Gorbals division voted for John Maclean.

1919 GORBALS, ENGLAND

For assaulting the Italian proprietor of an ice-cream parlour in Caledonia Road, a Gorbals man was fined the sum of £2. The Tradeston Temperance brass band entertained the inmates of Merryflatts poorhouse. Gorbals MP George Barnes suggested that 'there ought to be some world army to act as a sort of international police'.

The municipal ward of the Gorbals, with a population of 36,588, had eighty-eight licensed premises, including six licensed grocers. In spite of the plethora of orthodox drinking establishments in the area, there was an 'alarming' increase in the consumption of methylated spirits, known to addicts as 'finish'. At Gorbals public school, 75 per cent of the pupils were of the Jewish faith.

With highly contagious Spanish flu ravishing an exhausted and undernourished population, local chemists were inundated with requests for anti-influenza masks. By the spring, several hundred Glaswegians were dying of flu every week. By the end of September, over 17,000 Scots had succumbed to the global pandemic, which killed 250,000 people in Britain and fifty million worldwide. Local temperance campaigners were livid when it was suggested that flu victims might obtain some relief from doses of hot toddy. A man arrested for interfering with passengers leaving tramcars in Crown Street gave as his excuse that he had just returned from France after a cold journey and had 'taken some whisky to put some heat into him'.

For having loitered in a close in the Gorbals for the purpose of bookmaking, a man was fined a tenner; fifty-six betting slips were found in his possession. On the annual spring holiday, Glasgow Corporation provided a two-minute tramcar service to carry Gorbals families to the local beauty spot of Rouken Glen. For a 'cowardly assault' on two warders in the common lodging house in Buchan Street, Thomas Monaghan was sent to jail for twenty days.

Éamon de Valera, on the run from Lincoln jail, and shortly to become president of the first *Dáil Éireann*, was allegedly sheltered in the presbytery of St John's RC church in the Gorbals. For selling half-a-pound of currants at double the government-controlled price, a Gorbals shopkeeper was charged under the Profiteering Act and fined £2. At the Coliseum theatre, the Mary Pickford competition was won by Miss Babs Bowring, who vowed to pursue a career in films. For shouting 'To hell with the King and England' while the twelfth of July Orange procession passed along Norfolk Street, Robert Skelly was obliged to part with a guinea.

There were around six thousand Jews residing in the greater Gorbals. In the district's synagogues, Jews gathered to protest against anti-Semitic atrocities in Eastern Europe. In a typical Saturday night fracas in Main Street, the police 'came in for rather severe handling, and had the greatest difficulty in getting their prisoners to the police office'. Superintendent John Ord of the Southern police division authored *The Story of the Barony of Gorbals*. When not engaged in official duties, Ord was a keen amateur historian and a member of the Old Glasgow Club. Sarah Carroll, a 'dishonest Irish girl', was fined £5 or thirty days' imprisonment for purloining seventy yards of chiffon from her lodgings in King Street, Tradeston. A Gorbals man received a newspaper from New York addressed: 'Main Street, Gorbals, England'.

1920   GORBALS BEAUTY

The Gorbals was described as 'the polyglot quarter of Glasgow'. Gorbals girl Phyllis Nadell (20) told reporters that she intended to 'take up cinema work as a profession', having won Pathé's All-Britain film beauty competition.

With unemployment soaring, Gorbals left-winger Harry McShane and Clydeside revolutionary John Maclean addressed a mass-meeting of unemployed on Glasgow Green. Detective sergeant William Tait Brown of the Southern division was awarded a bar to his King's police medal for rescuing a woman who had jumped into the river Clyde from a Gorbals suspension bridge. John Campbell (10) was sent to a reformatory for nine years for stealing four boxes of chocolates and ten tins of condensed milk. Jewish children in the Gorbals were treated to an excursion to Rouken Glen to mark 'the restoration of Palestine to the Jews'. Britain controlled the country under a League of Nations mandate, and fewer than one hundred thousand Jews lived there, but in 1917 foreign secretary Arthur Balfour had promised to establish Palestine as the Jewish national home.

Disguised as 'a very hardworking engineer, with oily clothes and cap, and grimy hands', plainclothes constable MacKellar nabbed a bookie in a close in Surrey Street. A mirror, placed on a window sill in the police barracks in Nicholson Street, led to another bookie being caught in the act. The inhabitants of rat-infested Gorbals tenements were assured that Rodine rat poison was 'safe, sure and speedy'.

Temperance campaigners advised the inhabitants of the Gorbals ward to take advantage of local-veto legislation and vote for prohibition in the district. The drouthy Gorbalites voted instead for no change. Police sergeant John McAulay of the Southern division, who had won the Victoria Cross while serving with the elite Scots Guards on the Western Front, was presented with a parchment citation from the chief constable for seizing and holding a dangerous runaway horse in Govan Street. Katherine McLeary, a middle-aged woman carrying a baby wrapped in a shawl, appeared at the Southern Police Court charged with keeping a shebeen in Dale Street, Tradeston. Fined the hefty sum of £50 – a year's wages for some workers – she offered to pay the fine right away. On the twelfth of July Orange parade through the Gorbals, some of the female marchers sported 'orange coloured blouses made for the occasion'.

Thousands of ex-soldiers had come home to find a changed world in which they were unwanted. In Rose Street, unemployed war veteran George Watt was found dead in a gas-filled single end. The Glasgow Hebrew Boot and Clothing Guild took over three hundred poor Jewish children from the Gorbals district on a trip to bonny Drumchapel. Eglinton Street United Free Church

(1825) closed down, to reopen as the Bedford picture house. The Hutchesontown Prize Silver Band entertained the inmates of Hawkhead asylum. Robert Hunter got six months for burgling a Crown Street jewellers and making off with a hundred watches. At a children's event in D. H. Thomson and Sons' school of dancing in Cumberland Street, a collection was taken for the Broken Men's Fund.

At a large gathering in John Knox United Free Church in Surrey Street, Paddy Black, superintendent of the evangelical Dale Street Mission, received a public testimonial. Thomas Hart, described as an obstreperous army pensioner, was sent down for thirty days for assaulting a clerk in the Pensions Office in South Portland Street. The Duke of Atholl opened the Limbless Ex-Servicemen's Club ('non-political and non-sectarian') in Carlton Place. Two men, charged with attempting to break into a restaurant in Cumberland Street, pleaded that they were only trying to purchase fish suppers. George Barnes, the MP who had defeated John Maclean in 1918, was reported to be recuperating in Egypt. During a Bankruptcy Court hearing, it transpired that a Jewish credit draper in the Gorbals kept his business records in Yiddish.

1921 OPEN-AIR DANCING

IRA activist Frank Carty, alias Frank Somers, who had been arrested for murder in Ireland and had twice escaped from jail, was picked up by police in Glasgow. He was believed to have been hiding in a safe-house in the Gorbals. On 4 May, when the police moved Carty in a Black Maria from the Central Police Court in St Andrew Square to Duke Street prison, three parties of armed men ambushed the vehicle in broad daylight in High Street. Inspector Robert Johnson – the officer in charge of the armed police escort – fell from the Black Maria, shot through the heart. Detective-sergeant George Stirton, standing over the body of his colleague, fired back but was disabled by a shot through the wrist. Another member of the police escort, detective constable Macdonald, emptied his revolver at the assailants who, failing in their attempts to free the prisoner, scattered.

During the fierce gunfight, which lasted about three minutes, bullets ricocheted off the prison walls, but the driver managed to get his bullet-riddled van into Drygate and through the prison gates. By nightfall, the police had raided the homes of well known Sinn Féin sympathisers and arrested eighteen suspects, including a woman and a priest. Thirteen men were later tried at the High Court in Edinburgh. All were acquitted by the jury.

In thick fog in the Gorbals, a tram-car ploughed through a flock of sheep, killing six of the animals. At Hayfield Street school, during a miners' strike, nine hundred 'necessitous' children were fed in relays. Thirsty Gorbals men took Sunday charabanc trips into the country from Carlton Place so that they could qualify as bona fide travellers, the only people allowed a legitimate drink on Sundays. Patrick Gallacher was fined £2 or twenty days in jail for assaulting a woman in West Street and brandishing an open cut-throat razor 'to the danger of the lieges'. With the pig-iron market at a low ebb, Dixon's Iron Works in Crown Street closed for an indefinite period. Several hundred employees were thrown out of work.

Hundreds of unemployed Gorbals men queued daily to seek assistance from Govan Combination Parish Council in Carlton Place. For leading a march of unemployed men to the council chambers, and urging the unemployed to 'take food' rather than starve, Clydeside revolutionary John Maclean was jailed for sedition. At Gorbals public library, there was a rush of applicants for Corporation food tickets, which could be exchanged for basic groceries in local shops. A lucky Gorbals man won £3 a week for life, or £1,500 cash, for forecasting thirteen winners out of fourteen matches in a football pool.

Cumberland Street was reported to be a popular venue for open-air dancing. A Gorbals man was sentenced to three months' imprisonment for assaulting five police officers, including Sergeant John McAulay VC. For shouting 'Up Dublin!' in Hospital Street, a young Irishman called Owen Gillespie had to fork out five guineas. From premises in the Gorbals, Lithuanian immigrant

Zevi Golombok brought out the first issue of *Die Yiddishe Shtimme* (The Jewish Voice), a short-lived Yiddish and English monthly newspaper. In the Palace theatre, Main Street, a mass meeting was held under the auspices of the Ukrainian Jewish Relief Fund. Thomas McGuire (9), sent out to beg, collapsed from hunger at the door of a house in Rutherglen Road.

1922　GORBALS GOLD

During the general election campaign, posters and handbills printed in Yiddish appeared in the Gorbals. John Maclean, standing as the constituency's Marxist candidate, was defeated by Independent Labour Party stalwart George Buchanan. On a Scottish hunger march to London, there were contingents from the Gorbals. Many of the marchers were ex-servicemen. At the Great Synagogue in South Portland Street, there was unveiled the first Jewish war memorial to be erected in Scotland. The memorial tablet was inscribed with seventy names. A Gorbals man was sent to prison for thirty days for stealing a leather strap from a railway carriage. He probably wanted the leather to patch his boots; in defeated Germany, people pinched carriage straps for the same purpose.

A hoard of gold coins, locked up in a strong box, mysteriously disappeared from a house in Abbotsford Place, the address of many prosperous Jewish businessmen. A lady bookie, found in possession of 102 betting slips in a close in the Gorbals, was fined £10 with the option of thirty days in Duke Street jail. Supporters of Rangers and Celtic passed through the Gorbals in charabancs, 'and with flags, bugles and other instruments of torture, made themselves a perfect nuisance'. Gorbals music publisher Mozart Allan of South Portland Place composed an Arran Suite for the Scottish Players.

When Dr Chaim Weizmann – leader of the World Zionist Organisation – visited Glasgow, a procession of 'highly polished cars, bedecked with flags' accompanied him from Central Station to the Great Synagogue in the Gorbals. The Jewish special constables and the Jewish Lads' Brigade pipe band turned out for the red-letter occasion. The service concluded with the *Hatikvah* (a Zionist hymn) and 'God Save the King'. At the Southern Police Court, a man was fined £5 for inducing his pals to play a game of chance known as Crown and Anchor.

Harry McShane of the Glasgow Unemployed Committee led opposition to the eviction of a family in South York Street. For his pains, McShane spent seven weeks in jail awaiting trial for sedition. The verdict of the court was not proven. After the trial, McShane joined the Communist Party. Merryflatts poorhouse in Govan, final destination of many pauperised Gorbalites, was renamed the Southern General hospital.

1923   BOOTLESS BAIRNS

Young men from the Gorbals marched in the funeral procession that accompanied Scottish Workers' Republican Party firebrand John Maclean from his home in Auldhouse Road, Newlands to his last resting place in Eastwood cemetery. Five thousand took part in the march, which was led by the Clyde Workers' band. After the Bolshevik revolution, Lenin appointed Maclean to the post of Soviet consul for Glasgow. Maclean opened an office at 12 South Portland Street, Laurieston but mail addressed to him was not delivered because he wasn't recognised by the British government. At the Gorbals public baths, the privilege of free baths was extended to the unemployed. A young couple appeared in court charged with courting in a close in the Gorbals. Local police held a concert to buy footwear for the 'bootless bairns' of the area.

At the Coliseum, a company of 'coloured artistes' presented 'old-time darkie melodies'. Gorbals residents contributed to the Jewish Relief Fund for War and Pogrom Sufferers. Such was the success of the Kosher Food Protection Society of the Gorbals in supplying cut-price meat that Gentiles as well as Jews flocked to the society's shop in Rutherglen Road. The Temperance Crusaders held a series of well-attended meetings in the Coliseum theatre.

A black coal-merchant, described as 'a pure Nubian', plied his trade in the Gorbals. A melodrama entitled *The Rosary* was a big attraction at the Royal Princess's theatre. Devout Roman Catholics made Glasgow Fair holiday pilgrimages from the Gorbals to the Lourdes grotto at Carfin, a little mining community in Lanarkshire. Local Freemasons held their rituals in the Masonic Temple in Abbotsford Place. There were 62,644 unemployed men in Glasgow, many of them living in the Gorbals. In Rose Street, John and Mary Quinn threw pails of water over a sheriff officer sent to evict them. Wife assaults were reported to be 'getting very common' in the Gorbals. The Coliseum, doubling as opera house and cinema, featured the British National Opera Company's English-language version of Wagner's epic *Ring* cycle and a silent movie called *Flames of Passion*.

The Ardgowan picture house was opened in Weir Street, Tradeston. Fashioned out of a disused cork factory, it was dubbed 'the Corkie' by the locals. With wooden benches and gas lighting, the Ardgowan was scarcely state-of-the-art but it survived, with minor modifications, until 1963. Through the agency of the Guild of Aid, 150 'aged poor' of the Gorbals sat down to a substantial Christmas dinner in the Guild's South Coburg Street premises.

1924   NEW JERUSALEM

A Gorbals street vendor – a disabled ex-serviceman – was reported to be selling mechanical toys made in Germany. Two young men were taken into custody after constable George Shand was brutally assaulted by a gang of youths while patrolling his late-night beat in Surrey Street. Two public-spirited citizens took the unconscious policeman to the local police station, and from there he was conveyed to the Royal Infirmary. Riccardo Celli of Rutherglen Road was fined £1 for keeping his shop open after midnight and selling a girl twopence worth of chips. A plainclothes policewoman helped to convict a Gorbals woman who was using her tiny flat as an unlicensed dance hall.

The Gorbals was scathingly referred to as 'the New Jerusalem' on account of its large Jewish community. Mormons held religious services in a flat in Abbotsford Place. For stealing articles from a washing line in a back-court in Bedford Lane, a twelve-year-old boy was sent to Mossbank industrial school for four years. An elderly Gorbals woman denied being drunk and incapable on methylated spirits and blamed her condition on 'gey bad whisky'. Gorbals fish-and-chip vendors were rebuked for wrapping their wares in grimy old newspapers. John McCurdy was fined £10 with the option of sixty days' imprisonment for having made a brutal assault on a policeman in Rutherglen Road. John McNaught of the Gorbals Smithy, Hospital Street offered his services as a 'range repairer'.

Peter H. Duncan of Caledonia Road claimed: 'My special herbal treatment is the natural method of healing and has been successful in curing innumerable cases of disease, even of long standing.' Terence McLuskey was sent down for sixty days for brandishing a razor in a Crown Street shop and demanding money for beer. A Gorbals clergyman complained about the scarcity of Bibles in the homes of his parishioners. In Tradeston, three policemen had to struggle to retain custody of a prisoner after being set upon by 'a wild mob'. Charged with wife assault, a nostalgic Gorbals man told the court that the happiest time he had known since he was married was the four years when he was 'at the war'. Street collectors selling poppies on behalf of the Earl Haig fund met with 'a hearty response' in the Gorbals.

The Manxman bar in Gloucester Street, Tradeston advertised its strong points: 'good value, cleanliness, civility and personal supervision'. John Brown, pharmacist at Laurieston medical hall in Cumberland Street, promised: 'Whether National Insurance, or private physician's prescriptions, they will be compounded with equal care and precision.' Offering to patch up old clothes, Mr Shenkin described himself as the American Renovating Tailor and the Workers' Friend.

1925   SOCKS FOR LEPERS

Bad weather prevented Hutchesontown Prize Silver Band from parading through the streets on Ne'erday morning playing old Scots melodies, which they had done for the past sixteen years. A Gorbals undertaker advised customers to 'purchase British goods'. William Elky Clark, born in Mathieson Street, Hutchesontown, in 1898, won the European flyweight boxing championship by outpointing Michel Montreull of Belgium, the holder, in a contest over twenty rounds. The fight took place in Hengler's Circus, Sauchiehall Street. 'No love of the Jews in the Gorbals' was the excuse a local Protestant congregation gave for not taking a collection for missionary work among the Jews.

Socks knitted for lepers by members of the Girls' Guild of Hutchesontown were among items on show at a display of mission work. A ladies' hairdresser in the Gorbals reported a big demand for shingling and bobbing. A Gorbals wedding had to be cancelled at the last moment owing to the sudden disappearance of the bridegroom. The Coliseum theatre became a cinema, with a 'grand orchestral organ' and 'pretty girls dressed in bright green and gold'. On behalf of the Gorbals poor, the Guild of Aid operated five savings clubs and a day nursery for working women.

At a dance held in the Limbless Ex-Servicemen's Club in Carlton Place, music was provided by Smith's Ideal Jazz Band. Athlete Eric Liddell, who won a gold medal at the 1924 Olympic Games in Paris, and tossed away his chance of a second gold medal by refusing to run on a Sunday, conducted services in Hutchesontown Congregational church before leaving the country to take up missionary work in China. The Eglinton Electreum presented *The Perfect Flapper*, admission 4d. and 6d. At St Francis's church the May Queen 'presented quite a striking appearance with her maids of honour and attendants dressed in white for the occasion'.

A Gorbals clergyman discoursed on the subject of 'Ulster's enemies'. While walking along the pavement in Commerce Street, William Cameron (19) was bitten by a horse. The Judean Glee Party gave their first public concert in the Dixon halls, admission 1s. and 1s. 6d. Rose Street United Free Church was the venue for a 'six days Gospel Mission'. The Jewish Ex-Soldiers' Society held a grand concert in the Palace theatre in Main Street to help the widows and dependants of their fallen comrades. At the Labour Institute, Rutherglen Road, George Buchanan MP heard forty of his constituents complain about rack-renting private landlords. Max Goldberg, 'a Russian alien', was remitted to the Sheriff Court for failure to notify his change of residence from Govan Street to South Stirling Street. Walter Tennent of Cumberland Street was available for 'horse-shoeing and general smith work'.

Miss Danskin of the League of Nations Union addressed the Gorbals Junior Imperialists, the cadet branch of the Tory party. The congregation of the Beth Hamedrash Hagadol synagogue opened the New Central synagogue in Hospital Street. Graham's of Cathcart Road offered 'Bass's beer, six weeks in bottle', six shillings per dozen. Glasgow Corporation installed electric lights in the Adelphi Street tuberculosis dispensary. Thieves broke into a pub in Govan Street and stole 212 bottles of whisky. Hurrel's bar in Crown Street was one of over 130 pubs in the greater Gorbals.

1926   CHILDREN'S DEATH TRAP

The Gorbals was the scene of sporadic rioting and window breaking during the nine-day General Strike, which began on 3 May. During the strike, the city's trams, reduced to a skeleton service, were manned by students and blackleg workers. The Gorbals was spared the scale of disturbances which occurred in Glasgow's East End, where pickets at the Ruby Street tramway depot in Bridgeton were reinforced by 500 miners, shops and pubs were looted and the police made repeated charges with drawn batons.

In Rose Street, Gorbals, there were 943 people to the acre, compared with 57 for the city as a whole. The death rate was 32.2 per 1,000 against 14.8 for the city as a whole. The infant mortality rate was 190 per 1,000 against 107 for the rest of the city. Slums in an area bounded by Adelphi Street, Rose Street, Govan Street and Crown Street were described as 'a children's death trap'. The Gorbals Junior Imperialists were treated to a lecture on the fallacies of socialism.

There was a huge turnout for the funeral of Paddy Black of the evangelical Dale Street Mission in Tradeston, founded by Mr Black in 1873. His son James took over the post of superintendent and ran the Mission until it closed down in 1969. Gorbals coal merchants sold German-made briquettes stamped with the word 'Kaiser'. The chief templar of the Eglinton Lodge of Good Templars, a temperance friendly society, was fined £5 for conducting progressive whist drives. At a grand concert – held in the Coliseum cinema in aid of miners' wives and children – two safety lamps were auctioned and realised the sum of £29. Harold Hamilton of Crown Street sought bookings for his orchestra, The Friscos, 'terms moderate'. Levine's kosher restaurant was opened at 34 Govan Street. Rabbi Meyer of Berlin spoke at the Great Synagogue in South Portland Street and at the Talmud Torah Hebrew school in Elgin Street, which had seven hundred pupils on its roll.

The Gorbals branch of the Independent Labour Party provided a feeding centre so that miners, locked out of local collieries and denied parish relief in the aftermath of the General Strike, could be given one square meal per day. The canteen was set up in a hall in Errol Street belonging to the St Francis League of the Cross, a Catholic temperance society. An unemployed woman threw herself into the river Clyde from the Albert bridge. Her body was recovered by George Geddes of the Glasgow Humane Society. Gorbals justice of the peace Dr Thomas Colvin condemned proposals for the sterilisation of 'mental defectives'. Sopher's Emporium in Hospital Street promised 'better value and lower prices than in the city'. Sculptor Benno Schotz, whose first makeshift studio was in the Gorbals, had his first one-man exhibition in Reid's Gallery in West George Street.

After three children perished in a fire in a tenement in Thistle Street, the building was described as 'old, tumble-down, and crumbling, with the long dark passages, many doors, winding stairs and attics that belong to another age of architecture'. Local miners gave the bereaved parents £3 from their own depleted relief fund.

Patrick Lally – who later became a controversial Lord Provost of Glasgow – was born in a room-and-kitchen flat in Thistle Street. His parents were Irish Catholic immigrants from County Mayo. The Paragon picture house, Cumberland Street – located next door to St Francis's RC church – presented *Our Lady of Lourdes*, admission 3d., 4d. and 6d. Miss Torrance of Crown Street died leaving £13 in cash and over £3,000 (about £300,000 in today's money) in securities. Neighbours said that she had lived in abject poverty. The Gorbals Rambling Club reported a record attendance at their ramble to Baldernock Linn. The Workers' restaurant in Rose Street promised 'cheapness and quality'. The Gorbals was reported to be gradually losing its reputation as the Jewish centre of Glasgow.

1927 GORBALS DIEHARDS

After George Geddes of the Glasgow Humane Society found a woman's head on the north bank of the Clyde, James McKay was arrested and charged with murdering his mother, Agnes Arbuckle, in her flat in Main Street, Gorbals. McKay, an alcoholic, was also charged with stealing the woman's bankbook. At Glasgow's High Court, McKay lodged a special defence of insanity but Dr A. K. Henderson – physician superintendent at Gartnavel Royal mental hospital – who had examined the accused in Duke Street prison, testified that he was sane and fit to plead. After a trial that lasted three days, the jury took only twenty-six minutes to return a unanimous verdict of guilty of murder and robbery. Lord Ormidale assumed the black cap and sentenced McKay to death. As the prisoner turned to leave the dock he waved to a friend in the public area of the court and cried: 'Cheer up.'

In New York's Madison Square Gardens – while fighting Fidel a Barba for the world flyweight title – Gorbals-born Elky Clark, British and European flyweight champion, received the eye wound that ended his boxing career. When the King and Queen passed through Glasgow, Gorbals Cross was decorated with a banner bearing the legend 'Glasgow Jews welcome their majesties'. Three Gorbals boys played members of the Gorbals Diehards in a movie version of John Buchan's thriller *Huntingtower*, starring Sir Harry Lauder. Tenants were ordered out of a condemned tenement in Adelphi Street after the master of works inspected the building and found it to be in a dangerous condition. The tenants were rehoused by Glasgow Corporation, but a large number of lodgers were left homeless.

The Glasgow Jewish Board of Guardians opened a welfare centre in Thistle Street. Hundreds of 'necessitous' Gorbals mothers and children were treated to a steamer excursion to Ardgoil. In Erskine church, South Portland Street, Revd James Brishy discoursed on 'the results of Russian propaganda'. In the Palace theatre, the Carfin Players presented a Passion play. William Milligan and Margaret McLean were each fined three guineas for using their single-apartment flat as an unlicensed dance hall. When police arrived, there were forty people tripping the light fantastic in the single end, with nearly as many queuing for admission. Jane Perry and Jemima Cassidy each had to cough up £2 after police found 'a jazz band' playing in the bed recess of their single-end flat.

Veronica Mitchell, described as 'a middle-aged Jewess . . . an exceptionally wild woman when in drink', was found guilty of disorderly conduct in Crown Street and fined two shillings with the option of fourteen days' imprisonment. Fines ranging from 2s. 6d. to 3s. 6d. were imposed on several men found playing cards for money in Gorbals back-courts.

In the House of Commons, Gorbals MP George Buchanan described his constituency as 'perhaps the most poverty-stricken in the whole country with scarcely a well-to-do person within its boundaries'. A pardonable exaggeration in such hard times, but there were in fact a fair number of professional people living in comfortable circumstances in the area. In the Gorbals, however, four children died for every child in the neighbouring middle-class district of Cathcart.

The Cumberland Laundry, 103 Cumberland Street, urged:

'Save labour, time and clothes by making us your laundry men. A postcard will bring our representative.' St Francis's Boys Guild went to the Irish Free State for their annual camping holiday. The Southern Syncopators held their annual dance in the Progress café, Clarence Street.

Miss Marald Dingwall Grant was appointed warden by the 500-strong Guild of Aid, a post she held for thirty-eight years. One of her duties was to take Gorbals children on summer tramcar excursions (1d. tickets) to the local beauty spot of Rouken Glen. Thomson's Academy of Dancing in Cumberland Street featured the Michigan Novelty Band. At Gorbals public school in Oxford Street, the prize-winners included Jack Baskind, Samuel Citron and Sophie Arnstein.

Shopkeepers closed their premises and the police were called out in force during a twelfth of July clash between Orangemen and Catholics in Cumberland Street. The disorderly scenes – repeated in other parts of the city – occurred when the Orange contingents returned from a forty-thousand-strong rally at Dechmont Hill, outside Cambuslang. In Anderston, bottles and other missiles rained down on the marchers; there were serious disturbances in Partick and Springburn; and in Bridgeton a woman spectator was taken to hospital after being struck on the head with a spear.

The Gorbals Branch of the National Unemployed Workers' Movement voted to disaffiliate itself from the London headquarters to free the branch from 'political entanglements and interference'. In the Southern Police Court, the charge against Bertha Rosvana, accused of assaulting Fanny Kudlatz, was found not proven. The women were still in fighting trim when they left the court.

Local businessman John Grimmond organised a treat for 'the most deserving children in fourteen schools in the Gorbals area, without regard to denomination or creed'. Morrison & Company, gown designers of South Portland Street, promised patrons 'the most beautiful and authentic Paris models'. At the St Francis Catholic Young Men's Society dance in the League of the Cross hall, music was provided by the Riviera Orchestra.

1928 SOUTH SIDE STICKERS

James McKay, convicted of murdering his mother in her flat in Main Street, Gorbals, was executed in Duke Street prison. As was the custom crowds gathered outside the prison, but the practice of hoisting a black flag and tolling a bell to indicate that an execution had been carried out had been discontinued several years before. McKay had appealed against his sentence, and his appeal – which was dismissed – was the first to be heard under the Criminal Appeal (Scotland) Act of 1926.

William Watson Malone was charged with murdering his mother and father in their room-and-kitchen flat in Commercial Road. The couple had been struck with a hammer and their throats cut with a razor. Examined in Duke Street prison by professor John Glaister of Glasgow University, Malone claimed that he had been receiving 'spiritual messages by way of wireless'. Professor Glaister testified that the accused was subject to insane delusions of persecution and had more than once attempted suicide. Malone was declared insane and ordered to be detained during His Majesty's pleasure.

On Albert Bridge two rival gangs, the Gorbals-based South Side Stickers and the Calton Entry from the East End, fought a pitched battle with knives, bottles, stones and other missiles. During the fracas, James Tait (17) of Charlotte Street, Calton, was fatally wounded. At an identity parade held in the Royal Infirmary, the dying youth picked out the person who had stabbed him. At Glasgow High Court, James McCluskey of the Stickers gang was found guilty of culpable homicide and sentenced to five years' penal servitude. Four of his associates, one only fifteen, received sentences ranging from a year to eighteen months. During the trial, the accused youths lost their composure in the dock and 'wept freely, mopping their faces with their caps'. A witness told the court that the gangs had been quite friendly until there was a fight in a cinema over a girl.

Revd John Cameron Peddie, educated at Robert Gordon's College and Aberdeen University, came from Barrhead to take up his ministry at Hutchesontown parish church. The Coliseum cinema showed the silent movie *Kaddish*, 'a story of the ghetto with incidental folklore music by a Jewish male-voice choir'. The supporting feature was an Irish comedy called *Colleen*. Accused of being drunk and disorderly, a Gorbals man informed the magistrate that he had been washing windows with methylated spirits and had taken a drop out of the bottle.

Harry McKelvie, lessee of the Palace theatre in Main Street, gave a free pantomime matinée for old folks. There were fifteen primary schools in the Gorbals, with a total roll of 13,514 pupils. At Gorbals public school where the majority of the pupils were Jewish, two Jewish teachers were added to the staff. Miss Dora Stelmach MA and Mr J. Bernstein B.Sc had both been pupils at the school. A man with a wooden leg, George Devine, copped twelve months after being 'found with felonious intent' on a stair in Crown Street. In the Eglinton Electreum, Mrs J. R. Johnston Elliot spoke on Socialism and the Woman Worker. The James Rice Memorial Loyal Orange Lodge held a social in the Orange hall in Cumberland Street.

The *Jewish Echo* was launched from premises in the Gorbals. A weekly English-language newspaper, the *Echo* was founded and edited by Lithuanian-born Zevi Golombok (1880–1954). In its first year of publication, the *Echo* carried accounts of Nazi attacks on German Jews. A series of Gorbals gospel-tea-meetings were held in the Brass-finishers' hall, Main Street. Tenants were ordered out of a condemned tenement in Rose Street, certified as dangerous by the Dean of Guild. Nine families out of the thirteen were rehoused by the Corporation.

In the New Central synagogue, Hospital Street, Mr and Mrs Frutin presented a Sefer Torah (scroll of the law) to mark the occasion of their golden wedding. Having started from small beginnings in 1908, Bernard Frutin ran a show-business empire that included Glasgow's famous Metropole theatre. For converting a Main Street back-court into 'a palais de danse, with concertina music for jazzing', five men and a woman were each fined 2s. 6d.

The Coliseum presented a benefit for local hero Elky Clark,

flyweight champion of Great Britain and Europe, debarred from boxing because of an eye injury. Clark went on to carve out a new career for himself as a boxing reporter. Messrs Muer of Rutherglen Road were described as 'the only firm where the real Heimishe fish' were obtainable. Cohen's kosher delicatessen in Main Street advertised 'Russian Worsht direct from Kovno – a dish you enjoyed in the old home town'.

The Hutchesontown No-Licence Committee held an open-air meeting in Caledonia Road to campaign for a dry Scotland. Plans for a new public baths and steamie were delayed because fire had been raging for years below the selected site in Fauldhouse Street, Oatlands. Messrs Smith's Glasgow Crucible Works, Fauldhouse Street, blamed an escape of gas. At an Armistice Day service in the Great Synagogue in South Portland Street, Mr Sam Salberg DCM read aloud the names of local Jewish men killed on the battlefields. The silence was 'broken only by the pitiful sound of sobbing from the gallery'. A Jewish Lads' Brigade bugler played the 'Last Post'.

1929 KOSHER FOXTROT

Indian businessman Mr M. Kaka opened a wholesale warehouse in Brunswick Street, Laurieston, mainly to supply stock to door-to-door peddlers. Music dealer Mr Gabrilowitz of Hospital Street advertised a kosher foxtrot medley. The body of a stillborn baby boy was found in a back-court midden in Commercial Road. Police traced the mother of the child and she was removed to the Southern General Hospital for treatment.

At the Coliseum cinema, hundreds queued to see and hear the celebrated Jewish-American entertainer Al Jolson in the first full-length talkie, *The Singing Fool*. Tenants had to flee when fire engulfed a large warehouse in Oxford Street. The American Mineral Water Works in Dunmore Street prepared Passover soft drinks under the supervision of Rabbi Balkin and Rabbi Lurie. In Hugh Boyle's pub in Main Street, the special Passover bar was under the personal supervision of Mr Sam Salberg DCM.

James Tees of Cumberland Street and Bernard Taylor of Main Street sailed for Canada to work on a farm after four weeks training in a Ministry of Labour centre. Jacob Epstein was fined £1 for causing obstruction, nuisance and annoyance by playing a loudspeaker at the door of his Eglinton Street radio shop. Geneen's kosher hotel in Abbotsford Place charged 6s. 6d. for bed and breakfast. E & B Fastovsky of South Portland Place announced: 'loans granted daily'. The Coliseum cinema was the venue for a protest meeting against 'the massacre of Jewish settlers in Palestine'. A social and educational club for Jewish girls opened in Oxford Street. Solly Bunis advertised his 'new and up-to-date' hairdressing establishment in Bedford Street. Revd Fomin of Abbotsford Place offered circumcision consultations by special appointment.

Annie Dalgleish of Eglinton Street was admitted to the Victoria Infirmary after a hatchet attack by another woman. Riley's Bedford bar in Bedford Street offered 'Bass, Guinness and draught beer' and 'oldest proprietary whiskies'. The Guild of Aid in South Coburg Street ran a weekly dressmaking class known as the 'Busy Bees'. Madame Sher of Dunmore Street advertised her London and Parisian models. An 'Esperanto propaganda meeting' was held in the Brassmoulders' Union halls in Apsley Place.

1930   TOE DANCING

Revd J. Cameron Peddie of Hutchesontown parish church met members of the South Side Stickers gang and persuaded them to set up a non-sectarian and non-political club. Having personally investigated local conditions, Peddie was convinced that, contrary to popular belief, unemployment rather than religious bigotry was the main cause of gang strife in the Gorbals. Many young men had never had a job since leaving school.

James Ross retired after seventy-one years' service with Dixon's Blazes, the Govan Iron Works in Crown Street. When James first started work, he got 8d. (4p) for a twelve-hour day. Mr Sher Kader opened a grocery shop in Warwick Street, the first retail business in the Gorbals to be owned by an Indian. With unemployment soaring, local housewives were urged to 'ask first for home produce' and 'ask next for the produce of the Empire overseas'.

Gorbals Jews who were out of work were told by the Ministry of Labour that they wouldn't have to attend the labour exchange to sign the unemployed register on Rosh Hashanah (Jewish New Year) and Yom Kippur (Day of Atonement). Oberkantor Max Feder from Hamburg conducted services in the Chevra Kadisha synagogue in Buchan Street. The first Jewish lodge of the Antediluvian Order of Buffaloes was established in Abbotsford Place. The Palace theatre in Main Street, which had offered a mixed programme of cinema and live entertainment for many years, went over entirely to the movies. Several Gorbals families had to flee in their night attire when fire destroyed the premises of cabinetmakers Wolfson & Sons in Surrey Street. The work of the fire-fighters was greatly hampered by the location of the factory; in a back-court between two densely inhabited tenements.

At Gorbals public school, the prize-winners included Albert Zakharoff, Betty Kaplan, Sam Blumenfield, Sydney Goldberg, Sadie Solomon, Mendel Silver, Annie Labinsky, Bertie Cohen, Rose Daschovsky, Milly Bergson, Rachel Joseph and Celia Evsovitch. The old Crown cinema in Crown Street was replaced by a new 900-seat cinema equipped for the talkies. The Jewish Workers' Circle in Oxford Street had 102 members, the largest in its history. At a social-and-card evening, held in Mr and Mrs Joseph's house in Abbotsford Place, Miss Weistuch gave 'a very talented performance of toe dancing' and Mrs Bloom read cards 'in the approved gypsy style'. The Guild of Aid's day nursery in South Coburg Street cared for up to twenty-five babies and infants, who were brought to the nursery every day at 7.30 a.m. by working mothers. The charge was 1s. 6d. per week. Mr Weinstein of Apsley Place offered 'high prices for cast-offs'.

1931 PEEPING TOM

Grocery mogul Sir Thomas Lipton, who was born in Crown Street in 1850 to immigrants from Ulster – his father had a tiny dairy near Dixon's Blazes – was buried in the Southern Necropolis, Caledonia Road in the same lair as his parents and siblings. The cortège was led through the streets of Glasgow by a lone piper. The *Glasgow Herald* reported that Crown Street 'was deeply lined with people of the poorer classes', while 'every window and vantage point in the vicinity of the Necropolis was fully occupied'. The grave was piled high with floral tributes from all over the world. Lipton, a personal friend of King Edward V11, was knighted in 1898, having made his fortune by providing the working classes with wholesome food at affordable prices. Sir Thomas, whose estate was valued at over £1 million, left £80,000 'for the benefit of poor working class mothers and their children' and he also made many other bequests to city hospitals and institutions.

In a city-wide rationalisation of street names, Main Street, Gorbals was renamed Gorbals Street. Hundreds of Charlie Chaplin fans queued outside the Coliseum cinema in Eglinton Street for the first screening of his box office hit *City Lights*. After a spell with a travelling boxing booth, earning £1 a fight, Gorbals-born Benny Lynch (18), the son of a Donegal man, turned professional. The infants' percussion band of Gorbals public school broadcast from the Glasgow station of the BBC. The Bee-Hive bar in Govan Street announced: 'Family orders for Passover a speciality'. The Workers' Circle acquired new clubrooms in Gorbals Street. Robert Evans, described as a peeping Tom, was fined a guinea for spying on a Waddell Street neighbour. Nutkowitch & Sons of Gorbals Street offered made-to-measure suits from £3. 10s.

There were 39,712 one-apartment flats (single ends) in Glasgow, many of them in the chronically overcrowded Gorbals. Rosa Klar of Gorbals Street was admitted to the Victoria Infirmary with terrible head injuries afflicted by her husband, an unemployed cabinet-maker. In a case heard before the Southern Police Court, it was stated that some young Gorbals women were working full-time for ten shillings (50p) a week.

In the Coliseum cinema, Jews gathered to support Zionist demands that the British government honour the 1917 Balfour Declaration and turn Palestine into the Jewish national home. The Royal Princess's theatre featured a season of Yiddish plays. Maison Levey in Gorbals Street (proprietor Joe Levey) was touted as the last word in artistic hairdressing. The Workers' Circle hiking club went on a Sunday outing to Balloch. Two Gorbals bookies were each fined £10 with the option of sixty days' imprisonment.

1932 SUN-RAY BATHS

Over three thousand people gathered in the Coliseum cinema to hear Independent Labour Party stalwarts denounce the National Government's 'gross betrayal of the working people'. After entering office the previous year, the coalition government had denied benefit to a quarter of a million unemployed men and women. Other claimants had their paltry benefit reduced, and a stringent means test was applied to all applicants who had exhausted twenty-six weeks of unemployed insurance entitlement.

Communist activist Harry McShane – a resident of Lawmoor Street, Gorbals – and thirteen other members of the National Unemployed Workers' Movement (NUWM) were fined for marching through the district 'playing musical instruments, carrying banners and placards, and shouting slogans, with intent to provoke a breach of the peace'. Mr McShane organised the Scottish contingent on the 1932 national hunger march to London. The purpose of both national and local hunger marches was to draw attention to the scandal of the means test. At its peak in the early 1930s, the Gorbals branch of the NUWM, operating from Camden Street, had several hundred members and its own flute-and-drum band.

The Beth Din (law court) and Board of Shechita (slaughter of animals according to Jewish dietary laws) intimated that they were responsible for the kosher credentials of fowls killed in the Jewish community's poultry yard in Dunmore Lane. As a result of reforming chief constable Percy Sillitoe's reorganisation of the City of Glasgow Police, the old Southern division merged with Queen's Park division. The enlarged unit continued to be known as the Southern division, but the amalgamation resulted in the divisional headquarters and court relocating from Oxford Street to Craigie Street.

Gorbals cat burglar Johnny Ramensky was sentenced to eighteen months for cracking open a safe with explosives. The Jewish Workers' Circle presented a lecture entitled The Wonders of Heaven. Several persons were injured when rival gangs clashed in Rutherglen Road. A police constable, on duty at Gorbals Cross, apprehended a wild swan. Martin Hunt of Cumberland Street was fined £10 for loitering for the purpose of setting bets. A film show was given in the Coliseum in aid of the Fund for the Redemption of the Holy Land. Asian businessman Mr G. M. Sharif opened a wholesale warehouse in Oxford Street. At a community evening in Geneen's hotel, Hebrew songs were 'sung with great gusto'.

A court was told that 'a most obnoxious drink' made from methylated spirits, cheap red wine and vegetables was very common in the Gorbals. Nurse Livingstone of Abbotsford Place offered 'rooms for confinement' in 'the only Jewish nursing home in Scotland'. Gorbals municipal ward committee agreed to write to the Corporation requesting sun-ray baths for the Gorbals public baths. For breaking into a pub in Adelphi Street and stealing a quantity of spirits, Hugh O'Brien, 'unemployed and in receipt of relief', was sentenced to sixty days. The Economic Renovators of Crown Street offered to clean suits and coats for four shillings (20p). Glasgow Corporation health committee approved plans for a child welfare centre in Florence Street (formerly Rose Street).

The Bedford picture house in Eglinton Street was destroyed by fire. Nine months later, the New Bedford, a super-cinema in art deco style, with seats for 2,300 patrons, was opened in a blaze of publicity. Kapkin & Rabinovitch of Warwick Street stocked 'a large selection of ladies' gowns'. Mr Kallin recommended his ladies' tailoring establishment in Eglinton Street, La Mode de Paris. In Ballater Street, burglars raided a pub by excavating a hole in the wall of an adjoining tenement close.

To raise funds for the New Central synagogue in Hospital Street, Mr and Mrs Steinberg of Apsley Place held an 'at home' featuring 'Benny Lee, Glasgow's great small wonder'. Hislop's Stores in Main Street offered 'an extensive and varied selection of artistic wallpapers for the 1932 season'. Touting goods on hire purchase, house furnishers Green & Company of Eglinton Street declared: 'Don't be ashamed of your home. We make it easy for you to be proud of it.' The Ministry of Works was authorised to remove the fountain and clock at Gorbals Cross, a landmark in the district since 1878.

1933   PALESTINE WHISKY

Miss Edith White started a weekly dancing class for Gorbals children in the Guild of Aid hall in South Coburg Street. On the first day, crowds of poorly clad, barefooted children clamoured for admittance. Before the first class could begin, many of the weans had to be scrubbed clean and fitted out with clothing, socks and footwear. The classes were a great success, with Miss White giving twenty lessons each winter, sometimes to more than one hundred children. The annual dancing display in the Guild of Aid hall was going strong forty years later, with Miss White still in charge. A Gorbals wine and spirit merchant sold 'Palestine whisky' at 10s. 6d. (55p) per bottle. Athletic young Jews founded the Bar Cochba sports club, with premises in Turriff Street. The club took its name from an ancient Jewish warrior.

After Adolf Hitler was appointed German chancellor (30 January) the Coliseum cinema in Eglinton Street and the Crown cinema in Crown Street were venues for protest meetings against Hitlerism and the treatment of the Jews in Germany. The Sample Boot Store in Rutherglen Road advised customers to boycott German goods. Lord Provost Alexander Swan opened the new Gorbals public library. Situated at the corner of Norfolk Street and South Portland Street, the handsome modernist building contained an annexe for books and periodicals in forty foreign languages. The *Jewish Chronicle* noted that the new library had 'a fine section devoted to Yiddish and Hebrew literature, comprising a total of 1,000 books'.

Father Guardian treated the Boys' Guild of St Francis's RC church to a 'thrilling' lecture on his missionary experiences three thousand miles up the Amazon. In the Crown cinema, Lord Provost Swan was heckled while addressing unemployed Gorbalites. When he sat down, a large section of the audience began to sing 'The Internationale', a Communist hymn. The Lord Provost stood up and joined in the chorus. Family life in the densely populated Gorbals – difficult at the best of times – was breaking down under the pressure of mass unemployment. For throwing a kettle at his wife in their tiny Thistle Street flat, Alexander Lyon, an unemployed stone mason, was sent to jail for thirty days. Lyon was said to be 'quiet tempered when sober'.

The New Bedford picture house in Eglinton Street was the venue for a charity show in aid of German-Jewish refugees. The Carlton social club in Oxford Street was established to reduce the hardships endured by the residents of the grim common lodging house in Buchan Street.

The evangelical Paddy Black Memorial Mission arranged for three thousand Gorbals children to be taken on a day trip to Pollok Estate, country seat of the Maxwell family. The children travelled in lorries and horse-drawn carts and were accompanied by silver, pipe and flute bands. The Era bar in Gorbals Street offered to 'cater for all Jewish functions'. The St Vincent De Paul society presented 'a grand talking-picture entertainment' in the Coliseum cinema. A burglar blew open a safe in Co-op premises in Cumberland Street and escaped with £97. The pupils of Mrs Bessie Alexander of Abbotsford Place gave a dancing display in aid of the Glasgow Council for Community Service and the Unemployed.

After Gorbals Labour councillor James Strain was nabbed for soliciting a bribe from a market trader, Communist Party activist

Harry McShane stood for election and came second with two thousand votes. A smash-and-grab raider made off with over thirty rings from a pawnshop in Hospital Street. Frank Turetsky of Gorbals Street announced that he was a specialist in high-class remnants. Mr Ghulam Mohammed Sharif and Mr Ata Mohammed Ashraf opened a wholesale warehouse in Oxford Street. The Beth Din convened a meeting in Geneen's hotel, Abbotsford Place to discuss the supervision of kosher food in local cafés and restaurants.

1934 PARLOUR BOYS

Gorbals-born Benny Lynch fought and beat Jim Campbell to win the Scottish flyweight title. Sammy Wilson, who had 'discovered' Benny, was the manager of a Gorbals boxing club. Like his protégé, Sammy frequented Knott's restaurant, a very basic bistro in Florence Street. James 'Razzle Dazzle' Dalziel (35) of Surrey Street, leader of the mainly Catholic Parlour Boys, was hacked to death when the Briggait Boys and the Parlour Boys clashed in the Bedford Parlour dance hall in Kelty Street. At the High Court, James Collins (18) was found not guilty of Dalziel's murder, but along with four co-accused he was sent to jail for twelve months for mobbing and rioting.

Harry McShane of the Gorbals was in charge of the Scottish contingent on the national hunger march to London. Two policemen were forced to release a prisoner after being attacked by 'a disorderly and hostile mob' in Cumberland Street. Whitberg's Old Book Store in Gorbals Street offered Jewish devotional books at 'very low prices'. For attempting to break up a twelfth of July Orange procession in Gorbals Street and resisting arrest, Mathew Keith was sent down for thirty days. Malow and Lien of Gorbals Street advertised their 'best schmaltz herring'. Rose Cohen of Ballater Street announced that she had a display of all the latest autumn gowns. The Royal Princess's theatre presented 'Madame Fanny Waxman's Yiddish Repertoire Company'.

At the Jewish Passover, the Princess's bar in Gorbals Street (proprietor John Macdonald) went kosher with Palestine wines, spirits and liqueurs. For prudently clinging to a lamp post in Bedford Street while drunk and incapable, Andrew McKeefmey was fined five shillings. For breaking into the Poalei Tsedek synagogue in Oxford Street, James Daly got nine months' imprisonment with hard labour.

Gorbals cat burglar and expert safe-blower Johnny Ramensky became the first convict to escape from Peterhead prison. He was recaptured in Aberdeen twenty-nine hours later. During his chequered career as 'a one-man crime-wave', he would break out of top-security Peterhead no fewer than five times. At a treat for Gorbals mothers, held in St Mungo halls in Moffat Street, there was an outbreak of community singing. Pauper Frederick Hume was found drunk and incapable in Ballater Street, having rashly come out of Barnhill poorhouse in Springburn to have a look around.

Hutchesontown Home Mission to 'churchless' families resident in the Gorbals was reported to be an unsuccessful experiment. Mr Flacks of the Bar Cochba sports club, Turriff Street, advertised his 'ladies' classes for physical culture and acrobatic dancing'. Charged with breach of the peace in Carlton Place, war veteran David Hagen told the magistrate: 'I have a [silver] plate in my head, and when I take a little drink it upsets me.' Police, out to curb illegal drinking and gambling, raided the Abbotsford Street premises of the Antediluvian Order of Buffaloes.

At a meeting of the Gorbals ward committee, members were told about the appalling conditions in a tenement in Commercial Road: 'There were no lights on the landings, and you had to grope your way to the doors in darkness. There was one lavatory on the landing to serve fifteen adults and twenty-two children.' In Norfolk Street, Robert McKean committed a breach of the peace, under the influence of red biddy (potent red wine).

Accused of harassing Gentile women in Eglinton Street, Harry Herman explained: 'I like Christian women.' Sent to prison for an 'abominable' assault on his wife, Daniel McCaherty of Gloucester Street lamented, 'For the past five years I have had an awful time of it.' At the Southern Police Court, Eglinton Street was described as a 'happy hunting ground for beggars' who were 'often under the influence of methylated spirits'. Communist activist Harry McShane told the Gorbals ward committee that 'too many restrictions were being placed on working-class demonstrations'. The Mazel fish supper bar in Bedford Street was described as strictly kosher. At 'a fashionable wedding' in the New Central synagogue in Hospital Street, Miss Winetroble was married to Samuel Nutkovitch. Mr Kater Singh, charged with being drunk and disorderly in the Gorbals on Christmas Eve, was fined 7s. 6d.

1935 GORBALS AMAZON

Twenty thousand people packed the concourse of Glasgow's Central Station to welcome boxer Benny Lynch on his triumphal return from Manchester. On 10 September, Lynch had defeated Jackie Brown in Belle Vue stadium in a fight lasting only four minutes and forty-two seconds to become Scotland's first flyweight champion of the world. It was one of the greatest boxing performances of all time and Brown had no answer to the Scot's ferocious left hooks or to his trademark body shots. Such was his total dominance that Lynch actually dumped Brown onto the canvas eight times inside two rounds. Enthusiastic fans – five hundred of whom had accompanied him on the journey south – carried the champ on their shoulders across Gordon Street to a reception in the prestigious Grosvenor restaurant. Later that same evening, Benny and his trainer Sammy Wilson received a rapturous reception when they drove through the Gorbals in an open-top car. Florence Street, Lynch's birthplace, was decorated with bunting and placards reading 'Welcome Home Benny'. But Glasgow's city fathers, anti-boxing to the hilt, declined to honour him.

The novel *No Mean City*, set in a Gorbals of dire poverty and decaying slums, was published by Longmans. It was a collaboration between unemployed Gorbals baker Alexander McArthur and London based journalist Charles Kingsley Long, with the latter knocking McArthur's poorly presented manuscript into shape and receiving three-quarters of the royalties in consequence.

The book charted the rise and fall of a Gorbals gang leader, Johnnie Stark, who won the title of 'the razor king' due to his prowess in slashing the faces of his opponents. The character was based on a real East End gangster called John Ross. Known as the razor king, Ross, leader of the Billy Boys gang, had been sent to prison in 1930 for a brutal assault in a cinema.

The *Glasgow Herald* described *No Mean City* as 'a novel of tremendous power', and *The Scotsman* offered a fairly balanced judgement: 'Considered as a novel, *No Mean City* is not particularly distinguished, but from a social point of view it is important owing to the first hand knowledge of slum life it exhibits.'

Immediately banned by Glasgow Corporation libraries committee, *No Mean City* was serialised in the *Sunday Mail* and the first, hardback, edition had run to eight impressions by the outbreak of the Second World War. Sadly for the Gorbals, the misadventures of the novel's brutal protagonist were taken all too literally by readers who were unaware that the majority of the area's inhabitants were law-abiding. What singled the novel out from later imitations and ensured its enduring popularity was McArthur's vivid eyewitness descriptions of daily life in the Glasgow slums.

In a scene not unlike those described by McArthur and Long, Oxford Street in the Gorbals was the scene of a running battle between members of a local gang and invaders from the East End. Eleven men and four women were arrested after police raided a 'Gorbals den of iniquity' in Hospital Street. Drama, physical culture and public speaking were on the syllabus of the women's section of the Jewish Workers' Circle. There were eighty-seven pensioners on the roll of the Gorbals Benevolent Society. Three men and a woman, arrested for singing in Gorbals back-courts, were reported to be addicted to blue-flame cocktails, described as a concoction of methylated spirits and ginger beer.

As Orangemen and women returned to Glasgow from their annual July demonstration at Johnstone, there were severe disturbances in the city. The most serious outbreaks occurred in the Gorbals following the arrest of two young men. An attack was made upon the police and in the vicinity of Gorbals Cross, hammers, bottles, iron bars, pokers, stones and knives were among the weapons used in 'a series of wild faction fights'. The situation became so alarming that police reinforcements were called up and officers were forced to use their batons to restore order.

Three enterprising Gorbals youths were done for silverising farthings to give them the appearance of sixpenny pieces. Mary McFarlane of Norfolk Street, described as a Gorbals Amazon, was admonished on a charge of punching her husband. John Kane of Caledonia Road was fined a guinea after a 'Wild West' scene in an Eglinton Street pub.

Gorbals-born Isaac Wolfson, boss of Great Universal Stores, opened the new Jewish Institute in South Portland Street, formerly the MacNicol Memorial church. The refurbished building boasted a library, restaurant and ballroom and offered facilities for literary and debating societies, socials, weddings and bar mitzvahs. It soon became popular with Vic Oliver, Joe Loss and other top stars playing Glasgow's famous Empire theatre. Among 2,191 candidates competing for 344 bursaries in Glasgow, no fewer than 562 were pupils of Abbotsford and Gorbals public schools. To celebrate St Patrick's Day, a Cumberland Street shopkeeper gave away five hundred rabbits.

A Greenshirt (a member of the Social Credit Party) was fined £1 for defacing a wall in Ballater Street. He told the magistrate: 'We are starving in the midst of plenty.' At a meeting in the Workers' Circle hall in Gorbals Street, communist stalwart Willie Gallacher said that the capitalist system 'was the most fertile soil for the growth of anti-Semitism'. For trying to smuggle cigarettes and wine into Barlinnie jail, Peter Williamson of Crown Street was sent to that grim institution for twenty days. Milly Slotopolsky of Norfolk Street described herself as a 'chic milliner'. Three black men, all from Surrey Street, were fined for assaulting a neighbour in his single end in the same street. In a child-neglect case, heard before Sheriff Dods, a Centre Street, Tradeston tenement was described as a black hole. Professor Selig Brodetsky, grand commander of the Order of Ancient Maccabeans, addressed a Zionist demonstration in the Palace theatre, Gorbals Street. The purpose of the meeting was to promote further Jewish settlement in Palestine, where the Jews already accounted for 25 per cent of the population.

Three men were jailed for raiding Gorbals pubs by cutting their way through the floors of overhead flats. Glasgow Corporation opened a day nursery in Adelphi Street, 'nominal charge 6d. per day'. World flyweight boxing champion Benny Lynch, residing in Thistle Street, married Miss Anne McGuckian at Gretna Green. The couple set up home in a room-and-kitchen flat in Rutherglen Road, Gorbals, but separated after only four months. It was reported that many former Jewish residents of the Gorbals had flitted to King's Park, Giffnock, Merrylee, Clarkston and Mosspark.

1936 SOUR MILK AND PORRIDGE

Benny Lynch appeared at Glasgow's Central Police Court, charged with assaulting a woman in a Crown Street tenement and attempting to ravish her. His wife Anne, 'an attractive brunette', was in the court. The charge against the great boxer was later dropped. The reconciled couple moved out of the Gorbals to a house in leafy Burnside, a suburb of Rutherglen. Gorbals Communist activist Harry McShane helped to organise the national hunger march to London and led a contingent from Edinburgh. It was on the 1936 march that Ellen Wilkinson led the unemployed men of Jarrow, a scene captured on newsreel. With a population of 44,000, Gorbals ward had 121 pubs. The infant mortality rate in the district was 109 per 1,000 births, and no fewer than 13,220 people were on public assistance.

In a newspaper feature entitled 'Why I Wrote *No Mean City*', Alexander McArthur explained: 'I cannot and shall never claim to be a saint, yet I do have within me a desire to see all homes without lavatories abolished.' In Dunmore Street, a man was blown out of bed when thieves used explosives to crack a safe. Using 'cat-burglar tactics', four young men broke into a warehouse in South Portland Street and stole eight fur coats, 396 pairs of ladies' stockings and various other articles. There were 34,375 single ends in Glasgow, many of them in the densely populated Gorbals. At the Southern Police Court, fines and jail sentences were imposed on nine young men, all from Donegal, who had run amok in the Gorbals and assaulted police officers. At the Workers' Circle in Gorbals Street, Mrs Ockrent lectured on 'the Jews in the Soviet Union'. Avrom Greenbaum's Jewish Institute Players, founded in 1934, performed three one-act plays on an improvised stage in the new Jewish Institute in South Portland Street.

The Scottish Milk Marketing Board opened a milk bar in Crown Street. Children between two and five got a third of a pint for a half-penny, but the milk had to be consumed on the premises. One woman told the shop attendant that, apart from the fresh milk obtained in the milk bar, her children lived on a diet of sour milk, porridge, bread and tea. Kosher butchers Jacobs of Ballater Street promised 'something new in dainties at our delicatessen counter'. In Oxford Street, tenants had to flee their homes when fire swept through a warehouse belonging to Alexander Sloan & Company.

The Beryl Cigarette Manufacturing Company of South Portland Street were 'specialists in handmade Virginia and Turkish cigarettes'. William Dixon Ltd opened a new £250,000 coke oven plant, the first of its kind in Scotland, to enable the firm to produce a better quality of pig iron. An unlicensed dance hall in Mathieson Street was said to be frequented by the Gorbals Beehive Gang, which took its name from a warehouse in Cumberland Street. Female gang members were known as queen bees while junior adherents were called the wee hive. Isaac Glickman of Abbotsford Place advertised: 'Passover sweets prepared under the supervision of Rabbi Atlas'.

Phil Gillan of Fauldhouse Street, Oatlands (24), who had joined the Gorbals branch of the Young Communist League in 1931 and the National Unemployed Workers' Movement in 1932, arrived in Spain on 19 September, two months after the outbreak of General Franco's military rebellion – supported by Hitler and Mussolini – against the democratic Republican government. One of the first Scots to reach the war-torn country, he joined a unit named after Tom Mann (1856–1941), a veteran British Communist. Mr Gillan had his baptism of fire in November, at a place called the Hill of the

Angels. He was one of 476 Scots who served with the British contingent, which was made up of some 2,300 volunteers.

Alexander McArthur, having had 'enough of going about broke', pleaded for a job: 'I am the joint author of that notorious book *No Mean City*. The Town Council has banned *No Mean City*, and the Glasgow booksellers for the most part refuse to stock the book.'

1937 METHYLATED-SPIRIT DRINKER

Two young Gorbals men, Anthony Yates of Errol Street and John Connolly of Warwick Street, died in the battle of the Jarama Valley, where the British contingent of the 15th International Brigade suffered heavy losses. Of over 500 British volunteers killed in Spain in the course of the Civil War, 134 were Scotsmen. Phil Gillan, after helping to defend Madrid from Franco's troops, was badly wounded at Boadilla, hospitalised and repatriated back home, where he helped to organise food shipments bound for Spain.

In January at Wembley, despite his slide into alcoholism, Benny Lynch boxed brilliantly to outpoint Filipino Benjamin Gan, who fought under the name of Small Montana. Montana was the holder of the American version of the world flyweight title and by winning Lynch became the undisputed world champion. It was a miracle that the fight even took place; Lynch had arrived at his training camp in Buckinghamshire a full two stones over the flyweight limit only three weeks before. Then, in October, at Glasgow's Shawfield stadium, before a crowd of 45,000, he battered England's Peter Kane to defeat in thirteen rounds. The referee, W. Barrington Dalby, later wrote in his autobiography that it was the greatest fight he ever refereed, describing Lynch as a pocket Hercules with a phenomenal punch and the ideal personality for boxing: 'cold, calculating and merciless'.

The Jewish Institute in South Portland Street put on Sunday concerts featuring Hyman Winestone and his Swing Orchestra. Teitelbaum's of Gorbals Street offered 'all kinds of Vienna rolls made to order'. James Gabriel of Oxford Street was sent to prison for an anything but angelic assault on his wife. John Ross, a methylated-spirit drinker, was fined two guineas with the alternative of twenty days in Barlinnie for a breach of the peace in the Centre Street common lodging house. The New Central synagogue appointed Shmuel Aharoni of Palestine to the office of cantor.

Ibrahim Ashrif was enrolled at Gorbals public school, one of only two Asian boys on the school roll. He went on to get a Ph.D. from Edinburgh University. John McLean of the Robin bar in Norfolk Street stocked 'kosher wines for weddings and bar mitzvahs'. Rabbi Rogosnitsky of Leipzig delivered a Chanucah (Jewish winter festival) address in the Great Synagogue. Mr Bovilsky of Gorbals Street advertised his 'express radio service'. Glasgow Corporation opened 'a pioneer health centre' in Florence Street. Facilities included maternity and child-welfare services, a dental clinic and a tuberculosis clinic. The centre also treated patients suffering from trachoma, a highly infectious eye disease caused by low hygiene standards.

1938   GAS CHAMBER

Private James Shaw (23), a young regular soldier, collapsed in Ballater Street, bleeding profusely from a stab wound which had partially severed his jugular vein. He died in the Royal Infirmary. His assailant, Patrick Carraher (31), an habitual criminal who was unemployed and living in a Gorbals common-lodging-house, told a female confidante that he had stabbed the soldier because he had been very cheeky. Carraher had been involved in an altercation with several other men at Gorbals Cross when the ill-fated squaddie rashly butted in. Moved on by police, the men headed along Ballater Street, with the quarrelsome Shaw continuing to provoke Carraher, who earlier that night, the worse for drink, had threatened another man with a knife. At the High Court in Glasgow, a jury of fifteen men and women, by a majority verdict, found Carraher guilty of culpable homicide, in Scots law the equivalent of manslaughter. He was sentenced to three years' penal servitude.

At Kilmarnock Sheriff Court, Benny Lynch was fined £20 and banned from driving for a year. The fiscal told the court that the former champ had been zigzagging along the Irvine–Kilmarnock Road and had hit a telephone pole. A woman with a baby in a pram had a narrow escape. Addressing the great pugilist, the Sheriff said: 'Boxing and the bottle do not go together.' It was a disastrous year for Lynch. In June – prior to a world-title defence against American Jackie Jurich at St Mirren's Love Street stadium – he was stripped of his title when he failed to make the weight. The fight still went ahead and Lynch showed he was the better man with a twelfth-round knockout of Jurich. But he never seemed to recover from the disappointment of forfeiting his title. Later in the year at London's Earls Court, Lynch, sadly out of condition, was knocked out in three rounds by Romanian Aurel Toma, a man he would have wiped the floor with had he been fit. At the ridiculously young age of twenty-five Britain's greatest-ever boxer decided to retire to an Irish monastery to seek treatment for his chronic alcoholism.

For pinching six bars of chocolate from a stall in Billy Butlin's amusement park at the Empire Exhibition in Glasgow's Bellahouston Park – a show which attracted nearly thirteen million visitors – John Killen of Cavendish Street was fined £2 with the option of twenty days inside. The procurator fiscal argued that there was extensive petty thieving going on at the Exhibition and it required stiff sentences from the bench to stop the practice. Constable Robert Cairns – whose smartness and efficiency on points' duty at the junction of Bridge Street and Nelson Street had earned him the title of 'the lightning constable' – was promoted to sergeant. Five motor coaches were laid on for St Francis's Women's League of the Cross outing to Killiecrankie.

With Adolf Hitler threatening war over the Sudetenland of Czechoslovakia, there was 'a terrific rush for gas masks' in the Gorbals. At Hayfield Street school, seven rooms were put at the disposal of Air Raid Precautions personnel. For throwing half a pint of beer over a barman in a Gorbals pub, Annie Crawford, described as a public nuisance, was locked up for sixty days. In Gloucester Street, three policemen were besieged in a close.

At a demonstration of Gorbals Jewry in the aftermath of *Kristallnacht* – the Nazi pogrom directed at the Jews – a resolution was passed calling for the British government to boycott Hitler's régime. Kosher butcher Harry Lucas of Gorbals Street advertised 'salami wurst and beef Vienna' made by a Jewish refugee. The Knights of St Columba assembled in a flat in Eglinton Street for 'popular whist drives'. The Clock bar in Bedford Street stocked 'the best in kosher delicacies'. A Gorbals man who threw a flat iron at his wife while she was in bed with a broken leg was sent to Barlinnie for sixty days. Three men appeared in court after an affray in the common lodging house in Buchan Street.

Police searched for a hit-and-run driver in a sports car, who had knocked down and killed a woman at the junction of Centre Street and Nelson Street, Tradeston. The woman was identified as Jean Thomson by a pawn ticket. The Har Koah amateur-swimming-club held weekly meetings in the Gorbals public baths and offered 'expert instruction by the only Jewish fully qualified instructors in Scotland'. Police patrol cars rushed to Lawmoor Street when fighting broke out between two rival gangs. Gorbals Anti-Fascist Organisation ('non-party, non-sectarian') met in premises in Oxford Street to hear accounts of Jewish persecution in Nazi Germany.

A man who received fifteen shillings (75p) weekly dole from the Unemployment Assistance Board was sentenced to twenty-one days' imprisonment after being found begging in Norfolk Street. The Jewish Board of Guardians in Thistle Street received nearly three hundred applications for Passover relief of matzos and wine. Margaret Storrie of Warwick Street was fined 7s. 6d. for committing a breach of the peace by spitting at her Indian landlord, a student at Glasgow University.

Garment-factory worker Ralph Glasser of Warwick Street, who had left school at fourteen, won an Oxford University scholarship, an unheard of occurrence in the Gorbals of the 1930s. He cycled the four hundred miles south from Glasgow, carrying his worldly goods in a saddlebag and sending his books (all three of them) on ahead by post.

Margaret Stewart, a twenty-eight-year-old waitress, moved

into a room in Caledonia Road with her illegitimate baby boy Ian and advertised for someone to foster the child. John and May Sloan responded and the boy went to live with the Sloans in Camden Street. When he reached five, he was enrolled at Camden Street school. At sixteen he went to Manchester to live with his mother and in 1966 – by then known as Ian Brady – he was sentenced to life imprisonment for the 'moors murders' along with his accomplice Myra Hindley.

The former Southern police headquarters in Oxford Street (1895) was transformed into the City of Glasgow police training school for the purpose of training 229 probationary constables. The facilities included a gas chamber for training officers to deal with potential gas attacks by raiding enemy aeroplanes.

1939   NO FIXED ABODE

Benny Lynch was reported to be fighting in a Perth fairground boxing booth, a tragic end to a wonderful career. Police reported that, in the Gorbals, assaults were taking place almost daily. Local neds were accused of attacking 'innocent people against whom they have no grudge, but from whose sufferings they gain a sadistic pleasure'. Many victims were afraid to press charges: 'To inform the police is to invite another beating up – or even worse.' Three young Irishmen, who were said to have 'come all the way from the East End of the city to cause trouble in the Gorbals', were each fined 10s. 6d. Charged with assaulting his neighbour in a Devon Street tenement, Alexander Mills told the magistrate that the neighbour was 'knocking down with a fourteen-pound hammer' while he and his mates were having a drink. A radio which had 'almost been split in two by a bottle of tomato sauce' was produced in evidence of the destruction caused by Patrick Ormsby, a Gorbals man who ran amok in his home and threatened his wife with a poker.

For dossing on a stair in Centre Street, Tradeston James Harrigan of no fixed abode was fined a guinea with the option of fourteen days chokey. Three young Gorbals men walked forty miles to see the Hearts–Celtic cup tie at Tynecastle, Edinburgh. The financial position of the Great Synagogue in South Portland Street was described as precarious, owing to the migration of Jews from the Gorbals to attractive southern suburbs where new places of worship had sprung up. For embezzling Celtic supporter-club funds, James McManus of Surrey Street was sent to Barlinnie for fourteen days.

After the declaration of war on 3 September, air raids were presumed to be imminent. Local children had already been evacuated to the country. With the advent of the 'phoney war', during which, by mutual consent, hostilities were kept to a minimum, cinemas and theatres reopened and Gorbals pubs, which had closed at eight o'clock for several weeks, reverted to ten o'clock closing.

1940 MAD WITH DRINK

In Surrey Street, Laurieston sixteen people lost their lives when an explosion ripped through a starch factory. Employees fought their way through flames to the street, where several of them collapsed. An eyewitness said: 'I saw a flash, followed by a loud report. Looking out of a window I saw flames shooting out from all parts of the starch works, and in a few minutes it was blazing fiercely. At one window on the first storey an elderly woman appeared. Her clothing was on fire, and although people in the street shouted to her to jump for her life she turned back into the burning building.' A resident of a Warwick Street tenement who had just left his home as the factory erupted was turned into a human torch. All that remained of the factory after the inferno was a 100-foot chimney stalk. Rumours that the premises had been hit by a stray bomb were officially denied, and the tragedy was attributed to a boiler explosion.

At the height of the blaze, Archie Bowman of Surrey Street went from door to door warning his neighbours to flee their homes. He also made a return trip to his flat to carry his budgies to safety. Rescue squads expressed their gratitude to Mrs Strathdee, who ran a tiny grocery store in Surrey Street. As emergency workers toiled on the scene of the explosion she provided relays of tea and sandwiches, refusing payment. An air raid warden said: 'People have no idea how good she has been. After the "All Clear" has gone in every air raid Mrs Strathdee comes over with tea or coffee. She's an angel.'

Italian dictator Benito Mussolini declared war on the Allies on 10 May and, within hours, 'patriotic' looters had attacked Italian-owned shops and cafés throughout the city, especially in the poorest districts, where the lure of free chocolate and cigarettes proved irresistible. At the Central Police Court, James Thomson was charged with having, in the wee small hours of 11 June, kicked in the window of an Italian-owned shop in Crown Street, Gorbals. A fine of £1 was imposed. In the wake of the disturbances, naturalised Italians displayed placards stating 'We are British'. Lord Provost Patrick Dollan pointed out that the wave of vandalism would involve the city in claims for damages and compensation. He told his fellow citizens: 'If you want to fight fascism, join the armed forces.'

Gas respirators for babies were distributed from Gorbals public school. Private Dominic Docherty of Florence Street, reported missing in the aftermath of Dunkirk, was revealed to be alive and well in a German prisoner-of-war camp. Mrs Diana Cunningham of Abbotsford Place, whose first husband had been killed at Loos in 1915, was informed that one of her sons was a prisoner of war, while another son, reported missing, had returned, wounded, to the United Kingdom. Jean Brownlie of Cumberland Street was fined two guineas for stealing £5 from an English sailor in an Eglinton Street pub. The same penalty was imposed on a Crown Street shopkeeper who supplied a half-pound of mince without having obtained coupons from a ration book.

Glasgow's Dean of Guild Court granted Dixon's Iron Works permission to black out their coke ovens with a roof. William Paton and Alexander McDougall, 'mad with drink', assaulted two constables in Eglinton Street. In Gorbals pubs, the shortage of whisky was becoming 'acute', but some enterprising locals tried to make up for the deficiency. Eugen Junger (47), scroll-writer to a Gorbals synagogue, was fined £350 for having an illicit still in his flat in Warwick Street, Laurieston. Due to lighting restrictions, the kosher baths in Ballater Street were only open for four hours a day. Three men and three women, charged with a breach of the peace in Oxford Street, were said to 'congregate there to drink cheap wine, surgical spirit, and eau de cologne'. Some elderly Gorbals Jews – who had never become British citizens – were affected by a curfew order which obliged aliens over sixteen to be in their homes between 10.30 p.m. and 6 a.m.

Local Independent Labour Party members lodged strong objections when the police installed a revolver range in the police training school in Oxford Street. Police convener Gemmell explained that some officers had to be armed to guard vital install-ations against potential saboteurs. For firing his rifle in his home while the worse for drink, Gorbals squaddie Daniel McDairmid had to cough up a guinea. He told the magistrate that his family had only one room in a farmed-out tenement and as a result he had nowhere to keep his Army equipment.

1941 BIG MONEY

William Brennan, a thirty-two-year-old soldier, absented himself without leave and went home to Lawmoor Street, where he strangled his wife with an Army lanyard and took his own life by putting his head in a gas oven. Neighbours said the Brennans had been deeply attached to each other. When the Luftwaffe attacked Glasgow on the night of 14–15 March, bombs fell in the Gorbals in Logan Street, Rutherglen Road, Ballater Street and Chapel Lane. Unlike the raid of the previous night, when the bombers had concentrated on the shipbuilding town of Clydebank, the Glasgow raid was dispersed over a wide area, killing 647 people and injuring 1,680. The Paddy Black Memorial Mission in Tradeston was damaged by a parachute mine. Constables John Stirling and Joseph Park of D (Southern) division rescued a young girl from the rubble of a bombed tenement in Tradeston Street. Both officers were later awarded the British

Empire Medal. In Rutherglen Road, the Twomax clothing factory was set ablaze by incendiary bombs; the Lloyd Morris Memorial church was severely damaged, and Billdora – Bill and Dora Wolfson's hairdressing shop – was blasted. Crown Street residents took shelter in the basement of Hutcheson's boys' grammar school. With more air raids expected, the welfare department of Glasgow Corporation sought Yiddish-speaking staff for its emergency rest-centre at Gorbals primary school.

The Jewish Institute in South Portland Street was the venue for a variety show in aid of the Clydeside air-raid distress fund. At Glasgow Sheriff Court, a 'salutary' sentence of nine months was passed on Daniel O'Neil (19) when he pleaded guilty to mugging a sailor in Warwick Street. When O'Neil was arrested, two blood-stained £1 notes were found in one of his shoes. Every week, hail or shine, a priest from the Franciscan friary in Cumberland Street journeyed to Perthshire to say mass for Catholic evacuees from the Gorbals. For having been in possession of eight cigarettes and a match while in protected premises, Isabella Lamont of Cavendish Street was sent to prison for a month.

James Kinghorn of Abbotsford Place went to prison for fourteen days for assaulting his wife. He claimed that she had aggravated him. Local fish and chip shops had to close temporarily for lack of cooking fat. The League of the Cross hall in Errol Street was the venue for an Auxiliary Fire Service variety show. Proceeds went to widows of firemen killed in the Clydeside blitz. Patrick McCusker of Coburg Street was sent down for sixty days for assaulting his wife with his docker's iron hook. Asked what he had to say in his defence, the accused replied: 'My wife annoys me.'

In Gorbals pubs, whisky went up to 1s. 10d. (18p) a quarter gill. There was a 'rush for saccharin' following an announcement that no more sugar would be served with beverages in local tea-rooms and cafés. Angus Dickson and Thomas Berry were each fined 10s. 6d. for stealing fifty-six pounds of maize from premises in Gorbals Street where they were employed as fire watchers. The Jewish branch of the British Legion in Abbotsford Place sought 'comforts for serving men'. David Grimmond was charged with being drunk and incapable in Nelson Street. The fiscal remarked that the accused was 'earning big money these days'. The Picturedrome cinema and the Crown cinema gave Sunday shows in aid of local charities. Gorbals residents heard about plans for a 'mammoth housing scheme to be built at Castlemilk'.

1942   DAY OF MOURNING

As news of Nazi atrocities filtered out of occupied Europe, the Great Synagogue was the focus of a day of mourning. In the Coliseum cinema, at a meeting chaired by Lord Provost John Biggar, two thousand people heard speakers condemn 'the barbarous massacre of Jews in the enemy-occupied countries'. The Revd T. S. Stuart Thompson, representing the Moderator of the Church of Scotland, said: 'Scotland and Scandinavia are the only two countries [sic] in Europe which have never – and pray God never will – persecute the Jews.'

Gorbals café owners were livid when the Ministry of Food issued an order prohibiting the manufacture and sale of ice cream. Thomas Paterson of Portugal Street was fined £2 or twenty days in prison for threatening his wife with a cut-throat razor.

In Peterhead prison, where he was serving the last few weeks of a five-year sentence, Gorbals safe-blower Johnny Ramensky received a mysterious visitor who had come all the way from the War Office in London to invite him to join the Commandos and use his talents in the cause of freedom. Ramensky was later dropped behind enemy lines by parachute to open safes in Nazi-occupied Europe, and after D-Day he advanced with the Commandos, using his criminal expertise to crack safes and secure important documents for British Intelligence. When the Allies entered Rome, Sergeant Ramensky blew open the safes in fourteen foreign embassies in a single day.

Local doctors were kept busy vaccinating people against the dread scourge of smallpox, brought to Glasgow in a ship from Bombay. Within a month, more than 500,000 citizens had been vaccinated in an operation described as 'The largest mass vacci-nation campaign ever undertaken in the world.' Communist stal-wart 'Red Harry' McShane sought election to a municipal vacancy for the Gorbals ward. He promised to campaign against graft – the taking of bribes by local politicians. Over four thousand Gorbals residents signed a petition in support of McShane.

For seizing a conductress by the throat and throwing her off a tram in Eglinton Street, James Lavelle, a young Irishman, was fined £5. 5s. with the option of sixty days in prison. In his defence he claimed that the woman had thrown *him* from the tram and had then fallen on top of him. Admitting thirteen previous convictions, Peter Sutherland, fined £5 for creating a disturbance in Centre Street, mused: 'The best thing would be for me to join the Navy.' At the New Central synagogue in Hospital Street, a memorial service was held for Glasgow theatre entrepreneur Bernard Frutin. At the May crowning of the statue of Our Lady by Kathleen Milroy, St Francis's church in Cumberland Street was 'so densely crowded that many hundreds were unable to obtain admission'.

Gunner Nathan Zemmil of Crown Street was awarded the Military Medal for gallantry in the Middle East. A shebeen in Warwick Street, Laurieston was 'so well known that practically every Polish seaman who came to the city knew to go there for whisky or wine'. For resetting a large quantity of stolen goods, Bernard del Monte, a mantle manufacturer with premises in Gorbals Street, was sent to prison for six months.

Commenting on blackout attacks on local women, a police spokesman said: 'Women who are molested should use their feet. A well-directed kick has often more satisfactory results than calling for help.' At a 'musical treat' in John Knox church hall, Surrey Street, Revd Duncan Macpherson contributed no fewer than eight solos. For resetting 24,200 cigarettes, John Paterson of South Portland Street (33), a £7. 10s. per week tailor's cutter, was sent to prison for four months. The first Glasgow hostel for Catholic seamen of the Royal Navy and Merchant service opened in South Portland Street: beds, 1s. 6d. nightly; hot baths for 4d. The Gorbals baths in Gorbals Street, a designated gas-cleansing station where, in the event of a poison-gas attack, victims could be decontaminated, were open for public inspection. The 135-year-old Barony of Gorbals Benevolent Society expended the sum of £634 on pensions.

1943 SAVE THE CHILDREN

Gorbals recidivist Patrick Carraher, released from prison after serving a sentence for culpable homicide, appeared in court charged with slashing a man with a razor in a pub in the Townhead district of Glasgow. He was sent back to jail for three years. In Tradeston, Dr Wattie of the Corporation Public Health Department gave an address on venereal diseases, which had increased considerably owing to wartime promiscuity. Two babies were taken to Stobhill Hospital after being found abandoned in a pram in a Commerce Street tenement close. Small-time shebeener Alexander Lyon of Warwick Street, charged with trafficking in excisable liquors, was fined a fiver. Stated to have lifted a bottle in a shop in Gorbals Street, smashed the glass counter with it and challenged everybody to fight, Patrick McGowan (27) had to fork out a guinea or go to jail for fourteen days. Pilgrims from the Gorbals were among ten thousand Roman Catholics who took part in Lourdes Day at Carfin. After numerous complaints from workers who had had their pay packets stolen, William Cochran of Norfolk Street and Neil O'Donnell of Gorbals Street were each sent to prison for sixty days for loitering with intent to pick pockets. The men, both in their sixties and unemployed, seized their opportunity when workers were boarding trams.

Mrs Lena Zamansky of Rutherglen Road and Mrs Elizabeth McDougall of Cumberland Street received word that their husbands had been killed in North Africa. Edward Barron (74) of Abbotsford Place was fined £59 for having received cloth valued at £68. 10s. from Hyman Rimmer Ltd of Stockwell Street and Samuel Cohen Ltd of Claythorn Street without surrendering coupons. Mr Barron's agent said one of the accused man's sons had been lost in battle, another invalided out of the forces and a third had recently been awarded the Military Cross. In Cumberland Street, a man threw acid at a young woman and escaped through a back-court. The woman escaped serious injury.

After giving up work in a war factory owing to poor health, Margaret McGinn (48) of Adelphi Street bought a horse and cart and £3 worth of crockery. Fined £5 for overcharging for cups and saucers, in defiance of wartime regulations, she said in her defence that she was unaware that price controls were in operation. Geneen's kosher hotel in Abbotsford Place was the venue for a card afternoon on behalf of the Save the Children Fund to provide support for Jewish refugee children. By arrangement with the Government, the blast furnaces at Dixon's Iron Works – a gift to raiding Nazi planes – were closed down for the duration of hostilities.

Donald Steele of Florence Street, convicted of stealing furniture and clothing belonging to bombed-out families, was sent to prison for twelve months. The fiscal said: 'The furniture had been retrieved from blitzed houses and was being stored for the people until they got other houses.' The Jewish Institute in South Portland Street held a dance and reception for Lance Corporal Leslie Ferguson, who had returned from a prisoner-of-war camp. A dance-band musician in civvy street, he'd organised an orchestra among his fellow prisoners. Via a Christmas radio broadcast from Hitler's Third Reich, private Duncan Hannah of Weller Street, Tradeston – recently captured by the Germans – was able to let his sister know that he was fit and well.

1944   SLUMLAND COMMUNITY

A Sadlers Wells ballet called *Miracle in the Gorbals* – with music by Arthur Bliss and libretto by Michael Benthall – received its premiere in the Prince's theatre, London. An enthusiastic contemporary critic wrote: 'We are shown a slumland community in its dark cavernous dwelling among the Glasgow tenements. The sordid picture is lightened by the picture of the young lovers who seem unconscious of their surroundings. . . . Then a profound change comes upon the scene. A young girl is driven to suicide, an almost daily occurrence that scarcely finds its way into the newspapers. But this time a Stranger has come upon the scene and he brings the girl to life again.'

Police had to face a very hostile crowd several hundred strong when they intervened to stop four men fighting in the Gorbals. At the Southern Police Court, the fiscal explained: 'This was just one of the usual Saturday night brawls which take place in this particular area.' One of the street fighters, John O'Donnell (25), found guilty of breach of the peace and police assault, was sent down for thirty days. Mohammed Sarwar appeared at the same court charged with assaulting Sher Mohammed in Warwick Street. The complainant alleged that when he went into a grocer's shop owned by an Afghan, the accused began to shout and swear at him. The shopkeeper ordered them out, and on leaving the shop, Sarwar stabbed Sher with a penknife. The wound was superficial and Bailie Scot-Adamson fined Sarwar three guineas with the option of thirty days' imprisonment.

Geneen's restaurant prepared 'kosher food for members of HM Forces'. RAF driver Tommy Donnelly of Snowden Street, a parishioner of St Francis's RC church, spoke to His Holiness the Pope, having reached the audience chamber in Vatican City by a roundabout route, via the military campaigns in North Africa and Italy. In a letter to his aunt in Glasgow, Donnelly wrote: 'It was the most thrilling moment of my life. I shall never forget it.' In the Jewish Institute, Edward Warszawski, who had escaped from Nazi-occupied Poland, related his experiences in the Warsaw ghetto.

In the wake of the underground Polish Home Army's abortive uprising in Warsaw, the Catholic parishioners of St Francis's church joined in a novena for Poland and her people. The Muslim community of the Gorbals bought a tenement flat in Oxford Street and converted it into a mosque, the first mosque in the whole of Scotland. A restaurant in the Jewish Refugees' Society's premises in Abbotsford Place offered continental cooking with Vienna coffee and home-baked cakes.

1945

GORBALS VC

Gorbals-born private soldier James Stokes (29), of the King's Shropshire Light Infantry, won a posthumous Victoria Cross. On 1 March, at Kervenheim in the Rhineland, his platoon was pinned down by intense enemy fire. Private Stokes rushed forward, firing his rifle from the hip and reappeared, wounded, with twelve prisoners. Ordered back to the regimental first-aid-post, he refused to go and continued to advance with his platoon. As they approached their second objective, Stokes rushed forward through heavy fire, entered a farmhouse, and emerged with five more prisoners. Severely wounded, the diminutive soldier fell twenty yards from the final objective, firing at the enemy to the last. Private Stokes was buried in a military cemetery in Reichwald in northern Germany.

In a letter to Stokes's widow Janet – who was living in a single end in a rundown tenement in Clyde Street with her young son James and her brother and sister – his commanding officer wrote: 'His actions were those of a hero. Never have I been so proud of anyone under my command.' James junior received the medal at Buckingham Palace on his father's behalf. A pupil of St Luke's RC school in Ballater Street, Jimmy Stokes lost both parents at an early age and he was brought up in a Catholic boys' home. He was a keen Celtic fan and some local supporters' clubs were later named in his honour.

There were bonfires and impromptu street concerts in the Gorbals to celebrate 'Victory in Europe Day' (9 May). Schoolchildren were given a holiday to mark the occasion. Local ex-servicemen who survived the war returned to hideous conditions in a Gorbals of crumbling rat-ridden tenements, almost all owned by absentee landlords. A condemned tenement in Portland Street was described as 'a menace to life and limb'. Thirty-four families, comprising fifty-six adults and seventy-three children, were still living there. The Workers' Circle in Gorbals Street advertised a meeting 'of special interest to Jewish people who are more at home with the Yiddish language'.

After the company which owned the western section of the Southern Necropolis, burial place of generations of Gorbalites, went bust, vandals took possession and reduced the huge cemetery to 'a crazy panorama of violated graves'. Vandalism also 'reached a new peak' with the destruction of early memorial stones in the old Gorbals burial ground (1715) in Rutherglen Road. The railings had been removed for salvage during the war. An official said: 'Railings could not be replaced at present and when an attempt was made to build a wall, it was torn down as fast as it was being built.'

At a public meeting held in the Jewish Institute in South Portland Street, Zionist stalwart Professor Selig Brodetsky spoke on 'The lesson of Buchenwald and the German concentration camps.' The Royal Princess's theatre presented its last pantomime. After alterations, it reopened as the Citizens' theatre. In Ballater Street, two young men boarded a tram, held the conductress up at gunpoint and made off with her cash bag. In a house in Shamrock Street, Hugh Owens (45) stabbed and killed his prospective best man and brother-in-law, William Falkener (27). The latter was living with Owens's sister and the two men had quarrelled because the young woman had failed to put on a £13. 17s.10d. winning bet that Falkener had given her. Owens was subsequently executed.

1946 GORBALS FIEND

Gorbals teenager Joseph Hughes – serving with the Royal Army Service Corps in Hong Kong – was driving his three-ton ammunition lorry in a heavily populated area when the vehicle, part of a convoy, caught fire. He drove away from the convoy and fought the blaze with a fire extinguisher until the lorry exploded in a giant fireball. By his courageous action, hundreds of lives were saved. He was awarded a posthumous George Cross. Hughes was buried in the Chinese community's Happy Valley cemetery, and officers and men of his unit raised a subscription to erect a stone over his grave, which is honoured to this day by the people of Hong Kong.

At Glasgow High Court, Patrick Carraher, who had been jailed for culpable homicide in 1938, was tried for the murder of Seaforth Highlander John Gordon, a former prisoner-of-war who had been stabbed to death during a drunken scuffle in Taylor Street, Townhead, in 1945. Like Carraher's previous victim, James Shaw, Gordon bled to death from a neck wound. A witness told the court that, shortly after the crime had been committed, Carraher had danced around on tiptoe like a boxer and shown how 'he came down with the tool' – a woodcarver's chisel. Giving evidence for the defence, two leading psychiatrists told the court that Carraher, though sane and fit to plead, was psychopathic and abnormal, with a long history of alcohol abuse. After a three-day trial, the jury took only twenty minutes to return a unanimous verdict of guilty. An appeal against the sentence of death was dismissed and Carraher was hanged in Barlinnie prison on 6 April. Between the ages of seventeen, when he received his first jail sentence, and forty, when he went to the gallows, Carraher, dubbed 'the fiend of the Gorbals', had spent seventeen years in penal institutions. The chisel is on display in Strathclyde Police museum in Glasgow's Pitt Street.

After premiering Robert McLeish's four-act play *The Gorbals Story* in the unlikely setting of Buchanan Castle in Drymen, the Glasgow Unity Theatre presented the play in the Little theatre in the Pleasance in Edinburgh. A piece of social realism, set in a farmed-out Gorbals tenement, where eight families shared a kitchen, the play depicted the chronic overcrowding that had made the area a byword for squalor. The cast included Ahmed, an Indian peddler. A critic described the play as, 'A bitter comment on the housing of today, but the bitterness is seasoned with much genuine native humour, so that the rawness is often softened.'

A month after the premiere, Glasgow audiences saw the play at the Queen's theatre in Watson Street, near Glasgow Cross. A party of squatters, representing various camps in the Glasgow area, were in the audience as guests of the Unity Theatre players. The *Glasgow Evening News* described McLeish's play as 'people's theatre with a vengeance'. Born in Eglinton Street, Gorbals in 1912, the play-wright – the eldest in a family of eight children – worked as a plumber and heating engineer before getting a job as a cartoonist with a Glasgow newspaper. Due to the success of *The Gorbals Story*, which was performed more than six hundred times between 1946 and 1949, he was able to move with his wife and daughter from a room-and-kitchen flat in Eglinton Street to a villa in Langside.

Having lost his battle with alcoholism, Gorbals legend Benny Lynch (33) died of pneumonia in the Southern General hospital. Shortly before his death, Benny was boxing in fairground booths in Dundee, and he was last seen in a Glasgow pub inviting uninterested customers to punch a world champion for the price of a drink. His estranged wife Anne paid for his funeral and burial in St Kentigern's RC Cemetery, Lambhill. The man who made £30,000 in the 1930s from boxing – when a large detached house cost £2,000 – had no life insurance.

Young boys from Nazi concentration camps, recuperating at a convalescent home in Cardross, were given a reception in the Jewish Institute in South Portland Street.

1947   GOOD WIFE WHEN SOBER

Gorbals war hero Johnny Ramensky of Coburg Street, who won the Military Medal for his exploits behind enemy lines, was sentenced to five years' penal servitude for safe-blowing. Two policemen on beat duty near Rutherglen bridge came across Alexander McArthur (46), co-author of the novel *No Mean City*. He was unconscious on a footpath, some distance from his room-and-kitchen flat in Waddell Street, having drunk Lysol, a domestic disinfectant. McArthur, who had only $7^1/_2$ d. and a food ration-card in his pockets, died in the Royal Infirmary. Daniel Kelly, a casual acquaintance of the author – whose full name was Arthur Alexander McArthur – told a reporter: 'All he talked about was books and the success he might some day achieve as a writer. Whenever he had money he spent it quickly and freely.'

The Coliseum cinema showed *The Cantor's Son*, with Yiddish dialogue and English subtitles. Patrick Devine of Naburn Street was sentenced to seven years with hard labour for assaulting his wife Lily, who died from her injuries. Devine told the court: 'When sober, one could not find a better wife and her nature could not be improved upon. When in drink, she had a ferocious temper.' Beatrice Gowns of Oxford Street promised 'personal supervision of Marion Kinsell, proprietrix'. Glasgow had 11,982 notified cases of tuberculosis, one in twelve of them from the chronically over-crowded Gorbals.

With the division of the subcontinent into two independent and separate states, one Hindu and the other Muslim, most of the Indians in the Gorbals became Pakistanis. Edward O'Neil of Commercial Road had to have fifteen stitches inserted in wounds after being slashed with a razor in a Thistle Street pub. Two men brutally assaulted elderly tailor Zacharia Gaya in his one-man business in Caledonia Road and made off with a jacket and coat. In the Workers' Circle hall in Gorbals Street, veteran Communist Harry McShane lectured on Glasgow Jewry and Local Politics.

1948 SHADY RENT COLLECTORS

The influential mass-circulation weekly magazine *Picture Post* profiled the notorious Gorbals: 'In it, people live huddled together 281 to the acre. They live five and six in a single room that is part of some great slattern of a tenement, with seven or eight people in the room next door, and maybe eight or ten in the rooms above and below. The windows are often patched with cardboard. The stairs are narrow, dark at all times and befouled not only with mud and rain. Commonly there is one lavatory for thirty people and that with the door off.'

In addition to highlighting deplorable living conditions, the magazine carried pictures of Gorbals folk at play in Frank Judge's bar and Diamond's dancing academy ('a bright respectable place with a goodish if decorous band'). The grimmer aspects of life in the Gorbals weren't omitted. It was observed that, 'The Gorbals has no large industries and few small ones, where its residents may find work. . . There are always a lot of Gorbals residents on Public Assistance, either through sickness or in the interval between one short job and the next.'

One girl told the *Picture Post* man: 'I hate it in the Gorbals. If I meet anyone new I have to give a false address.' Another girl said: 'We're eight in the one room. We go to bed in relays. My elder brothers walk around the back-court while we girls undress. Then they come back and kip down on their mattresses on the floor beside us. The cat sleeps with us. If a rat runs over the blankets, he springs out and has it.'

The magazine also noted that in the football-mad Gorbals, the dream-team was Celtic: 'Inside Gorbals houses, the commonest pictures are of the Sacred Heart and the Celtic team.' Ironically, of the photos by Bert Hardy taken to illustrate the feature, the editor omitted the one which has since become a Gorbals icon – the picture of two scallywag pals in Warwick Street!

Gorbals and Hutchesontown housing association (membership around one hundred) alleged that 'shady rent collectors' were 'backed up by razor gangs'. Tenants paying extortionate rents for rat-infested slums risked being beaten up or scarred for life if they took cases to rent tribunals. Madame Ashe of Gorbals Street announced the arrival of 'the newest and smartest collection of gowns'. Mrs Alice Cullen succeeded George Buchan as Labour MP for the Gorbals.

Revd Fomin of Abbotsford Place, cantor of the Great Synagogue, advertised his proficiency as a *mohel* (a religious functionary who performs circumcisions). For Passover, Gorbals pubs stocked 'Shield o' David, the original kosher Scotch whisky'. At the Jewish Institute, Miss Berg of Tel Aviv gave lessons in modern Hebrew, the language of the newly created state of Israel.

Robert McLeish's critically and popularly acclaimed play *The Gorbals Story* was put on in London at the Garrick theatre, Charing Cross Road with Roddy MacMillan and Russell Hunter in the cast. The theatre critic of the *Observer* newspaper got the message: 'The moral of it all is that no reform is any good until we get houses, houses, houses.' One woman, leaving the theatre, was heard to remark: 'You'd think they would do something about everybody getting drunk and girls marrying Indians.'

Tommy Docherty, who spent his early years with his father, mother and sister in a cramped single end in the Gorbals, signed for his boyhood heroes Celtic. He was paid £9 a week, a fortune compared to his pay in the forces and the unskilled manual work he found after being demobbed. He later admitted that the money was a secondary consideration: 'I was so keen to play for them I would have gone for nothing. My mother was pleased too. She was a staunch Catholic and loved Celtic.' But within a year Docherty had become disillusioned with life at Celtic, where he played second fiddle to halfback Bobby Evans, one of the club's greatest-ever players. So he signed for Preston North End, helping the team get to Wembley for the FA Cup final in 1954. He was awarded his first cap when he turned out for Scotland in 1951, and his progress was such that he was honoured with the captaincy of Scotland in 1957.

1949 INFANT RAFFLES

Admonished on a charge of breaking into a Gorbals bank with intent to steal, an eight-year-old boy was described as 'not so much an infant Raffles as a child imbued with the spirit of Alice in Wonderland'. At the junction of Gloucester Street and Paterson Street, Tradeston, a young man fired a small-bore rifle at May McBride (21) and escaped in a car with four other youths. Miss McBride told the police: 'The man behind the driver came out of the car and shouted "What the hell are you looking at!" and fired a gun straight at me.'

After workers ripped off the roof and removed all doors and windows from a condemned tenement in Shamrock Street, fourteen families remained in the building. They had nowhere else to go. The squatters included a blind girl aged four. Isaac Wolfson, chairman and managing director of the £36 million Great Universal Stores, was reported to have 'a big grip on the hire purchasing furnishing business throughout the country'. Wolfson had his bar mitzvah in the Chevra Kadisha synagogue in the Gorbals, where his father Solomon led the congregation. The Gorbals Talmud Torah had 550 pupils on its roll.

Decades of neglect by absentee landlords were taking their toll of decrepit Gorbals tenements. John Bell of Mathieson Street looked out of his window and heard the ominous rumble of falling masonry. He instinctively caught hold of a little boy who was standing on the pavement and pulled him against the wall, saving him from serious injury as pieces of jagged stone crashed to the pavement.

In her maiden speech in the House of Commons, Gorbals MP Alice Cullen spoke of the dreadful housing conditions in her constituency. Two ten-year-old Gorbals boys, placed on probation for slashing children with razor blades, denied that they had been 'playing at gangsters'. Broken bottles were used in a vicious and unprovoked attack on a pedestrian in Ballater Street. The perpetrators – three young men – made 'a clean getaway'. Cavendish Place, a tiny cul-de-sac in Laurieston, became 'a roaring riotous bedlam' when policemen tried to make an arrest. The plainclothes officers were pelted with bricks and stones.

1950 EARTHY LANGUAGE

At Glasgow High Court, James Ronald Robertson, a thirty-three-year-old police constable in the Cumberland Street area of the Gorbals, went on trial, accused of murdering unmarried mother of two Catherine McCluskey (40) of Nicholson Street, Laurieston, by stunning her with a rubber cosh and running over her body in a stolen car in Prospecthill Road, a few hundred yards from Hampden Park. John Glaister, professor of forensic medicine at the University of Glasgow, testified that the horribly mangled corpse was consistent with the dead woman having been run over several times. Some months before her death, Ms McCluskey had given birth to an illegitimate baby boy. She had refused to divulge the identity of the father to welfare officials but had told her closest friend that he was a police officer who had agreed to pay eight shillings a week maintenance for the baby's support. Robertson, who had joined the police force in 1945, faked an entry in the log book in his Gorbals police box, claiming that he had seen Ms McCluskey knocked down by a hit-and-run driver. But, after a trial lasting seven days, the jury, by a majority verdict, found him guilty. The accused, described as 'a devoted husband and father, teetotaller and non-smoker', showed no emotion and stood to attention when sentenced to death. After an abortive appeal and an equally unsuccessful application for a reprieve, Robertson was executed in Barlinnie prison. The padre who accompanied him to the gallows later confided that he had faced death with composure.

The people of the Gorbals were reported to be 'ashamed and fed-up with their district being branded in ballet, ballad and story as the home of the razor kings'. The local ward committee petitioned Glasgow Corporation to have the entire greater Gorbals renamed Laurieston. Anthony Currie, chairman of the ward committee, explained: 'Because of books like *No Mean City* and plays such as *The Gorbals Story*, depicting us as living immoral lives in tumble-down tenements, visitors to Glasgow shun the district. It is true we have slums, some very bad, but compared with other parts of the city we are by no means the worst off.'

John Longmuir (21) suffered cuts to his hands when he went to the assistance of a woman who was being attacked by a man in a Nicholson Street back-court. The woman was taken to the Royal Infirmary with a severe throat wound. After the incident, David Barr was found dead with his throat cut open in a close in the same street – a short distance from the Glasgow police training school in Oxford Street.

At Buckingham Palace, two Tradeston men, John Johnston of Ardgowan Street and John McIndoe of Weir Street, received George Medals for their bravery in averting catastrophe at the British Oxygen Company's factory in Helen Street. The men had dragged a smouldering acetylene cylinder into the factory yard and dived for cover shortly before it exploded.

The Coliseum cinema was the venue for the Scottish premiere

of the film version of *The Gorbals Story*, made on a shoestring budget by New World Pictures Ltd at Merton Park studios in London. Before the film – starring Russell Hunter, Roddy MacMillan and other members of the Glasgow Unity Players – was released, censors 'got to work on the earthy language of the Gorbals', and the movie was consequently described as slow, jerky and dull. It did however contain one gem of *cinéma vérité*; Roddy MacMillan washing his feet in a kitchen jawbox (sink).

The overcrowded slums of the Gorbals and other deprived districts of Glasgow had 2,829 new cases of pulmonary tuberculosis, the highest number since 1910. Two men, one armed with a handgun, the other brandishing a cut-throat razor, menaced Lilian Ross in her father's pawnshop in Houston Street, Tradeston, making off with £20. A 'shop bandit' who demanded money in Elizabeth Ford's general store in Hospital Street, Hutchesontown took to his heels when attacked by Brownie, her seven-month-old dog.

At the general election, William McGuinness stood in the Gorbals as an Irish anti-partition candidate. Bailie William Samuels was given a rough ride while campaigning for the Tory cause in the district. Praising the pre-NHS provision of medical care, Bailie Samuels said: 'We built wonderful hospitals.' A heckler replied: 'Aye, and Barnhill, the poorhouse.' Undeterred, Samuels went on: 'We built splendid housing schemes for the working class between the wars.' A heckler retorted: 'Aye, in Mosspark. In Giffnock. How about the Gorbals?' The seat was held for Labour by Mrs Alice Cullen, Britain's first woman Catholic MP.

In a post office in Eglinton Street, a man tried to pay for two ten-shilling postal orders with 'a split pound note', which consisted of only one side of a conventional Treasury note. Thieves hid in the George cinema in Crown Street, waited until it closed for the night, then blew open the safe, escaping with nearly £100. Among the most popular Gorbals watering holes were the Seaforth bar in Gorbals Street, the Victoria bar in Crown Street and Vogt's bar in South Portland Street.

1951 BLISTERING SORE

Ordered out of condemned tenements in Cavendish Street and Cavendish Place, twenty Gorbals families carrying babies, bedding and furniture forced their way through barbed wire into Cowglens military hospital and took possession of empty huts. The squatters were driven out by Royal Army Medical Corps camp police with Alsatian dogs. Mrs Isa Gregory complained that her twenty-month-old daughter was asleep in her cot when the soldiers burst into the hut and began to remove beds and chairs. Alexander Dalrymple claimed that he was kicked and beaten when he tried to prevent the soldiers from removing his wife and five-year-old son from a hut. The squatters reported that a young squaddie who refused to help evict them from the camp was marched off to the guardroom. After the families had been packed into buses and sent back to the Gorbals, soldiers patrolled the grounds with dogs in case any squatters had stayed behind.

Glasgow Corporation refused to bow to a request by the Gorbals ward committee and rename the greater Gorbals district 'Laurieston', in spite of the area's fearsome reputation. The Gorbals ward had a population of around 36,000 with an average housing density of 154 persons per acre. Nearly 42 per cent of the population of the area were living more than two per room. Less than half of the houses had an indoor lavatory and less than one in ten had a plumbed-in bath. Councillor McPherson-Rait, Glasgow's housing convener, described the Gorbals as 'the blistering sore in the heart of Glasgow' and promised the people of the district 'modern, multi-storey flats with central heating, lifts, plenty of space for the children to play and tree-lined streets'. Mrs Cissie Leitch of Commercial Road said: 'It would be heaven to live in such flats. We would be proud to live in the new Gorbals.'

Gorbals war hero Johnny Ramensky was jailed for five years for blowing open a safe in Cardonald post office and stealing £410. Mr Ramensky explained that he needed the money to pay for his forthcoming wedding to attractive Gorbals widow Mrs Lily Mulholland.

After successive waves of vandalism, the historic Gorbals burial ground in Rutherglen Road was reported to be 'more like a battlefield'. Iron memorials to Waterloo veterans had been 'smashed to smithereens'. With 90 per cent of memorials beyond repair, Glasgow Corporation decided to turn the graveyard into a 'garden of rest', with some eighteenth-century stones preserved around the retaining wall. Harry Cowan, a small trader with premises in Hospital Street, was fined £10 for overcharging on hire-purchase transactions. In his defence, Cowan told the court that he had to cover his risk: 'One woman actually took five years to pay for a rug.'

At Glasgow Sheriff Court, police sergeant Andrew Hislop told how a nineteen-year-old girl had been found with a bayonet beneath her coat after rival gangs had run amok with knives, bayonets and bottles in Abbotsford Place, Bedford Street and South Portland Street. Sergeant Hislop said: 'It is sometimes the custom of people engaged in gang fights to pass on a weapon to a woman to keep it out of sight.' During the mêlée, the neds assaulted several innocent bystanders, including a twelve-year-old girl, who had seven stitches inserted in a head wound. One of the accused, Christina Boyle, the mother of a child of eleven months, admitted that she'd been 'pretty well-on' after drinking whisky, beer and 'cheap red wine'. She was sent to prison for six months, while sentences of up to two years were imposed on four youths.

Old Gorbals boy Tommy Docherty was awarded his first cap when he turned out for Scotland at Hampden Park against Wales. Glasgow Corporation decided to close the grim model-lodging-house in Portugal Street because it was 'the most uneconomic one to run' and was 'in a very poor state'. One councillor described the Portugal Street dosshouse as 'the last stage of moral degradation'.

1952 MUSICAL MENORAHS

Mrs Jean Dunn of Ballater Street won a coveted television set in a competition organised by the Scottish Co-op Wholesale Society. A twelve-inch telly cost around £67, with many working men taking home a wage of less than £7 a week. A fifteen-year-old youth, described as a 'scar-faced razor slasher from the Gorbals', was sentenced to two years' detention – the maximum sentence possible at his age – for three razor attacks. The youth waved cheerily to his friends as he went from the dock to the cells. Thieves stole a lorry loaded with eight cases of rationed tea from the Clyde Shipping Company, Carlton Place. Four men had to receive hospital treatment after rival gangs fought with bayonets and chisels in Gorbals Street. The Talmud Torah in Turriff Street invited students to 'Learn Hebrew and forge a link with Israel'. Whitberg's of Gorbals Street offered for sale 'musical menorahs' (seven-branched candelabra). The Great Synagogue in South Portland Street was described as a stronghold of religious orthodoxy.

Gorbals recidivist Johnny Ramensky escaped from top security Peterhead prison with his memoirs – written in school exercise-books – tucked inside his shirt. He was at liberty for only forty-seven hours. Sentencing Michael Duffin to thirty days in prison for throwing a bottle at a busload of Rangers supporters at Gorbals Cross, the magistrate said: 'You are the kind of man who is just a perfect pest, a man who is not a sportsman but thinks he is.' Marie Josephine Daniels of dilapidated Crown Street married James Morgan McKelvie, son of an American millionaire. After word got out that he practised faith-healing, Revd John Cameron Peddie (65), famous for his work with pre-war Gorbals gangs, was deluged with requests for help. Revd Peddie said: 'I don't want this publicity. But it has not quenched the spirit. The healing will go on.'

1953 QUEEN OF FLORENCE STREET

A self-styled housing official called on Mrs Mary Duffy of Hospital Street and promised to 'put a house her way' for £10. Mrs Duffy raised the money, and the 'official' handed over a key to a house in a new council scheme. The key fitted the lock and Mrs Duffy moved in, only to be ejected later when the 'official' turned out to be a crook. Martin Tait was jailed for eighteen months for 'cruel' frauds on people who were desperate to escape from the slums. Tait left his Kirkcaldy home every day to carry out his scam in the most deprived areas of Glasgow.

Five men died when fire swept through Leon & Company's upholstery warehouse in Ballater Street. Four of the men, including the managing director, had tried to reach the roof to fight the fire with extinguishers when they were trapped in a blazing hoist. For their heroic attempts to reach the doomed men, officers of the Glasgow fire brigade received three George Medals and two British Empire Medals. In Portugal Street, two young women – one armed with an axe, the other wielding a bottle – joined three male accomplices in chasing six or seven youths towards Gorbals Cross. Sentencing one of the girls to fourteen days, Bailie John Mains said that the axe was 'a well-known weapon in the Gorbals'.

Housing officials planning slum clearance and redevelopment in Hutchesontown and Gorbals were uncertain what to do about the district's pubs; since the 1890s, the city fathers had refused to allow pubs in municipal housing developments. A score of families were warned out of their tenement flats when fire swept through the Coutts Gordon paper store in Tradeston Street. Communist stalwart 'Red Harry' McShane, who led hunger marchers through the Gorbals during the grim years of the 1930s, resigned from the party after having been a member for over thirty years. Said Mr McShane: 'For quite a while now I have been dissatisfied with the way things are being run in the Scottish Communist Party.'

In the House of Commons, Gorbals MP Mrs Alice Cullen demanded that steps be taken to stop the sale of single ends in condemned tenement properties. People bought the tiny flats in order to jump the housing queue. Armed with a bread bin, Mrs Elizabeth Moffat fought off a housebreaker who'd broken into her ground-floor flat in Gorbals Street and seriously injured her elderly and partially blind mother. The man escaped but was later apprehended by police.

In preparation for the Coronation celebrations, the men, women and children of Kinning Street, Tradeston scrubbed graffiti from grimy tenement walls and decorated the bleak street with fairy lights and bunting. A Bridge Street hire-purchase firm promised to deliver and install television sets 'up till six p.m. on Coronation Eve'. Eight-year-old Margaret Turnbull was crowned queen of a Coronation street party attended by 120 children in Florence Street. In Norfolk Street, Laurieston a woman passenger on a Riddrie-bound tram was attacked and beaten by four women who had boarded the vehicle in Tradeston. The ladies from hell jumped from the tram, hailed a passing taxi and made a clean getaway.

With the Gorbals Jewish community shrinking in size, the Beth Jacob synagogue in Abbotsford Place closed and the congregation merged with that of the Chevra Kadisha synagogue in Buchan Street. The Indo-Pakistani communities of Glasgow numbered about five hundred, of which around four hundred lived in the Gorbals. Over 90 per cent of the immigrants were engaged in the drapery business.

After climbing forty feet onto a garage roof to retrieve a football, ten-year-old Jimmy McMenemy of Commerce Street had to be rescued by firemen using a turntable ladder. Having toured the slums of the Gorbals and other inner-city black-spots, an English tuberculosis specialist said: 'It struck me that many of the people living in those houses might just as well be housed in a coal mine. I shall never again wonder why Glasgow has the health problem that it has.'

1954 GORBALS VAMPIRE

In Thistle Street, two small children, Billy and Christina Quinn, were buried under plaster and soot when a chimney stack tore through the roof of their bedroom during a ninety-seven miles-per-hour January gale. A neighbour, fifteen-year-old Sam Nichol, tunnelled his way through the debris and rescued the infants.

Residents in Caledonia Road called police to complain about a disturbance caused by hundreds of children pouring into the Southern Necropolis in Caledonia Road in search of 'a vampire with iron teeth', which they believed had killed and eaten two wee boys. Nine-year-old Margaret Boyle of Caledonia Road said that she was told by bigger boys that a monster was roaming in the graveyard. Some of the children were so upset that their mothers had to give them sedatives to put them to sleep. Constable Alex Deeprose said afterwards: 'When I appeared I felt like the Pied Piper of Hamelin. All shapes and sizes of children streamed after me, all talking at once, and telling me of the "vampire with the iron teeth". This I could handle, but when grown-ups approached me and asked earnestly, "Is there anything in this vampire story?" it made me think.' Mr Edward Cusick, headmaster of St Bonaventure's RC primary school in Braehead Street, gathered all the pupils together to reassure them that the vampire story was absurd. Bailie John Mains claimed that American horror comics such as *Tales from the Crypt* were responsible for the 'vampire' scare.

Ian Brady, the future 'moors murderer', reared in the Gorbals by foster parents, appeared at Glasgow Sheriff Court on nine charges of housebreaking and theft. He was put on probation on condition that he went to live with his natural mother in Manchester. He duly arrived on her doorstep with his personal belongings, which included Nazi memorabilia and books on the occult.

Children, described as the pick of all the Sunday Schools in the Gorbals, broadcast a BBC children's hour concert of hymns from the partly-blitzed Lloyd Morris Memorial church in Rutherglen

Road. James Stuart, the Tory secretary of state for Scotland, refused a Labour MP's invitation to tour the slums of the Gorbals.

Members of Glasgow housing committee, led by deputy town clerk William Gordon and city architect and planner Archibald George Jury, travelled to Marseilles to inspect Le Corbusier's controversial high-rise flats with a view to building something similar in the Gorbals. Mr Gordon said: 'We are going with quite an open mind and have decided nothing in advance.' The deputation decided that the Frenchman's *Unité d' Habitation* wasn't quite what they had in mind but they didn't rule out skyscraper flats entirely.

Ann Howat, fifteen, of Lawmoor Street, out for a walk with her three-year-old sister Helen, was dragged into a Fauldhouse Street, Oatlands, back-court and beaten unconscious by a gang of teenage girls. In populous Tradeston Street, quick action by firefighters prevented a fire from reaching vats of oil in the Anchor Oil Works. Three men, armed with a gun, razor and crowbar, burst into Sultan Asari's shop in Nicholson Street, Laurieston and bludgeoned his nephew and shop manager Wali Mohammed. The men bound and gagged Mohammed and a girl assistant and escaped with £700. A model of the proposed new Hutchesontown-Gorbals went on show at the Modern Homes Exhibition in the Kelvin Hall.

1955 JUST ANOTHER RAMMY

Jimmy Cairns (89), known throughout the Gorbals as Papa, died when fire gutted his tiny flat in Surrey Street, Laurieston. Born of Irish parents in the US state of Missouri, he came to the district in the 1900s and, with his brother Johnny, went on stage as the Brothers Emmett, a blacked-up minstrel act. Every Fourth of July, Papa Cairns hung out Old Glory in the Gorbals to celebrate Independence Day.

In Rutherglen Road, a policeman and a policewoman chased a borstal escapee who appeared to be armed with an automatic pistol. The youth fired several shots before he was cornered in a Florence Street back-court. The gun proved to be a starter's pistol loaded with blank cartridges. Policewoman Isabella Rankin was awarded the British Empire Medal for her part in the arrest.

Six hoodlums called at an address in Nicholson Street and seriously injured John Lynn, a young unemployed man, with broken bottles. Lynn's wife Cathie tried to come to his rescue but was knocked semiconscious to the ground. The men escaped before police reached the scene. In the Mayfair café in Caledonia Road, a young ned smashed a bottle over proprietor Peter Gizza's head and snatched a few coppers from the till. In a café in Gorbals Street, three young tearaways fought with broken bottles. The youths did a bunk before the police arrived, but they were nabbed when they turned up at the Royal and Victoria infirmaries to have their injuries patched up. In Camden Street, thugs slashed a young woman on both cheeks and robbed her of £150. At Glasgow High Court, a witness described a bottle assault in the Gorbals as just another rammy. In Thistle Street, fourteen young thugs attacked two women who had ignored their whistles and catcalls.

Hugh Payne of Abbotsford Place told a reporter how a huge chunk of plaster fell from the ceiling and came within inches of hitting his two-year-old son, who was asleep in his cot. Payne, an ex-Seaforth Highlander, said: 'I'm desperate for a decent home for my wife and kids and I'm willing to pay for it. Until recently I was paying over £1 a week for this sublet until we went to the rent tribunal. It now costs eight shillings. We're frightened to go to bed at night for the rats and the chance of part of the ceiling falling on us.'

Gorbals-born tycoon Isaac Wolfson – boss of Great Universal Stores and one of eleven children of Solomon and Necha Wolfson, who had emigrated to Scotland from Bialystok in the Ukraine – established the £6 million Wolfson Foundation to fund education projects and medical research. When Wolfson was only nine years old, his father declared: 'I am not much good at business but I have a son who is a financial genius.'

A Gorbals woman who gatecrashed a wake in a South Portland Street house had to fork out £2 with the alternative of ten days in jail. In Florence Street, David Alexander, alone in his fish-and-chip shop, was punched and kicked by three thugs who made off with

£16. Mr Alexander heard one of the men say: 'I can't find the cash, use the razor on him.' In Nicholson Street, two hoodlums assaulted Indian peddler Naka Alm and escaped with £3. Tram conductress Cathie McGloin was punched and kicked by a passenger as the tram was passing Thistle Street. Two policemen saw the incident, hopped on the vehicle and arrested the attacker, who had told Cathie that he didn't like her Irish brogue.

Safecracker Johnny Ramensky and two confederates raided a bank at Oban and got away with £8,000. Ramensky gambled away his share of the loot and, within weeks, received a ten-year sentence for a raid on a bank in Rutherglen. Police sought a 'mystery boy', after four-year-old Bernadette Sweeney of Marinch Street, Tradeston drowned in the Kingston Dock. Lorry driver John Bell – a non-swimmer – risked his life in a vain attempt to save the little girl. At Govan Juvenile Court, a nine-year-old boy 'with fair hair and rosy cheeks', charged with murdering Bernadette by pushing her off the quay, was remitted to Glasgow Sheriff Court.

In Hutchesontown, 87 per cent of the flats had only one or two rooms. Only 3 per cent of the houses had a fixed bath and less than a quarter had an internal water closet. In the general election, Mrs Alice Cullen held the Gorbals for Labour with 22,567 votes. The Communist candidate came second with over 11,000 votes.

1956   RAT HUNT

After a rat bit six-year-old Annette Wilson in a condemned Florence Street tenement, her mother said: 'I've lived in this house for fourteen years, and the place has been infested with rats all that time. My husband has caught more than forty rats in the house.' Camden Street tenants' leader Robert Miller complained that Alice Cullen MP had done nothing to 'clear the street of its army of rats'. An angry Mrs Cullen retorted that the only way the rats could be eliminated was by demolishing the slums. Four teenage residents of Florence Street – John Kinnaird, Michael McDonald, William McMann and Dicky Dawson – organised a rat hunt and the children of the area killed 119 rodents. One wee boy told a reporter: 'I hadn't anything to hit them with, but I got three with my feet.'

Bank manager Dan McKellar described the Gorbals as the Soho of Glasgow and enthused: 'I've got clients from Israel, Ireland, Austria, Latvia, India, the Lebanon, Italy and Pakistan.' With the Jewish population of the area in terminal decline, the New Central synagogue in Hospital Street closed and its congregation merged with that of the Great Synagogue in South Portland Street to form the Great Central Synagogue. A spokesman for Glasgow Corporation announced that in the rebuilt Hutchesontown-Gorbals – the city's 'future dream town' – only 57 shops would be provided in place of the existing 440. There would be only 9 pubs in place of the existing 47.

Police stepped up patrols in the Gorbals after James Patrick Lavelle (53) was murdered in the flat behind his tiny newsagent's shop in Caledonia Road; as a result, the tough district was reported to be silent and law-abiding. When found by his elderly father, Mr Lavelle was bound head and foot. Detectives discovered that the intruders had missed £50 hidden under floorboards and about £20 concealed in Mr Lavelle's bed. Five local men were charged with robbery and murder and committed to Barlinnie but were later set free. In the wake of the murder, described as the climax to a year of violence in the Gorbals, local shopkeepers sent a telegram to Sir Anthony Eden, the prime minister, urging the retention of the death penalty. Gorbals traders told reporters that they lived in fear of hoodlums who operated a protection racket. One shopkeeper said: 'I have been threatened about six times, and each time I have told them to clear off. On one occasion several weeks ago a man returned to my shop and broke the windows.'

The death was reported of former British and European flyweight boxing champion, William Elky Clark. Born in Mathieson Street, Gorbals in 1906, he suffered a severe eye injury in 1927 while challenging Fidel a Barba for the world flyweight title in New York's Madison Square Garden, but carved out a new career for himself as the boxing correspondent of a Scottish daily newspaper. The women's section of the Jewish Institute in South Portland Street sought donations of clothing for North African immigrants travelling to Israel. In Gorbals Street, cinema crowds scattered as rival gangs fought with bayonets.

BBC producer David Thomson came to the Gorbals to record local children reciting 'their own native rhymes and jingles' for the Third Programme. Said Mr Thomson: 'The subjects ranged from Teddy Boys to bicycle-chain gangs.' After John Kerr was fined £15 for using his Nicholson Street flat as a shebeen, his wife told a reporter: 'For a while everybody was happy. Some of the people around here said it was great. If they had a "big head" on a Sunday, they were able to come here and get something to cure it.'

In Thistle Street, policemen were besieged by a hostile crowd in a police box after making several arrests. When a Black Maria arrived, it was pelted with bricks and bottles. The crowd managed to free a woman from the vehicle.

1957 ROCK 'N' ROLL SOCKS

Hutchesontown-Gorbals – where the population density was 458.6 persons per acre – became a Comprehensive Development Area, at 111 acres the largest in the United Kingdom. Prominent architects Robert Matthew and Basil Spence were appointed as design consultants, working in collaboration with Glasgow's city architect and planner, Archibald George Jury. The redevelopment was scheduled to take place in five phases.

BBC television's *Panorama* featured 'the £13 million Gorbals of the future' and interviewed one of forty-seven local publicans whose livelihoods were threatened by redevelopment. Representatives of Gorbals shopkeepers, schools and churches complained that the programme only showed 'the seamier side' of life in the district.

It was reported that, in a condemned tenement in Carnoustie Street, Tradeston the residents were plagued by rats and thieves: 'The rats terrorise the kids and women. The thieves steal lead piping and cause flooding.' In Camden Street, an elderly lamplighter encountered three rats on a stairhead landing. He threw his boots at them. When that didn't work, neighbours summoned passing beat policemen. The cops tucked their trousers into their boots and waded in with their batons. When Mrs Alice Everett of Thistle Street got up in the wee small hours to prepare milk for her baby, she found a live baby rat inside the bottle. Her screams woke her husband, who disposed of the rodent.

The Martin family of Elmfoot Street, Oatlands were able to exchange houses with a family who had stayed only one month in Castlemilk before deciding that they loathed the brand new peripheral housing estate. In the Paragon in Cumberland Street, an irate film fan attacked the pay box with a knife when told by the cashier that the cinema was full.

At a garage in Adelphi Street, work on a pit for a hydraulic car-lift was suspended when human remains were unearthed. Suspicion of foul play was allayed when detectives discovered the site had formerly been occupied by the graveyard attached to St Ninian's hospital for lepers, founded around 1345. In Rutherglen Road, a trendy young man held up a girl shop assistant at knife point and made off with two pairs of rock 'n' roll socks.

In a tenement close in Portugal Street, Laurieston a young boy watched helplessly as a gang of men attacked his father with bottles, struck him to the ground and kicked him senseless. In Rutherglen Road, a tenement stair was littered with broken glass after a 'terrific rammy'. Scores of policemen were rushed to Florence Street and Caledonia Road as the Gorbals experienced 'the worst night for gang warfare since the early nineteen-thirties'. An eyewitness, Mrs Martha McVenna, said later: 'One man with a bayonet ran through the close with four policemen after him. They caught him in Crown Street.'

The Gorbals Group, an experimental evangelical outreach to the people of the area, led by Geoffrey Shaw, a young Church of Scotland minister, was formally inaugurated at a communion service in a tenement flat in Abbotsford Lane. Born in 1927 to wealthy parents in Edinburgh, where his father was a pioneering plastic surgeon, Shaw had worked with drug addicts in the slum ghetto of New York's East Harlem.

Sadie McGuire of Abbotsford Place won a free ticket for rock 'n' roll sensation Bill Haley's live appearance on stage in the Odeon cinema, Renfield Street. On the first day of Glasgow's five-week campaign to screen citizens for tuberculosis using twenty-eight mobile X-ray units scattered throughout the city, priority was given at Hutchesontown to an eighty-year-old woman whose husband and son had died of the disease.

Pupils of Adelphi Terrace secondary school gathered to watch a fight between two of their schoolmates. The boys were armed with a hatchet and an iron bar. The arrival of a police patrol car put paid to the junior gladiatorial combat. In Shearer Street, Tradeston, hundreds of people had to flee their homes in the middle of the night when fire engulfed Scotland's largest flour mill, property of the Riverside Milling Company. James Kerr was enjoying a cup of tea in his Gorbals Street flat when a bottle crashed through his window. Said Mr Kerr: 'I ran down the stairs and saw a man whose face was very badly slashed. Another man came over and joined him. He had been slashed too. I advised them to go to the police.'

1958   ALL-ELECTRIC HOUSES

After a magistrate in Nairobi, Kenya, made a scathing reference to 'Gorbals gangsterism', Revd John Cameron Peddie of Hutcheson-town parish church, who knew more about Gorbals gangs than most people, said: 'I am going to write a polite letter to this man and put him right on a few points. His remarks are a slur on the area. There is no more gangsterism in this part of Glasgow than there is anywhere else in the country.' Writing in a Warsaw newspaper, an imaginative Polish Communist claimed that in the Gorbals he had found 'rows of murky tumble-down huts, lacking water and even the most primitive amenities'. At Glasgow Sheriff Court, an unemployed labourer of South Portland Street was jailed for nine months for stealing gas meters from tenement houses in Helen Street. To remove the meters, he cut the gas pipes, endangering families in the buildings.

In Kidston Street, a large crowd watched impassively as a gang of youths beat up two policemen. The cops were attacked because they tried to move along a crowd of jivers who were dancing in the street. Only one man tried to help the police: Roderick Charles, a black man known locally as Black Bob. He shoved his way into the mass of flailing arms and legs and helped the officers into a tenement flat, from where they were taken by ambulance to the Victoria Infirmary. Afterwards Mr Charles said: 'I have no real love for the police. But I couldn't stand by and see them battered like that.' Three of the attackers were caged for a total of twenty-four years. For keeping the young thugs at bay with his baton while his colleague – constable Bernard Thompson – lay unconscious, constable William Hazleton was later awarded the British Empire Medal.

Alice Cullen opened Hutchesontown Area A, the first stage of the Hutchesontown-Gorbals redevelopment. The 'modern, all-electric houses', in Ballater Place and Commercial Road, were described as 'a revolution in council design'. Mrs Isabella McHale couldn't believe her good luck: 'After twenty years of sharing an outside lavatory, I'm in seventh heaven at the very thought of a bathroom to ourselves.' Mrs Mary McFadyen agreed: 'I just can't believe it's true.' Glasgow Corporation approved Sir Basil Spence's 'revolutionary' scheme for high-rise blocks in the Gorbals. The city's housing convener said: 'There is no design like this in this country or anywhere else.' The fashionable architect enthused: 'When all the washing is out it'll be like a great ship in full sail.'

In a crumbling tenement in Thistle Street, a seven-month-old baby boy had a narrow escape when plaster rained down on his cot. A budding slum landlord who lived in a Drumchapel council house purchased a condemned tenement in Camden Street, Gorbals – for £5. In a Florence Street back-court, fifty teenage boys and girls watched two boys fight with studded belts. A police spokesman said: 'These kids come from a nearby school and the fight between the two neds was probably to see who would boss the school gang.'

Old Gorbals boy Tommy Docherty was transferred from Preston North End to London giants Arsenal for the not inconsiderable sum of £27,000. After five thugs brutally attacked a man as he walked through the Gorbals, police described the incident as 'the worst assault for some time'. Mrs Marjory Park of Florence Street sent her four young children to live with relations and neighbours because her house was infested with rats. Said Mrs Park: 'They have beaten me, and now my family is split up.'

Following in the footsteps of many other Glasgow Catholics, Gorbals-born Pat Crerand signed for his beloved Celtic. Reared in a room-and-kitchen flat – where he shared a bed with three siblings – Pat was brought up single-handedly by his mother, his father having been killed in an air raid during the Second World War. For the young man life in the Gorbals was often less than idyllic. Sickening violence, he later recalled, was commonplace: 'there were public houses on nearly every corner and when men came out of them at night they stood around, they argued and they fought . . . with fists, or bottles, hatchets or knifes.' And the violence was compounded by deep religious divisions: 'The first thing you learned was that were two kinds of people in the world – Catholics and Protestants', a point that was driven home when he worked as an apprentice welder in Fairfields shipyard, a place racked by sectarian strife.

Despite these problems Crerand retained great affection for the Gorbals of his childhood: 'There were many wonderful people in the Gorbals. They would give you their last penny; they would do anything for anyone in trouble.' It was a lesson Crerand learned well and, after he became famous, he often tried to help those less fortunate than himself. On one occasion he went to Glasgow's notorious Barlinnie prison – with the great Jim Baxter of Rangers – for a football quiz with prisoners. To his astonishment, Crerand discovered that he knew most of the inmates from the old days in the Gorbals.

After a jewel robbery in Ayr, the car used in the crime was found parked in Camden Street in the Gorbals. When a detective inspector and three other officers entered one of the houses in the street, they discovered three men and the stolen jewellery. In the fierce struggle that ensued one of the men fired a revolver, wounding a policeman. Six men later appeared in the High Court; three were found guilty and received sentences of nine, eight and seven years.

Safe-blower and war hero Johnny Ramensky, who'd been

sentenced to ten years 'preventive detention' in 1955, made three escapes from Peterhead prison. In all, he had broken out of the top-security nick five times, the first occasion being in 1934. The John Knox Free Church in Surrey Street – the church of Revd John Buchan, father of the famous novelist – was up for sale described as 'suitable for storage'. The Paragon picture house in Cumberland Street, opened in 1912, closed down. There were around twenty Indo-Pak drapery warehouses in the Gorbals.

Frank Kerr (71), a local character known as Lord Mayor of the Gorbals, died after being attacked in the close leading to his Thistle Street flat and robbed of £4. 16s. His assailant was never brought to justice. Blast-furnace operations at Dixon's Iron Works in Crown Street were suspended and three hundred men were made redundant because of reduced demand for pig iron consequent on the fall in demand for steel.

1959   DANDY MACKAY

Hundreds of fans greeted the new British middleweight boxing champion John 'Cowboy' McCormack when he arrived home to his tiny Florence Street flat, which was only yards from Benny Lynch's old home. Rows of flags were strung across the street, and pride of place went to a huge 'welcome champion' banner. McCormack won the title at Wembley, when Londoner Terry Downes was disqualified in the eighth round.

Gorbals-born career criminal Samuel 'Dandy' Mackay, awaiting trial in Barlinnie prison in connection with a £38,000 bank robbery, escaped from the hospital block by cutting through an iron bar with a hacksaw blade and went 'underground'. A life of crime had taken Mackay from his bleak Florence Street birthplace to a luxury bungalow in Netherlee, Renfrewshire. The Gorbals Group, led by Revd Geoff Shaw, turned the Kingdom hall, an old Jehovah's Witness hall in Abbotsford Lane, into a multi-purpose clubhouse for local people. A newly-born baby girl, found lying on the floor of a communal water closet in a condemned tenement in Sandyfaulds Street, was taken to the Royal Maternity Hospital, Rottenrow.

Adelphi Street residents had to walk almost a mile for their mail because postmen refused to wade through stagnant water to reach their homes. Bill Harris told a reporter: 'Sanitary officials have been here, but nothing has been done. And for this I am paying a rent of £4. 2s. 6d. a month.' Lily Robertson said: 'I have lived here all my life. Once it was a building anyone would have been proud to live in. Now it is a nightmare.'

In Camden Street, two thugs forced their way into David Schumaker's flat, tied him up, and made off with £40, the takings from his fruit shop in nearby Thistle Street. Detectives raced to the Diamond dance club in Gorbals Street after a young man was found seriously injured in a cloakroom. Crumbling Gorbals tenements, neglected by absentee landlords, were becoming a menace to life and limb: in Eglinton Street, a young policeman was seriously injured when a chimney stack crashed to the pavement. When Jimmy Murphy (74) returned to the Gorbals from a convalescent home, he found that neighbours had refurnished and redecorated his Caledonia Road flat with funds raised from dances and whist drives. Two skiffle groups, performing on the back of a lorry on a vacant site in Thistle Street, raised £28 to help pay for a pensioners' bus trip.

In Hallside Street, twelve angry families who had been without water for a week appealed to their MP. Spokesman Robert McLellan said: 'Already one child has been taken to hospital with dysentery.' The Govan Iron Works in Crown Street – also known as Dixon's Blazes – which had illuminated the night sky over the Gorbals for 120 years, closed down for good. Founded in 1839 by industrialist William Dixon, it was the last blast-furnace plant to operate within the city boundary. In Cumberland Street, neds mugged peddler Mohammed Ismail as he walked home to Abbotsford Place and made off with his case of samples. Mr Ismail said: 'Three men came running up behind me and I was punched on the back of the neck. I fell down and they snatched my case and ran through the closes in a condemned building.'

Hutcheson's boys' grammar school, founded in 1650 by two Glasgow worthies, George and Thomas Hutcheson, and situated in Crown Street, Gorbals, since 1841, moved to the pleasant southern suburb of Pollokshields. Among the old boys of the school were novelist John Buchan and Independent Labour Party stalwart James Maxton. William Cowan, a street busker, was playing Christmas carols on his accordion in Crown Street when thugs attacked him and all but severed his jugular vein.

1960 GORBALS BEATNIKS

Denying reports that there was a colour bar in Glasgow, Allister McLeod, headmaster of Gorbals primary school said: 'There is certainly no discrimination. The chief reaction of the white children is to help the others.' Purnam Singhpall of Logan Street agreed: 'My children are loved by their schoolteachers. They're happy and have the chance of a good education.'

Two members of the Gorbals Cumbie gang were sent to jail after gang members, brandishing hatchets and bottles, 'cut a swathe of terror' through the district. A police spokesman said: 'There are about forty members in the Cumbie gang, and most of them live in the area. They hang about Cumberland Street and cause trouble. There are times when they try to extort money from betting shops, but with little luck. But they extort the occasional fiver or tenner from street bookies as "protection".'

Revd Geoff Shaw, described as a secular Gorbals monk, moved into a two-room-and-kitchen flat in a dilapidated tenement at 74 Cleland Street. Soon local people were beating a path to his ever-open door, and the flat became 'one of the busiest addresses in the west of Scotland'. With other members of the evangelical Gorbals Group, Revd Shaw helped to halt evictions and organise rent strikes to force landlords to carry out essential repairs. Like fellow minister Revd Cameron Peddie in the 1930s, he also worked with local juvenile delinquents.

Thomas Ward, fifteen months, and his sister Elizabeth, eight, were rushed to hospital after being bitten by rats while they slept in their Mathieson Street home. A neighbour, Mrs Annie Gill, said: 'When I look out of my window it's like a scene from the Dark Ages.'

Mrs Lillian Hill, a sixty-three-year-old widow, was watching telly when her top-floor home in Gilmour Street, Oatlands, began to tumble about her as the walls collapsed. Tenants had to move in with friends and relations as workmen prepared to demolish the dangerous tenement property. A reporter took a Sunday-morning stroll through the Gorbals just as people were heading for church. He saw 'numerous well-scrubbed children with white socks and gloves and noted that the accompanying parents were 'correspondingly neat and clean'. Two Gorbals men, Edward McNulty of Buchan Street and Alexander Gallacher of Thistle Street, lost their lives while working on the new Clyde tunnel. Mr McNulty, nicknamed the 'tunnel tiger', died of a broken back, while his colleague was buried by a rockfall some eighty feet below the surface.

Police made a dawn swoop on a luxury bungalow near Dublin and arrested Samuel 'Dandy' Mackay. At Glasgow High Court, Mackay was sentenced to ten years imprisonment for his part in a Shettleston bank robbery. Sent to Craiginches Prison in Aberdeen, he went on hunger strike before settling down to work in the prison kitchen. Gorbals constable Willie Hazelton, holder of the British Empire Medal and with twelve commendations for police work, quit the force after twelve years on the beat because of low pay. Said Willie: 'I could only average £13 a week as a cop. Now I'm fixed up with a TV firm with almost double the wages – and a car into the bargain.'

After an intruder broke into the clubhouse of St Francis Boys' Guild in Errol Street and smashed a television set, Father Aquinas O'Connel said: 'It took the boys almost two years to raise the seventy-five guineas for the set. I hope that the boys will show the same spirit as in the past and some day they might be able to buy another set.' Giving evidence in Glasgow Sheriff Court, after a gang of 'Gorbals beatniks' ran amok in the district, a detective said that the beatniks were 'dressed in dark jackets, with denims, and long untidy hair'. In West Street, three teenage girls threatened a shopkeeper with an axe and made off with a collection box. The conscience-stricken tearaways later walked into Gorbals police office and gave themselves up. In thick fog in Camden Street, a ned grabbed fifteen-year-old Margaret Muirhead's shopping bag, punched her in the face and made his escape with her family's £10 housekeeping money.

Learning that hole-in-heart girl Helen Cumstie of Devon Street needed thirty-six pints of blood, while blood-bank supplies were running low, her neighbours asked the Blood Transfusion Service to send a mobile unit to Abbotsford primary school, where 120 people turned up to donate blood. Police had to call out reinforcements when a free-for-all fight broke out at Gorbals Cross. Gorbals licensed grocers sold 'Melroso, the full strength wine with the rich, deep-down glow of pleasure'.

1961 NEW-LOOK GORBALS

Glasgow Corporation handed out a £1.3 million contract for Sir Basil Spence's 'new look Gorbals'. The top architect had made a special trip to Marseilles to glean ideas from Le Corbusier's *Unité d'Habitation*. A Corporation spokesman said: 'These flats can be taken as the key style of the new Gorbals.'

After it was announced that the Queen would pay a visit to 'the showpiece section of the Gorbals', MP Alice Cullen suggested that the monarch should 'see the worst as well as the best' part of the district. Mrs Margaret Kilpatrick, aged seventy, who had been rehoused in a three-apartment maisonette after spending forty-five years in a tenement in Lawmoor Street, said: 'I'd be delighted to meet the bonny lass and tell her what a wonderful place the Gorbals is.'

When word got round that the Queen was likely to visit a condemned tenement in Sandyfaulds Street, women scrubbed out closes and removed graffiti from walls. The monarch looked round Catherine Dempsey's tiny single end in the street and asked in astonishment: 'Is this all you have?' Mrs Dempsey, whose husband was a machine operator in a brick-works, later said: 'I think she was amazed at the smallness of the house.' In another single end in the same street, Mrs Elizabeth Meek told the Duke of Edinburgh that the floorboards were giving way and warned him to take care. The Duke looked around Mrs Jean Percy's living room in a new all-electric flat in Commercial Row and asked: 'Is this all on the never-never?' Proudly Mrs Percy replied: 'Not at all, everything is paid for.'

The Queen was shown a model of Sir Basil Spence's Area C high-rise development, consisting of a single and two linked slab-blocks, and told that every family would 'have a garden at their back door, even at twenty-storey level.' As the royal party toured the area, a snotty young equerry remarked: 'We'd all heard so much about the Gorbals. We imagined we'd be walking through three feet of mud.'

Unveiling plans for a new industrial estate on the site of the Govan Iron Works, better known as Dixon's Blazes, Harold McCue, chairman of Taylor Woodrow Industrial Estates, announced that the name would be retained because 'it has been used by generations of Glasgow people and is too striking to lose'. Endorsing the project – which it was hoped would provide factory units employing up to ten thousand local people – councillor George Robertson, the city's planning convener, said it was 'an answer to those who said that industry was being driven out of the city by overspill'.

After ten-months-old Elizabeth Walsh was bitten by a rat in her home in Thistle Street, her father said that it was not unusual for rats to come out and watch him eat his lunch. When a police officer visited the flat, a rat scampered across the floor in front of him. The constable threw his baton at the rodent, but missed.

There were 98.9 persons per acre in the Gorbals, compared with 11.9 in Pollokshields and 18.7 in Kelvinside. After 'pep pills' were consumed at a party in Nicholson Street, a teenage boy died and six people were rushed to the Victoria Infirmary. The dead boy's mother said the pills had been circulating in the Gorbals for months: 'They've been taken by people who are out of work and can't afford to buy drink.' After neds wrecked the Maccabi Jewish youth club in Turriff Street, its chairman Josh Khan said: 'We don't think the vandals had any spite against the Jewish community. The types who wrecked this place would wreck anything.'

Ex-Gorbalite Tommy Docherty became player-coach of Chelsea FC at the age of thirty-three. Under his tutelage, the team won the

League Cup and also reached the FA Cup final and the semi-final of the UEFA Cup. After veteran Gorbals GP Dr Gladstone Robertson claimed that the people of the district were too lazy to get rheumatism, Mrs Ellen McMurry of West Street, Tradeston, who raised eight children and had worked during the Second World War cleaning buses in all weather conditions, said: 'I've had rheumatism ever since.'

1962 HANGING GARDENS

After a gale-blown chimney stack crashed through the ceiling of their home in South Portland Street, Mr and Mrs Black had to distribute their family of four sons and two daughters among relations and neighbours. The Blacks had been on the Corporation housing list since 1946. The Lynch family had to vacate their flat in Norfolk Street and move in with relations while men from the Corporation's sanitary department tried to deal with a plague of rats.

Opening a high-rise block in Adelphi Street the Tory secretary of state for Scotland, Michael Noble, said: 'People in Glasgow have a picture of the Gorbals. It is often a bad one and a wrong one. Here, ladies and gentlemen, the world is going to see the real miracle of the Gorbals.' Norway's King Olav, on a state visit to Scotland, insisted on seeing 'the slums of Glasgow's Gorbals'. The King looked on benignly as an old Gorbals tenement bit the dust, a few yards from Sir Basil Spence's rising slab blocks.

As buildings were demolished all around him, Hugh Fyfe (82), a First World War veteran, refused to move out of his home in a partly demolished tenement in Mathieson Street. Hugh said: 'The Jerries couldn't scare me, and neither can the Corporation.' In South Portland Street, twenty people barely escaped with their lives when the rear wall of a condemned tenement split in two, sending tons of masonry crashing to the back-court. Seven families made homeless by the collapse were taken to Foresthall, a former poorhouse.

Sir Basil Spence OM – Britain's most successful modern architect – defended his controversial Gorbals slab blocks, where large balcony spaces were provided so that the tenants could have 'hanging gardens in the sky'. He said: 'I aimed at houses where each had its own garden, no matter how high.' The hanging gardens never materialised, and fortunately Sir Basil – a bon viveur who loved big cigars and vintage wines – never had to live in the slab blocks, which soon became a nightmare for residents. When an Edinburgh property company revealed plans for a shopping centre, to be built at the foot of the Area C development, local people were distinctly underwhelmed. Bus driver John Trainer of Cumberland Street said: 'It's a liberty. They give you a choice of flats when they throw you out. Take it or leave it.'

Released from prison on five days' parole under a training-for-freedom scheme, Johnny Ramensky – who had spent thirty years of his life behind bars – went home to his wife's flat in Eglinton Street. Born into a Lithuanian immigrant family in 1905, he had moved to the Gorbals with his mother and sisters during the inter-war depression and then drifted into a life of crime. The Glasgow Jewish Blind Society was established in Thistle Street to offer 'comfort and friendship' to sightless and partially sighted people of the Jewish faith. Old Gorbals boy Isaac Wolfson, described as one of the greatest living philanthropists, was honoured with a baronetcy.

After twelve years on the Corporation housing list, Bill and Catherine McCafferty moved with their three children from a tiny room-and-kitchen flat in a crumbling tenement in Pine Street, Hutchesontown, to a flat in a seventeen-storey block in Commercial Court. Mrs Jean Cairney, a middle-aged woman of no fixed abode, was found battered to death in a derelict tenement in Adelphi Street, overlooking the river Clyde at Albert bridge. A police spokesman said that the condemned building 'may have been used for hooch parties'. On the day Mrs Cairney's body was discovered, a man jumped to his death from the Albert bridge and his body was recovered by Ben Parsonage of the Glasgow Humane Society.

Peddler Bashir Mohammed was rushed to the Victoria Infirmary after being stabbed in the back outside his home in South Portland Street. After Scotland beat England 2–0 at Hampden, Celtic halfback Paddy Crerand paid tribute to his pal Jim Baxter of Rangers, saying: 'He was tremendous. Jim was the best player on the park.' In

Frankfurt, West Germany, John 'Cowboy' McCormack retained his European middleweight title, beating his opponent on points.

After the congregation of the 106-year-old Caledonia Road church dissolved, the Glasgow presbytery of the Church of Scotland asked Glasgow Corporation if they were interested in purchasing the category 'A' listed building, the work of world-famous architect Alexander 'Greek' Thomson. The Coliseum cinema, which had started life as an upmarket music hall, became Scotland's only Cinerama theatre with a super-wide, wrap-around screen.

1963 GORBALS HERMIT

While out for an evening stroll with their baby son, Donald and Patricia Kesson of Norfolk Street were attacked by a razor-wielding thug. The Kessons were rushed to the Victoria Infirmary with face wounds. Their attacker escaped. A police spokesman said: 'This was a savage crime, apparently without motive.' The evangelical Gorbals Group took over the disused St John's RC primary school in Nicholson Street and turned it into a youth centre, with facilities for arts and crafts, sports and games.

In Riddrie cemetery, there was a large turnout for the funeral of Mrs Sophie Geneen (74). She was the widow of Lewis Geneen, one of the four *shochtim* who were engaged in providing the kosher meat and poultry requirements of the Jewish community. As a special mark of respect, Mrs Geneen's coffin was carried into the Great Central Synagogue in South Portland Street, an honour usually reserved for rabbis. Mr Solomon Yaffy, a regular patron of Mrs Geneen's famous hotel and restaurant in Abbotsford Place said: 'She was a wonderful woman. I remember once she told us of a man who had both his legs amputated. Within a few minutes £800 had been collected, a large part of it from Mrs Geneen herself.'

Jimmy Boyle (18) of Sandyfaulds Street, a member of the Young Cumbie gang, was sent to borstal for two years for running amok through the Gorbals and slashing innocent pedestrians. Violence flared in Cumberland Street and Crown Street after Rangers beat Celtic 3–0 at Hampden Park. The worst disturbance took place when rival factions clashed on board a steamer bound for Ireland; eighty policemen were rushed to the Broomielaw and twenty-five men later appeared in courts charged with breach of the peace offences. Samuel 'Dandy' Mackay, serving a ten-year sentence in Gateside Prison, Greenock, lost nine months' remission for trying to smuggle a letter out of jail.

Fogell's of Hospital Street advertised their 'separate Passover bake-house'. The Jewish Board of Guardians, Thistle Street, announced a 'boot and clothing distribution'. Sculptor Benno Schotz, who launched his career in the Gorbals, was appointed Sculptor-in-Ordinary to the Queen.

At Glasgow High Court, Patrick Gilgun was sent down for four years for the homicide of Bill 'Smiler' Bryden. The men had fallen out in the Diamond bridge club in Gorbals Street. Gilgun's agent told the court: 'When the two came face to face outside the club, Bryden had a knife. Gilgun managed to get hold of it, although he had a wound in the face which later needed forty-three stitches.' Willie Clark of decrepit Thistle Street – an £11. 10s. a week shipyard labourer – won £72,358 on Littlewood's treble-chance football-pools. His wife May told a reporter: 'When the man from the pools came, we told the kids it was to see about getting us a new house.'

When Benny Lynch's son John appeared in court charged with punching his three-year-old son Benny, his wife Susan pleaded for a custodial sentence 'to keep him from drink'. The Sheriff obliged with six months. Benny Lynch's ex-wife Anne said: ''Drink ruined Benny. It put him right in the gutter.'

Having played for Celtic for six years, Pat Crerand went south to join Manchester United, his transfer fee being in the region of £50,000. After only three months at the club he played the starring role in a classic FA cup final at Wembley, in which Manchester United beat Leicester City by three goals to one. Crerand, a tough-tackling halfback, would later win two league championships and a European Cup medal with the Old Trafford side. He also played sixteen times for Scotland, but believed that he would have got more caps if he had not been a Catholic who had once turned out for Celtic!

The Labour Party put on an open-air concert of rock 'n' roll and Irish dancing in a Thistle Street back-court. A spokesman said: 'The site was chosen in the Gorbals because of the community feeling there.' Mademoiselle Anne of Norfolk Street offered 'cocktail dresses at greatly reduced prices'.

After his neighbours moved to new houses from a condemned rat-infested tenement in Surrey Street, Tom McGuire (70), described as the hermit of the Gorbals, decided to stay on in the crumbling building, which had been his home for over forty years, rather than be sent to the Foresthall centre for the homeless. A Corporation spokesman remarked: 'In the case of an old person it is very difficult. We do all we can for them.' By filling a giant whisky bottle with 7,440 pennies, the patrons of Mike Herraghty's pub in Oxford Street raised £31 for spastic children.

Glasgow Corporation bought Alexander Thomson's famous Caledonia Road church for £3,700 after the congregation moved out because it could no longer afford repairs to the building, which had been listed category 'A' three years earlier. Monumental sculptors Lipton and Sons of Bedford Lane promised 'first-class work by Jewish craftsmen'. The death was reported of old Gorbals boy Avrom Greenbaum, tailor, playwright and founder of the Jewish Institute Players.

1964 BEATLE BOYS

The Hutchesontown Area B development of medium-rise and high-rise flats between Ballater Street and the river Clyde – dubbed Riverside by the planners – was completed to the designs of Sir Robert Matthew, Johnson-Marshall and Partners. The new development included the four tower blocks of Commercial Court and Waddell Court. Jewish community leaders expressed concern that elderly families – rehoused in outlying housing schemes such as

Priesthill and Nitshill – were 'living in virtual isolation from the rest of the community'. An official of the Jewish Board of Guardians said: 'When the redevelopers clear places like Thistle Street, Rutherglen Road, Ballater Street, South Portland Street and Gorbals Street, the problem may well become more acute.'

Two-thirds of the Gorbals families who had been rehoused in the Ballater Street-Commercial Road area petitioned Glasgow Corporation for a ban on pubs in the area. Said local councillor Frank McElhone: 'This was meant to be the new Gorbals, with the old stigma removed. Only nine public-houses are being allowed back into the area, instead of the previous forty-seven. But putting the first two on this site, beside a housing estate for the elderly and large families, a playground and a nursery school, is ridiculous.'

After defeating a Nigerian boxer in just over two minutes in Govan town hall, ex-British and European middleweight champion John 'Cowboy' McCormack said: 'If I'd lost or failed to win convincingly I was going to announce my retirement from the ring.' In impoverished Hospital Street, neighbours got a big surprise when they heard that Miss Jean McColl (76), an elderly recluse, had left over £12,000 in her will.

Hours after sixteen families were given twenty-four hours to vacate a dangerous tenement in Thistle Street, part of the building collapsed. One young newly-married couple escaped with only minutes to spare, but lost all their furniture. Councillor Frank McElhone said: 'None of the families will be homeless. I promise they will be rehoused.' After moving with her family from a crumbling tenement to a new Gorbals high-rise block, Mrs Frances Smith complained that her five-year-old daughter Donna was a prisoner in the multi-storey. Said Mrs Smith: 'How do you explain to a wee one that she can't go out to play anymore? I wish I was back in my old tenement. At least the children were happy there. They had freedom. We are so high up it would take ages to get down if the children were in any danger.'

Sir Basil Spence's Queen Elizabeth Square slab blocks were sixteen months behind schedule. Unimpressed by the architect's avant-garde vision, one local said: 'They're an eyesore. They don't look like houses at all. And what about that colour scheme: blue and orange. That's going to cause trouble for a start.'

In Surrey Street, on a quarter-acre site surrounded by condemned tenements, variety star Jimmy Logan opened a Scandinavian-style adventure playground. The long-established Guild of Aid allowed the Laurieston-Gorbals nursery school to be set up in their Coburg Street meeting hall. The Guild continued to operate homes for the aged, thrift clubs, an over-sixties choir and dancing classes for children. Rumanian-born rabbi A. F. Herling was appointed to the Chevra Kadisha Beth Jacob synagogue, one of the two remaining Jewish places of worship in the Gorbals. After long-haired 'Beatle boys' were told to wear bathing caps in the Gorbals baths, Alex Carroll of Commercial Court said: 'This action seems unnecessary but I'd wear a cap rather than give up swimming.'

1965 PLAY PARADISE

The new Gorbals adventure playground was described as a play paradise. It was staffed by a full-time youth leader, two part-time play organisers and voluntary helpers. Play organiser, folk singer Matt McGinn, said: 'My job here is not to tell the children to do this or do that, but to be there if they want help. Another important, if unofficial, job is to give them lights for their fags.'

Geneen's kosher restaurant, which in its heyday had been patronised by big names in the entertainment business – including Joe Loss, Richard Tauber and Larry Adler – closed down. During Jewish festivals, the restaurant had delivered kosher food to prisoners in Barlinnie. The *Victor* comic for boys featured on its front cover, 'The soldier who would not give up' – Gorbals war hero James Stokes VC.

In March, at Glasgow High Court, Jimmy 'Babyface' Boyle (21), was charged with murdering John Lynch, a middle-aged man, in a Gorbals back-court the previous year by stabbing him repeatedly with a knife. But he walked free after a Crown witness, who had picked Boyle out in an identity parade, changed her evidence.

George Forbes, a leading Scottish crime reporter, wrote: 'His reputation as the man who could freely commit murder, his place of honour in the underworld, had now been achieved. He was fêted in Gorbals pubs by all the villains of the day, held in awe by the weak, spoken respectfully to by the cautious, the darling of the girls, the king of the hoodlums.' Two months later, Boyle was charged with stabbing an eighteen-year-old youth to death. Since witnesses could not be persuaded to come forward, the capital charge was later withdrawn, but in July the Gorbals gangster was sent down for two years for two vicious attacks involving broken bottles in which one of the victims lost an eye.

Forbes described how ex-borstal boy Boyle, a former member of the Young Cumbie gang, gravitated from a local protection-racket to the role of chief heavy for a gang of loan sharks, known as the 'tallymen'. Forbes wrote: 'Boyle was the perfect strong-arm man for the gang, even if he went about his task too enthusiastically at times. Only he knows how many customers he beat up, brutalised and terrorised at this time, and, naturally enough, he is not saying.' The journalist put the number of assaults at between eighty and a hundred and asserted that Boyle had also been in demand as an out-of-town hitman for the notorious London-based Kray twins.

After a group of doctors, social workers and clergymen gathered in an Abbotsford Place flat to inaugurate the Christian Action (Glasgow) housing association, with the intention of buying and renovating old tenements, the group's chairman, Richard Holloway, minister of St Margaret's and St Mary's Episcopalian church said: 'I've married young couples who were obviously very much in love, and then seen that love wither simply because of the conditions they had to live in.'

Glasgow Corporation earmarked £34 million for the Laurieston-Gorbals CDA, designed to provide 'broad streets, multi-storeys, tree-lined avenues, open spaces, modern highways and play areas'. Enthusiastic planners envisaged 'a South Bank development' featuring 'a broad tree-lined promenade with restaurants, Continental-style cafés and amusements'. The project, to be spread over twenty years, called for the razing of 5,671 houses, 429 local industries, 625 shops and pubs and four primary schools. No less than 30 per cent of the existing houses had shared water closets and only 11 per cent had plumbed-in baths. Councillor Matthew Reilly, planning sub-convener said: 'This is going to rid us of some of our worst slums. Everyone will be thankful to see the start made.'

After six terrified families fled their Nicholson Street homes when a huge crack appeared in the tenement, a sanguine Corporation official examined the building and told the residents: 'It's safe to go back, phone if you see it moving.' John Marley, a father of three, said: 'They will never convince me that this is safe. Our lives are one long nightmare. There are more than thirty children in our close and many more round about. We'll have to wait until the building falls about them before the authorities act.'

As the old Gorbals was gradually bulldozed out of existence, the Jewish Board of Guardians set up a house-purchase scheme to help the area's remaining Jews to move to more attractive parts of the city. Caledonia Road church, a unique category 'A' listed building, designed by 'Greek' Thomson, was left a smoking shell after an attack of vandalism.

Four committee members of the newly-opened Close theatre club – an intimate venue next door to the Citizens' theatre in Gorbals Street – pulled the plug on a production of Christopher Marlowe's *Doctor Faustus* because producer-director Charles Marowitz refused to change a scene in which Sloth, one of the seven deadly sins, was played by an actor wearing a mask depicting the Queen's face. Actor Duncan Macrae, a director of the club, said: 'Mr Marowitz has gone beyond his rights. You must have something to portray Sloth in the text, but he has chosen quite arbitrarily to portray the sin as being connected with the Queen.'

1966   SKYSCRAPER BLUES

Giving evidence during a trial in Glasgow Sheriff Court, Barlinnie warder Douglas Birnie claimed that 40 per cent of the jail's inmates were either from the Gorbals or had relations there. After ten months in South Africa, Patrick and Doreen Donnelly became so homesick for the Gorbals that they stowed away, along with their baby son Pat, on a liner bound for Southampton. On arrival, they were fined £20 each. Waiting for them when they got home to the Gorbals was Patrick's mother, Mrs Mary Donnelly of Kidston Street. Patrick told her: 'You live in the most wonderful place in the world. I'll never know why we left it.'

With women in Glasgow's high-rise flats reported to be suffering from 'skyscraper blues', Gorbals MP Mrs Alice Cullen suggested that more day nurseries and playgrounds should be provided for multi-storey families. Mother of three Mrs Rodgers, on the top floor of a multi in Rutherglen Road in the heart of the new Gorbals, had nothing but praise for her home. She said: 'I wouldn't change my new flat for anything. The children are not allowed to play in the corridors but they have a swing park opposite the building. At first I didn't want to live so high, but we have such a marvellous view. I wouldn't swap my flat now for one any lower.'

Work began on the Scottish Special Housing Association's Hutchesontown-Gorbals Area D development, which included four 24-storey blocks. After inspecting the Gorbals adventure playground, Glasgow councillors expressed their disapproval of the unconventional play area by cutting its £1,000 a year grant. Councillor Gordon Rennie opposed the cut: 'Since the playground started two years ago there has been considerably less vandalism in the area of rebuilding around it. I am sure that is a direct result of the freedom of expression allowed the children in the playground.' Housewives complained that in award-winning Waddell Court, a seventeen storey multi in Hutchesontown, they had to use their verandas as 'makeshift washing greens' because vandals and thieves had wrecked the building's coin-in-the-slot drying cupboards. Resident Michael Heneghan said: 'Most of the tenants here have a real pride in their homes. We don't like to see them looking like slums with washing hanging from every window.'

In Thistle Street, twenty-nine families, backed by Revd Richard Holloway, went on a rent strike to force private landlords to improve their abysmal living conditions. A spokesman for house factors Stobbs and Sons said: 'If the tenants hold back their rents we will serve them with eviction notices.' Shortly after the rent strike was announced, Glasgow's public-health department declared the slum tenement unfit for human habitation. Revd Holloway said: 'This is wonderful. It looks as though we have won the first round in this battle. It could mean that the families will be rehoused by the Corporation in the near future.'

Gorbals-born John Duddy (37) – wanted along with Harry Roberts and John Witney in connection with the murder of three London policemen – was arrested in an armed-police raid in Calton in Glasgow's east end and flown to London under Scotland Yard supervision. During the flight south, Duddy allegedly told police: 'I just grabbed the gun, ran to the police car and shot the driver through the window. I must have been mad. I wish you could hang me now.'

At Cheshire Crown Court, after a trial lasting fourteen days, Ian Brady was found guilty of murdering two children and a seventeen-year-old youth. His co-accused, Myra Hindley, was found guilty along with Brady of murdering two children. Brady and Hindley were sentenced to concurrent life sentences. Born out of wedlock in 1938 – the son of waitress Mary Stewart and a Glasgow newspaper reporter – and reared by foster parents in the Gorbals, Brady had shown sadistic tendencies at an early age and had buried a cat alive at the age of ten. The 'moors murders' – the child victims had been tortured and killed, then buried on Saddleworth Moor in the Pennines – had shocked a nation as yet unused to serial killers.

After a much-criticised BBC television programme about Glasgow's teenage gangs, Lord Provost John Johnston took BBC chairman Lord Normanbrook on a tour of the city. The Lord Provost said: 'We are not trying to cover up anything, the Gorbals is included in the tour to show him our difficulties as well as our achievements.' Glasgow Corporation obtained a compulsory purchase order for the Palace bingo hall in Gorbals Street – opened in 1904 as the Palace Theatre of Varieties – planning eventually to demolish it to make way for a flank of the inner ring road (M8).

1967   SING SING BLOCK C

At the heavily-guarded High Court in Glasgow, Jimmy 'Babyface' Boyle (24), previously acquitted on two separate murder charges, was sent down for a minimum of fifteen years. After a trial lasting three days, it took the jury forty-five minutes to find Boyle guilty of murdering William Rooney in his home in Kinning Park. Rooney, a 32-year-old labourer, who owed moneylenders £7, was stabbed in a 'frenzied' manner on the face, neck and chest. Having butchered Rooney, debt collector Boyle got rid of the murder weapon and headed for London where, according to top crime reporter George Forbes, his pals the Kray twins hid him in a safe house. But detective superintendent Elphinstone Dalglish of the Glasgow CID led a police posse, which nabbed Boyle in a London pub frequented by the underworld.

Police witnesses told the court that William Mackie and his wife Helen, Rooney's terrified neighbours, had been rehoused in another town for their own protection. The police had even done the couple's flitting so that no removal van would lead Boyle's associates to their new home. Mrs Sadie Cairney (21), Rooney's girlfriend, said that she had lived in fear since the murder and had fled to Manchester and asked for police protection, explaining that there was 'a team from Glasgow' looking for her. A detective described Mrs Cairney as a very frightened woman and added: 'Her whole worry was that the man Boyle would get to her.' Another Crown witness, Edward McGill (15), stabbed by Boyle four months previously, told the court that days before he was due to give evidence, gelignite had been exploded outside his home in Hutcheson Court, Gorbals. Lord Cameron said that the case had been heard against 'a sinister background of terror and intimidation' and described Boyle – who had fifteen previous convictions – as a dangerous menace to society. As the Gorbals hoodlum began his life sentence, witnesses were still under police guard. A detective said, 'they will be given protection for as long as necessary'.

Gorbals safecracker Johnny Ramensky was sent down for four years for raiding a bank in Rutherglen. In concentrating on opening the safe, 'Gentle Johnny' had ignored a drawer which contained £80,000. Gorbals MP Alice Cullen voiced her strong opposition to a proposal to remove the Gorbals from the electoral map and rename the constituency 'Hampden'. Zubaidah Hussain of Eglinton Street beat her sister Kaneneza by one mark to become the dux of Adelphi Terrace secondary school. The evangelical Gorbals Group published the first edition of *Gorbals Voice*, described as 'Britain's first community newspaper'. Editor John Harvey promised to focus on poor housing conditions and social deprivation in the area.

During a tour match in Bermuda, the manager of Chelsea FC, ex-Gorbalite Tommy Docherty, blotted his copybook when he took exception to a decision made by a black referee and told him: 'You should be swinging from a tree, not refereeing.' Docherty was obliged to resign, but went on to manage a string of clubs over the next four years including, infamously, Queen's Park Rangers, where he lasted only twenty-eight days after a bust-up with the chairman.

At St Francis's RC church in Cumberland Street, Linda Mullen was the May Queen and took part in the crowning of Our Lady. The traditional procession through the district had to be abandoned on account of redevelopment. It was reported that disillusioned residents of Sir Basil Spence's high-rise development in Queen Elizabeth Square had given each of the blocks a nickname: Alcatraz for Block A, Barlinnie for Block B and Sing Sing for Block C. Vandalism in the Gorbals was blamed on 'the complete lack of amenities for young people'. Gorbals inhabitants described the allocation of Corporation houses as a very hazardous scheme and complained that they were being treated as 'second-class citizens'. A planning official described deck-access housing – scheduled for the new Hutchesontown Area E – as 'still very much at the experimental stage'.

Top art dealers in London and Paris anxiously sought the whereabouts of seventy-eight-year-old Gorbals-born Scotty Wilson (Louis Freeman). A friend said: 'He never was one to leave a forwarding address.' At the age of fifty, Scotty – described as a wizened eccentric – had discovered his ability to draw. He once hawked his surreal drawings to passers-by in London's Piccadilly at £1 a time; half a mile from a Mayfair art gallery selling his drawings at £250 each.

The Gorbals Boy Scouts launched a recruiting campaign to attract Indian and Pakistani boys to their ranks. An official said: 'There is only one Scout troop in the Gorbals, a Roman Catholic one. We would like to see a new troop which will integrate the Indian and Pakistani lads.' With the Gorbals adventure playground – popularly called the Venny – threatened with closure, some five hundred kids sporting home-made banners marched to George Square to present a petition to the Lord Provost. As a result, the Corporation provided funds to keep the Venny functioning.

Around a thousand Indians and Pakistanis lived or worked in the Gorbals, running twenty wholesale warehouses, fifteen grocery shops and eight clothing factories. In addition to thrift clubs, the Guild of Aid – a feature of Gorbals life for eighty years – ran the roof-garden club and the over-sixty club.

In Cumberland Place, Mrs Nancy Coyle's four children died when fire swept through a brand-new maisonette flat. The blaze started in the kitchen, where a paraffin heater was knocked over. The flats had off-peak electric storage heaters, which few tenants could afford to use. Two firemen collapsed while fighting the blaze and were rushed to hospital. One of them, station officer William Clark, was dead on arrival.

James Shearer and family got their 'best Christmas present ever' – the keys to a flat in Hutcheson Court. Mrs Margaret Shearer felt that the best features of the new house were the bathroom and the kitchenette. The Shearers counted themselves extremely fortunate since thousands of families were desperate to leave the old tenements. Interviewed in her rat-infested single end in South Portland Street, Mary Galloway (80) said the rodents didn't bother her: 'It's not the four-legged rats that scare me. It's the two-legged ones I hate. They're more dangerous.'

After convicted murderer Jimmy Boyle assaulted the assistant governor of Barlinnie, he was taken from the Bar-L to Glasgow Sheriff Court in a high-security operation, remanded in custody and whisked back to prison. Armed police ringed the court and the proceedings were held in a cell, since police had been tipped off about an underworld plot to set the young killer free.

A million slates, rescued from demolished Gorbals tenements, were recycled in the modern retirement village of Crookfur, near Newton Mearns. Gorbals-born shop manager Pat Lally, a Labour councillor, was heavily criticised for selling blood-red ties emblazoned with the words 'Ya Bass', the slogan of the Tongs gang. An unrepentant Mr Lally said: 'They are only frivolous. Anyone who thinks otherwise is adopting pompous and moral attitudes.'

1968 GORBALS GROUPIES

After Hurricane Low-Q hit Scotland on 14 January – killing nine Glaswegians and leaving whole streets looking as if they had been blitzed – absentee private landlords in the Gorbals were castigated for 'shirking their responsibilities' and leaving tenants to live 'in almost primitive conditions'. In a Thames Television feature shown on Scottish Television, leaders of Glasgow's teenage gangs boasted about the 'territories' they controlled. For the benefit of viewers, female groupies from the Gorbals chanted bloodcurdling gang slogans.

Angry residents of Battlefield and Langside were up in arms because the Parliamentary Boundary Commission proposed to merge their attractive residential districts with the Gorbals constituency. A spokesman for the good people of Battlefield said: 'We don't want public houses, betting shops and the like, which are the way of life in the Gorbals.' One anti-Gorbals protester opined: 'The kernel of the matter is the name. It stinks all over the world.' Objecting to the proposal, Revd Geoff Shaw told the Commission that 'the name of Gorbals had a long, glorious and honourable historical tradition'.

On a visit to his native Glasgow, tycoon Sir Isaac Wolfson (70), now head of an empire worth £400 million, went to the Gorbals to see his old school – Gorbals public school in Oxford Street – and the Chevra Kadisha synagogue in Buchan Street where he sang as a choirboy. Refusing to enter the buildings, Wolfson said: 'A man can only look back so far.'

At Glasgow High Court, after a trial lasting nine days, Gorbals-born Frank 'Tarzan' Wilson, crooked lawyer James Maxwell Latta and John 'Bandit' Rooney were sent to prison for a total of twenty-four years for trying to terrorise witnesses prior to the Jimmy Boyle murder trial of the previous year. Wilson lamented: 'This is what you get for trying to help that bastard Boyle.'

An English tabloid newspaper – *The People* – serialised the story of Pat Crerand in a piece entitled, 'From the Slums to Soccer Greatness'. Mrs Alice Cullen (76), MP for the Gorbals since 1948, announced her intention to stand down at the next general election. Mrs Cullen, who joined the Labour Party in 1916, said: 'People have been phoning asking me if it's true I intend to retire. They forget you're not Methuselah.' The tenants' association in the Queen Elizabeth Square tower blocks ran a petition for prepayment electricity meters. Chairman Joe Moore explained: 'People are paying two to three times the rent and rates they used to. Now they get electricity bills every quarter, instead of putting a shilling in the meter. They get caught and their electricity's cut off. No fire, no cooking, no light – the houses are all-electric.'

Pamela Stringer of Abbotsford Place, a typist with furniture manufacturers Stragowitz and Gillman, Surrey Street, complained that the 'new' Gorbals lacked entertainment for young people. In Bedford Street, Mr Ellis, owner of a small shop, lamented that he 'was losing customers steadily, and no new ones were replacing them'. Mrs Doris Seidlin, owner of Vanity Fashions in Cumberland Street, was concerned that her shop 'could be demolished at a month's notice'. She felt that shopping habits had changed, since high-rise dwellers 'didn't come down so often to shop'.

A Coburg Street man was fined £25 for breaking into a Gorbals butcher's shop and stealing live hens. The court was told that it was a religious custom for Indian and Pakistani residents of the Gorbals to buy hens live and slaughter them themselves. Revd John Cameron Peddie, who became a legend in the Gorbals during the dark days of the inter-war depression, died in an old folk's home.

1969 WORLD SHOWPIECE

At Edinburgh High Court, Paddy Meehan, a small-time Gorbals crook, was sentenced to life imprisonment for the murder of wealthy pensioner Rachel Ross. Bludgeoned in her home in Ayr, Mrs Ross (72) had died in hospital. Meehan told the court: 'You have made a terrible mistake.' He appealed against his conviction, but the appeal was dismissed. Paddy Meehan spent seven years in solitary confinement in Peterhead prison before receiving a free pardon and a substantial compensation payment. The real killer – violent psychopath William 'Tank' McGuinness – was never brought to justice.

Transworld Publishers, under whose Corgi Books imprint *No Mean City* had sold hundreds of thousands of copies, brought out a cheap paperback edition of *No Bad Money*, written by Peter Watts and based on fragmentary papers of Gorbals author Alexander McArthur, whose first-hand knowledge of life in the Gorbals slums had made *No Mean City* an enduring success. Since McArthur's death in poverty in 1946, many authors had cashed in on the Gorbals gangland genre.

A birth-control clinic for Asian women – with leaflets about the oral contraceptive pill printed in Urdu – was opened in Florence Street under the auspices of the Family Planning Association. After two public inquiries, the Battlefield area of Cathcart constituency and the Gorbals constituency were joined together to form the new parliamentary constituency of Queen's Park. Lord Mountbatten of Burma opened the Glasgow College of Nautical Studies in Thistle Street, the subject of a Civic Trust award. The College, which featured a domed planetarium, soon had students from all corners of the globe. The Cumberland arcade, a tiny shopping centre containing thirty-seven shops and one small supermarket, was opened under the shadow of Sir Basil's Spence's Queen Elizabeth Square slab blocks. Before the Second World War, the Gorbals had over a thousand shopkeepers, including purveyors of Eastern European delicacies and dressmakers who kept abreast of the latest Parisian fashions.

The Ben Cluach pub was the last surviving howff in Florence Street, birthplace of boxer Benny Lynch. As the street's tenements were razed one by one, each local resident was promised 'a palace of baths and hot water and space'. Mother of nine Mrs Chrissie Lee said: 'I'm glad the place is getting pulled down at last. But I would really like to be rehoused in the neighbourhood. The Gorbals will be a world showpiece.'

After the death of Mrs Alice Cullen MP, described as tireless in her zeal for the downtrodden, Gorbals Labour Party chose Frank McElhone – who lived in leafy Pollokshields but was born, raised and married in the Gorbals and had a shop in the district – as their candidate. Revd Geoff Shaw, who had criticised separate Roman Catholic education and was therefore anathema to devout Catholics, put his name forward as a candidate and was rejected by a narrow margin. In the increasingly depopulated Gorbals, it was alleged that 'the rats outnumbered the voters'. Councillor Tom Brady, the SNP candidate, took a caged rat into a packed committee meeting and said: 'I decided to do something drastic after a Gorbals family complained to me about rat infestation in their house.' In the by-election, Frank McElhone held the seat for Labour with a majority of 4,163, while Matthew Lygate polled seventy-two votes for the Workers' Party of Scotland.

Contractors Gilbert Ash (Scotland) Ltd began work on the Hutchesontown Area E development of multi-storey blocks and deck-access flats, using a prefabricated system pioneered by a French construction company working in the arid climate of Algeria. Hutcheson's boys' grammar school in Crown Street (1841), a handsome listed building which had been derelict and a target for vandals for some time, fell to the bulldozers. With great reluctance, the secretary of state for Scotland Willie Ross, no fan of tower blocks, gave the go-ahead for a new £6 million multi at Gorbals Cross. Mr Ross said he was worried about the lack of amenities for families with young children and described the high-rise block as 'expensive and not as well designed as I would have liked for the city's redevelopment'.

The Twomax clothing factory in Old Rutherglen Road, located in an old cotton spinning mill, sought 'trainees, aged 15–25'. The products of the factory were sold as far afield as Sweden. Pakistani and Indian children in the Gorbals were enrolled for special language tuition at Centre Street primary school, which also had Greek, Hungarian, Venezuelan, Chinese, Polish, Spanish, Japanese and Egyptian pupils on its role. Mr Ajit Singh appeared before Glasgow Sheriff Court, having passed a bus driving-test while holding a forged driving licence, purchased in the resourceful Gorbals for £17.

After the pupils of Abbotsford primary school saw a television transmission of the Apollo Twelve moon landing, nine-year-old Maxwell Logan said: 'I want to go to the moon and get a big piece of it to throw at Rangers supporters.'

The Paddy Black Memorial Mission in Tradeston Street closed down after sixty-six years' service to the community. Started in 1903, the Mission grew to such proportions that it boasted its own Sunday school, Girls' Guildry, Boys' Brigade, penny savings bank and silver band. As thousands of Gorbalites were rehoused out of the area in the various housing schemes, the Mission haemorrhaged supporters. At the closing social, however, a great many of Paddy Black's old friends and helpers were present to ring down the final curtain. The last superintendent, James Black, was the son of the Mission's founder.

Frank McElhone MP accused Glasgow's Tory-Progressive alliance of not laying a single brick in the Gorbals since they won control of Glasgow Corporation. Four hundred students drank dry the Mally Arms, Eglinton Street. The students consumed 112 gallons of heavy ale, 132 gallons of lager, 45 gallons of stout and 23 gallons of export.

1970 GENTLE JOHNNY

By affecting a French accent and inventing an affluent lifestyle of country-house parties and holidays in exotic locations, Mrs Barbara Morrison, a Gorbals mother of eleven children, conned people into believing that she was the abandoned daughter of Margaret, Duchess of Argyll. One of Mrs Morrison's victims said: 'She seemed very plausible and I liked her as a person. She spoke with a foreign accent and looking back on it, she was a very good actress.' Convicted murderer Jimmy Boyle (27) had six months added to his sentence after he pleaded guilty to assaulting the governor of Porterfield prison, Inverness.

Scotland's best known safecracker – Johnny Ramensky of Queen Elizabeth Square, Gorbals – appeared in court in a wheelchair and was jailed for two years for trying to carry out a job in Stirling. 'Gentle Johnny' – who had spent most of his life behind bars but had eschewed violence throughout his criminal career – had fallen off a roof and was seriously injured.

Dr George Gladstone Robertson published his memoirs, *Gorbals Doctor*, the story of forty-seven years in general practice in the greater Gorbals area. Dr Robertson began work in the district in 1923, assisting his uncle with his practice in Abbotsford Place. In a three-apartment flat in Centre Street, Tradeston the young medic delivered a woman of her twenty-second child. In all, the woman had twenty-six pregnancies, and four miscarriages. Dr Robertson claimed that in all his years of practice in the much-maligned Gorbals, he had 'only once seen a street incident where a number of youths were involved and never witnessed more than one or two broken shop windows at any one time'. He had however 'attended a considerable number of women with signs of bruising on their faces and bodies attributed to their husbands'.

When the Close theatre, a private club in Gorbals Street, pre-sented *The Cenci*, a romp through one of the nastiest segments of Italian history, civic chiefs queued up to condemn the production as 'disgusting' and 'utter filth'. Shelter, the national campaign to house the homeless, chose a 'shocking' picture of a Gorbals back-court to launch a fund-raising drive. In Nicholson Street and Abbotsford Place, the few remaining residents endured dawn-to-dusk pile-driving.

Despite encroaching redevelopment, the Gorbals still had some fine old traditional pubs, including the Turf bar in Hospital Street, the Braeside bar in Rutherglen Road (known to regulars as 'Hurrel's'), the Tavern in Ballater Street, the Kilorn bar in Eglinton Street and the Blarney Stone in Caledonia Road. At Glasgow Sheriff Court, an Asian wholesaler from the Gorbals, described as one of the ringleaders in a passport racket to bring illegal immigrants into Britain, was jailed for eighteen months. The court heard that passports bought for £15 in this country fetched up to £400 in Pakistan.

Oatlands (1870–1900) was declared one of Glasgow's first Housing Treatment Areas and – with public opinion veering away from wholesale demolition and towards architectural conservation – the local authority expressed hopes that some of the district's structurally sound tenements might be renovated. In the general election, John Kay, the Communist candidate for Queen's Park, which took in the Gorbals, called for a basic old-age pension of £8 per week. Gorbals adventure playground had to move from Surrey Street to Lawmoor Street to make way for new high-rise flats.

After a tenement gable-end collapsed in Caledonia Road, it was disclosed that MP Frank McElhone had called for special patrols to be set up to keep watch on dangerous buildings. At a fund-raising dance in the Plaza ballroom, Eglinton Toll, Madge Gillespie (21) was crowned Miss Gorbals 1970. The winner of the contest didn't live in the Gorbals, but in the far more salubrious district of Pollokshields.

1971   SOME GOOD, SOME BAD

Ex-Gorbals boy Sir Isaac Wolfson, born in a Hospital Street tenement in 1897, was made a Freeman of the City of Glasgow. Sir Isaac, described as the epitome of the successful Jewish businessman, lived in a Georgian town house in London's Portland Square. He told a reporter: 'I just lead a simple Glaswegian way of life'. By 1971, through the Wolfson Foundation, the tycoon had reputedly distributed over £17 million to groups and institutions all over the world.

A life-size mural painting of world flyweight champion boxer Benny Lynch was discovered beneath six layers of wallpaper in the Norfolk bar in the heart of the Gorbals. 'Old timers said there should be a painting of him somewhere in this pub', said bar manager Dick Gilmour. 'Imagine putting wallpaper on a painting of Benny Lynch, a Gorbals hero.' A pub regular said: 'Benny Lynch used to drink here when he was finished with fighting.' Lynch's son John was found dead in a burn in the grounds of Woodilee hospital, where he was being treated for chronic alcoholism. He was thirty-four, a year older than Benny when he died of an alcohol-related illness.

In North Portland Street, Laurieston a dozen of Glasgow's longest-serving lamplighters watched Lord Provost Sir Donald Liddle light the city's last gas street-lamp, the sole survivor out of 24,000. Antique street lamps from the Gorbals had been sold worldwide. Families were evacuated from a dilapidated Ballater Street tenement when fire engulfed an adjoining church designed by world-famous architect Alexander 'Greek' Thomson. The derelict church had last seen use as a cork works. The Royal Scottish Academy in Edinburgh was the venue for a retrospective exhibition of the work of eighty-year-old sculptor Benno Schotz, who began his artistic career in the Gorbals.

Gorbals-born Tommy Docherty got a call from the Scottish Football Association and became manager of the national team. He revitalised the side and, in twelve matches under his stewardship, Scotland won seven and lost only three, and those were against very strong opposition in the shape of England, Brazil and Holland. Residents of tower blocks in Hutchesontown complained that 'noise from jet planes has become a real nuisance, particularly in the small hours of the night'. Gorbals primary school in Oxford Street, opened in 1885, closed down. The school's last headmistress, Mrs Lillian McCallum, said: 'I have no illusions about the people in the Gorbals at all. Some are good, some bad, but there is an essential warmth and friendliness that I shall never forget.'

Gorbals Fair, the brainchild of folk singer Matt McGinn, Revd Geoffrey Shaw and several other enterprising citizens got off to a tentative start, lasting only a weekend. Some tenants of Scottish Special Housing Association houses in Hutchesontown were 'spoiling the appearance of the property' by hanging out washing on their balconies. Yankel's kosher restaurant in Coplaw Street was 'open on Saturdays' and 'under the sanction of the Glasgow Beth Din'. Enthused by MP Frank McElhone's 'sponsor a pensioner' scheme, an anonymous donor presented Gorbals pensioner Mrs Isabella Weston with a food parcel on her ninety-fifth birthday.

1972   SLUDGE BOAT

Seven firemen lost their lives in a spectacular blaze at a cash and carry warehouse in Kilbirnie Street, Tradeston owned by Rafiq Sher and his four brothers. Six of the seven were searching for a trapped colleague when a section of the blazing roof collapsed. Among the dead was fireman William Hooper (44) of Centre Street, who was married with five children. In all, eight children were orphaned by the fire. Five of the dead firemen were from B division headquarters in Centre Street, which had also lost five men in the Cheapside Street whisky-bond fire of 1960. A spokesman for Sher Brothers said: 'The partners are too upset to talk about this tragedy.' Six of the firemen were buried in the Glasgow Necropolis beside the nineteen firemen and salvage officers who lost their lives in the Cheapside Street disaster.

War hero Johnny Ramensky was arrested a considerable distance from his flat in a Gorbals multi – on a roof in Ayr. Since his first conviction in 1917, he had been sentenced to a total of fifty-six years in jail. Solicitor Joe Beltrami said: 'He has been on more roofs than the famous fiddler.' The sixty-seven-year-old recidivist was jailed for a year. Matthew Lygate, who had stood for election in the Gorbals in 1969 and polled seventy-two votes as the candidate for the Maoist-style Workers' Party of Scotland, was jailed for twenty-four years for his role in three armed bank raids which, if successful, would have raised over £13,000 for party funds.

Families in condemned tenements in McNeil Street and Ballater Street wanted to be rehoused in the new Gorbals and complained that Glasgow Corporation housing department officials were using 'bullying tactics' to make them move out of the area to the peripheral housing estate of Castlemilk. A Queen's Park firm of property agents asked £86 rent per annum for a tiny gas-lit single end in a crumbling tenement in Crown Street. Abbotsford Place, Laurieston, a wide street of run-down Georgian terraces, fell to the bulldozers. Praising the so-called 'miracle of the Gorbals', a journalist expressed astonishment at the transformation: 'Grass is growing everywhere. And who would have thought that one day there would be anything like that in the Gorbals?'

Johnny Ramensky was acquitted on a safe-blowing charge for the first time in his lengthy career of crime. But 'Gentle Johnny' didn't walk out of court a free man, as he was already serving a twelve-month sentence. The first flats in the Hutchesontown Area E complex were opened by the Queen, who presented Mr and Mrs Gerald Johnson with keys to a house in Pine Street. Severe condensation and water penetration turned the £7.2 million development – consisting of two 24-storey blocks and 759 deck-access flats – into instant slums, which were soon nicknamed 'the Dampies'. In no time at all, tenants' brand-new furniture, carpets and wallpaper were ruined by fungi.

Constable David Peterson (36) was overcome by smoke and died after he went up to the eighth floor of a Queen Elizabeth Square slab block to warn residents to leave their homes. Firemen wearing breathing apparatus located the unfortunate policeman by means of the signal from his pocket radio.

Tommy Docherty landed the biggest job in football: manager of Manchester United. Under Docherty's stewardship, the team reached the FA Cup final in 1976, but lost to Southampton, and again in 1977, when Liverpool were beaten 2–1. With the cup safely ensconced in the Old Trafford trophy room, Docherty seemed to have the football world at his feet. But when his clandestine love affair with Mary Brown – the wife of the club physiotherapist – became public knowledge Louis Edwards, the devout Catholic chairman of Manchester United, unceremoniously sacked him.

The death was reported of ex-Gorbalite Scotty Wilson (Louis Freeman). The youngest of six sons of a labourer, Scotty emigrated to Canada shortly before the Second World War. In a Toronto boarding house, he began to make highly original pen-and-ink drawings which secured him a niche in the art world. On Laurieston tenants' association cruise 'doon the watter' on 'the sludge boat' – the vessel used to transport Glasgow's treated sewage out to sea – the members enjoyed deck quoits. With the old Guild of Aid hall in Coburg Street showing its age, the foundations were laid for new premises in Oxford Street, a stone's throw from the original building. Lord Provost John Mains – born and reared in Waddell Street in the heart of the Gorbals – complained that city planners had created high-rise 'communities without a community', leaving people 'more and more in isolation'.

The Pig and Whistle bar in McNeil Street promised 'personal supervision from Rose and Jim'. Among the new pubs that were rising from the rubble of the old Gorbals was the appropriately-named Phoenix in Old Rutherglen Road. The language centre in Tradeston Street celebrated the Chinese New Year with 'dances with a dragon of papier-mâché'. The Chevra Kadisha synagogue in Buchan Street, in use since 1899, closed down.

Johnny Ramensky died of a brain haemorrhage after being rushed to hospital from Perth prison. Born in 1905, the son of a Lithuanian miner, he followed his father into the Lanarkshire pits, where he learned to use explosives. After his father's death, the young Johnny moved with his mother and sisters to the Gorbals. Detective chief superintendent James Binnie, head of Glasgow's CID, said: 'Although he was a criminal he was the type of man for whom you had to have a certain respect and fondness.' Crowds gathered to give 'Gentle Johnny' a good send-off after a funeral service in St Francis's RC church, Cumberland Street.

1973 FRANK'S BANK

Jimmy Boyle was sentenced to an additional six years inside for his part in a riot at top-security Porterfield prison, Inverness in which a young prison officer lost an eye. In the Glenbervie bar in Gorbals Street, four men and two women finished their drinks at closing time, then beat up and robbed the manager. The New Bedford cinema, opened in 1935, became a bingo club. Of the three thousand Pakistanis in Glasgow, around a thousand lived in the Gorbals and Govanhill. After a distinguished career as a metallurgist, old Gorbals boy Monty Finneston was appointed chairman of the ailing British Steel Corporation. The historic Citizen's theatre was badly damaged by water and smoke when the adjoining 150-seater Close theatre was destroyed by fire. Ten families had to flee their Gorbals Street homes at the height of the blaze. In Crown Street, sanitary officials insisted on examining bed linen before giving residents the go-ahead to move to houses in the new Gorbals.

In a brand new multi-storey block at Stirlingfauld Place, the first stage of the Laurieston-Gorbals redevelopment, 'high-living' got the tenants down when a main fuse blew, stopping lifts, blacking-out stairs and halting the water-pumping system. One angry housewife said: 'It isn't the first time that the lifts or the heating have broken down.'

Jane Finlay, a young American volunteer worker at Gorbals adventure playground, had difficulties understanding the local patois. She told a reporter: 'One child asked me to "geez a coaxie" [give me a piggyback ride]. It took me a while to figure out what he was saying.' Granada Television's award-winning *World in Action* team made a documentary about MP Frank McElhone's Saturday surgery, known throughout the Gorbals as Frank's Bank. A spokesman for *World in Action* said: 'We didn't choose the Gorbals because of the usual "No Mean City" angle. We were there to praise Mr McElhone's work in his constituency and pose relevant questions. There is a strong political line to the programme and we will be asking why the Government cannot make sure every MP in the country has a surgery.'

Jimmy Boyle and Larry Winters – two of the four so-called hard men responsible for the riot at Porterfield prison – were reclassified as psychiatric prisoners and transferred to the newly opened Special Unit at Barlinnie jail. Nicknamed the Nutcracker Suite, it was designed to house long-term prisoners who were prone to violence.

1974 CHÂTEAU WINDSOR

Gorbals police promised a glue-sniffing probe after James McCafferty (18) of Commercial Court, Hutchesontown, was found dead with a polythene bag over his head and a tin of glue beside his body. Within a few years, solvent abuse would be a big problem in Glasgow's underprivileged communities.

Evelyn Cowan authored *Spring Remembered*, a celebration of the close-knit Jewish community of her Gorbals childhood. Born in 1921, and reared in a tenement in Apsley Place, she was the youngest of eleven children. Her father, a self-employed tailor, died only months after her birth, leaving her mother to bring up the large family single-handedly. Ms Cowan's highly readable book contained memorable vignettes of Jewish life in the Gorbals, including a description of a bar mitzvah ceremony in the old South Portland Street synagogue.

Phil McCall played a Jewish barber from the Gorbals in Bill Bryden's play, *Benny Lynch, Scenes from a Short Life*, staged by the Royal Lyceum Company. The play, based on the career of Scotland's first world champion boxer, also starred Roddy MacMillan and Rikki Fulton. Andrew Byatt, a nineteen-year-old actor from Maryhill, was cast as the eponymous hero and had to lose more than seventeen pounds before matching Benny's fighting weight of eight stones. Mrs Anne Duchen, Benny's widow, flew three thousand miles from Canada to Glasgow to see the play, but she was deeply disappointed and slammed the playwright for his 'inaccuracies'. Anne claimed that Benny, unlike his stage persona, never swore in her presence during their brief married life together. 'It's about time the real story of Benny was told,' said Mrs Duchen. 'I can't defend him on his drinking, but far too many myths have grown up about him. The play gives a completely wrong impression of him. If it weren't so tragic, I could laugh at all the inaccuracies.'

The play resulted in a flood of reminiscences from old-timers who had known Benny in his heyday. John Devine, the boxer's sparring partner at the height of his glory, told a reporter: 'I knew Benny inside out in bad and good moments during his profess-ional career. I can tell you Benny was a wee gem in every way. Benny was a kind-hearted guy and never turned his back on a hard-luck story.'

Grandmother Jessie Grant, known as 'the saint of the Gorbals', retired after twenty-four years' service as sub-postmistress of Bridge Street post office. Locals told how Mrs Grant, who won a bravery award for thwarting an armed robbery, had 'dipped into her own purse' to help OAPs and 'made them tea in her little dingy back room to cheer them up'. Jessie told a reporter: 'Like the old tenements here, I've got to go, but I'm really sad to leave.' Gorbals parish church (1810), one of the jewels of Regency Laurieston, bit the dust in a crass act of official vandalism.

Geoff Shaw (47), the charismatic Gorbals clergyman who had become a household name in Scotland for his outreach activities in the tough district, was elected convener of the newly-created Strathclyde Regional Council, which had responsibility for half the population of Scotland. In an Ibrox tenement, Gorbals-born policeman and boxing legend John 'Cowboy' McCormack, helped to deliver a baby girl.

A reporter visited lifer Jimmy Boyle in the Special Unit at Barlinnie Prison and found the convicted murderer painting 'murals of his old Gorbals streets'. Boyle said: 'If I hadn't been moved here from the prison jungle I was used to, either I would have been dead by now or other people would have been.' There was a storm of protest when it was revealed that Boyle had been released from the Unit to visit an Edinburgh art gallery where a piece of his sculpture was on exhibition. A police spokesman said: 'we are yet again flabb-ergasted by the amounts of money being spent in the rehabilitation of thugs, gangsters and neds rather than on the victims.'

The Great Central Synagogue (1901) in South Portland Street, the last Jewish religious building in the Gorbals, closed down. For Passover, Tempo off-sales in Govan Road offered 'Château Windsor kosher red wine' at £1 per bottle.

When young 'shop raiders' entered a small general store in Commercial Court, they were put to flight by three battling housewives: shop assistants Mrs Anna McMahon, Mrs Agnes Robb and Mrs Martha Laird. At Sothebys in London, an American art dealer paid £7,500 for an album of photographs by Glaswegian Thomas Annan, including an 1868 view of Main Street, Gorbals. Glasgow Muslims estimated that it would cost at least £500,000 to build a new mosque on land in Adelphi Street, near Gorbals Cross. Lacking the necessary funds, they continued to hold religious services in a dilapidated tenement in Oxford Street.

1975   SANCTUARY FOR SINNERS

In the New Year's honours' list, a knighthood was conferred on scientist and industrialist Dr Monty Finneston, chairman of the British Steel Corporation between 1973 and 1975. Born the fifth son of a Jewish haberdashery salesman, he began life in poor circumstances in the Gorbals. The general assembly of the Church of Scotland paid tribute to Revd Geoffrey Shaw, whose two-room-and-kitchen flat in Cleland Street, Gorbals, had for many years been 'a sanctuary for misfits and sinners and seekers after truth'. A fellow minister praised Revd Shaw for his 'constant concern for the underprivileged' and cited his 'battles with sanitary inspectors, factors and insensitive landlords'. Shaw wasn't present to hear his praises sung by the assembly; he was at his desk in Glasgow where he was convener of Strathclyde Regional Council.

Addressing a large meeting of local politicians at the opening of a new £250,000 community centre, councillor Patrick Lally – born in a Thistle Street room-and-kitchen flat – said that the centre would provide 'a social heart for the Gorbals and Hutchesontown'. The building, the first of the city's community centres to be named after an individual – John Mains, a former Lord Provost and Gorbals worthy – provided facilities for such activities as table tennis, judo, yoga, drama, dressmaking and painting.

The last structure at historic Gorbals Cross, an underground gents' lavatory, disappeared. The Eglinton Electreum picture house, opened in 1911, closed down. Glasgow Corporation had to pay builders Crudens Ltd nearly £280,000 compensation because ten Gorbals families refused to vacate their old tenement homes despite several offers of rehousing. A councillor said: 'We could have moved these families into a top-class hotel for a year until suitable houses could be found. In fact, it would have paid us to give them £15,000 each and told them to go and buy bungalows.'

Tenants of Hutchesontown Area E deck-access blocks in Cavendish Place complained that dampness had 'reached alarming proportions'. An official of Glasgow Corporation's pest control unit said that tiny beetles in the flats 'were feeding on the dampness or the condensation'.

1976   GORBALS YO-YO

After William 'Tank' McGuinness, who'd murdered Mrs Rachel Ross in 1969, died in a Glasgow hospital, his wife Agnes came forward with her husband's confession. As a result, Paddy Meehan walked out of Peterhead prison with a royal pardon. He later received compensation of £50,500. Interviewed in her flat in Old Rutherglen Road, Gorbals, Paddy's ex-wife Betty – who had fought to clear his name – said: 'I owe Agnes McGuinness a real debt of gratitude.'

Former Glasgow dockhand Mark McManus, later to become famous as the eponymous hero of Scottish Television's hugely successful *Taggart* crime series, sweated for hours in the gym to lose weight, dyed his hair black and learned basic boxing skills to play Gorbals legend Benny Lynch in a Granada television drama. Mark said: 'My mother listened on the radio to the commentary when Lynch took the title from Jackie Brown. He was to her what he was to a great many people – a hero.' Mrs Anne Duchen,

Benny's widow, who had remarried and gone to live in Ontario, Canada asked the television company to leave out references to her and to Lynch's womanising.

Journalist and novelist Chaim Bermant, a graduate of Glasgow University and the London School of Economics, saw the publication of his autobiography *Coming Home*. Born in Poland in 1929, he arrived in the Gorbals at the age of eight. His father, an ex-rabbi, was the local *shochet* (slaughterman). Recalling the Gorbals of his childhood, he wrote: 'There were Yiddish posters on the hoardings, Hebrew lettering on the shops, Jewish names, Jewish faces, Jewish butchers, Jewish bakers with Jewish bread, and Jewish grocers with barrels of herring in the doorway.'

At Norfolk Court, near Gorbals Cross, residents of a brand new 24-storey block complained that 'people have gone up and down like a yo-yo for five minutes before the lift will open at a floor.' By pulling out high-tension electric cables in a lift in a Caledonia Road high-rise block, vandals turned the lift cage into 'a death trap'. Gorbals-born tycoon Sir Isaac Wolfson set up the Wolfson (Scotland) Trust to serve educational and artistic activities in Scotland.

Jim and Muriel Peebles of Camden Street were among four hundred families in the Hutchesontown Area E development who banded together to refute Glasgow District Council allegations that their new homes were affected by condensation rather than damp. When James and Margaret Carlin of Sandiefield Street complained to the Council, they were told that the dampness in their flat was caused by 'heavy breathing'. Jim Friel, a tenants' spokesman, told a Shelter (Scotland) conference that the blocks were known locally as the fungus flats. 'When you go out to meet your friends,' said Jim, 'you know you stink.' Mr Friel said that the tenants were pinning their hopes on legal action, backed by fourteen local general practitioners who were willing to testify that conditions in the flats constituted a health hazard.

Offering to give lifer Jimmy Boyle a £2,000 a year job when he eventually left Barlinnie's Special Unit, Edinburgh art impresario Richard Demarco said: 'I am not defending Boyle, because his crimes were heinous. I would like to have him work as the director of a gallery in the Gorbals, where he could help Glasgow shape its future.' In McKinley Street, five families who were facing eviction from a condemned tenement threatened to barricade themselves in their homes. The families had turned down offers of alternative accommodation in outlying housing schemes because they wanted to be rehoused in their old community. Mrs Patricia Collins said: 'I bought this house less than a year ago and was told it would stand for six to ten years. I won't give up without a fight.'

Writing in the *Jewish Echo*, old Gorbals girl Muriel Goodwin, reared in Rutherglen Road, recalled the colourful Jewish community of her childhood: Phineas Sofer's cheder [religion class] with 'Parla Esperanta' over the door; Harris's and Bakun's delicatessen with its barrels of herrings, gherkins and black olives; and the Eglinton Electreum cinema where, according to Muriel, 'three jam jars guaranteed a seat'. In the Riverside tavern, a modern lounge bar in Waddell Court, Hutchesontown, customers had to put ten pence into a swear box every time they uttered an expletive. The money was used to buy treats for local old folk.

At Craigton crematorium, there was a large turnout for the funeral of James Black, who'd been superintendent of the Paddy Black Memorial Mission in Tradeston from 1926 until 1969. The Coliseum cinema in Eglinton Street banned children under sixteen after juvenile punch-ups disrupted movies.

1977 BIRDS BEHIND BARS

Labourer Ronnie McLachlan (23) averted carnage in ex-boxer Derry Treanor's pub in Cathcart Road, Gorbals, when he kicked a gelignite bomb out of the lounge bar, which was full of people enjoying a Saturday night singsong. The bomb – which had been hidden in a Celtic FC sports bag – exploded in the street, shattering the pub windows. McLachlan, knocked unconscious by the blast, was rushed to the Victoria Infirmary.   Five people were injured in the explosion, which followed a Celtic–Rangers game at Parkhead. As he left hospital, Mr McLachlan said: 'I am no great hero. Anyone would have done the same.' Mrs Patricia Yuill had been sitting with friends at a table near the door when she noticed the bag, which smelt of burning and was making a strange sizzling noise.

The Protestant paramilitary Ulster Defence Association denied responsibility, and the Special Branch admitted that they found the attack 'puzzling'. Mr Treanor, who once fought for the British featherweight title, blamed the attack on 'Protestant extremists' but said that the bombers hadn't done their homework: 'My pub has the reputation of being an Irish shop. But 80 per cent of my customers are Scots and many of them are Protestants.'

After lifer Larry Winters died from an overdose of barbiturates in the Special Unit at Barlinnie prison, the Scottish Office probed claims that inmates had access to sex, drugs, drink and gourmet foods. Among the allegations, made in letters smuggled out of the Bar-L, was the assertion that Gorbals-born convicted killer Jimmy Boyle had a Polaroid camera and handed round photos of himself 'as if he was a Hollywood star'. A prison officer said: 'They have female visitors in their cells. There is nothing they could get on the outside that they cannot get here.' Inmate Hugh Collins, jailed in 1975 for a gangland murder, later claimed that the social workers, psychiatrists and lawyers who visited the Unit were like groupies: 'They got a thrill from being near you. Some of the women who visited the Unit would even sleep with you.'

Douglas Andrew Fraser (60), whose family left the Gorbals in the early 1920s for Detroit, was described as one of the most powerful and influential union figures in America. In 1970, when Mr Fraser returned to the Gorbals in search of his roots, he discovered that his old tenement home in Cumberland Street – last seen when he was six – had been bulldozed. During a nationwide strike by fire-fighters, soldiers and sailors using elderly Green Goddess fire engines fought a spectacular fire which destroyed the historic Cunninghame church in Ballater Street.

At a meeting with housing supremos in the city chambers in George Square, members of the Gorbals Anti-Damp Campaign produced bottles containing water beetles to highlight dreadful conditions in the Hutchesontown Area E development of two 24-storey multis and 759 deck-access houses. Confronted by representatives of angry families who were desperate to get out of the damp-riddled flats, Scotland's housing minister Hugh Brown promised the tenants top priority on the city's overloaded housing list. MP Frank McElhone backed the tenants in their campaign to have the rateable value of their homes reduced to nil and said the new flats, known locally as 'the Dampies', were worse than the slums the families had moved from.

Families in Cathcart Road were evacuated to a hostel when their condemned tenement began to collapse. Glasgow District Council officials had expected the tottering building to stand for another two years. The fire damaged Palace bingo hall in Gorbals Street, originally the Indian-themed Palace Theatre of Varieties, was bulldozed out of existence. Some of the exotic interior fittings, including four elephant heads, were salvaged, to be installed in due course in the revamped Citizens' theatre.

In a high-rise in Norfolk Court, near Gorbals Cross, firemen rescued twenty-two people trapped between floors in two lifts. Mrs Teresa Lynch said: 'There was hardly any air in the lift, and the longer we were trapped the hotter it got. We could hardly breathe.' Members of Strathclyde Region's social work committee made a surprise visit to 'the Venny' – the Gorbals adventure playground – and decided to axe it as 'a threat to children's lives'. At Glasgow High Court, a sixteen-year-old Gorbals youth was sentenced to be detained indefinitely for knifing a youth to death. The court heard that the teenager became 'a crazed killer' after drinking beer left in the pipes of a derelict Gorbals pub.

Among the few remaining Jewish business enterprises in the Gorbals were Cohen's Delicatessen Stores in Main Street, Wholesale Hosiery in Gorbals Street and monumental sculptors Lipton and Sons of Bedford Lane. The Riverside tavern in Waddell Court featured 'professional cabaret' and a 'ladies only evening'. The Mally Arms in Eglinton Street was described by real-ale aficionados as a pub of real character with an excellent pint.

1978 WHISKY GALORE

Revd Geoff Shaw, CND activist, champion of Gorbals delinquents, convener of Strathclyde Region and one of the most influential clergymen of his generation, collapsed and died of heart failure in Glasgow's Royal Infirmary. Thousands lined the streets outside Glasgow Cathedral, where a memorial service was held. Shaw had spent seventeen years in the Gorbals and there was a large turnout of local people at Linn crematorium. The *Catholic Observer* praised Shaw, an unorthodox Church of Scotland minister, as 'a man who saw his ministry in terms of service to everyone who needed his help – in whatever way.' The BBC chose six boys from two hundred hopefuls in schools all over Scotland to play the Gorbals Diehards in a six-part television serialisation of John Buchan's thriller *Huntingtower.* None of the lucky six hailed from the Gorbals.

Refusing to admit design defects in the damp-riddled Hutchesontown Area E flats, Glasgow District Council launched an £8,000 leaflet blitz to convince tenants that their lives were being blighted by 'condensation'. Fire-fighters who rushed to a blaze on the fifth floor of a block of flats in Queen Elizabeth Square found every smoke door lying open. A fire service spokesman said: 'If the people who live in high flats nullify fire safety precautions then a terrible tragedy could occur.' Tenants in Waddell Court, a Hutchesontown high-rise block, complained about the pungent aroma emanating from the neighbouring Strathclyde distillery, which produced several million gallons of grain whisky per year.

Campaigning for former Gorbals gangland enforcer Jimmy Boyle's early release from the Special Unit, Boyle's lawyer described his client as 'an accomplished sculptor'. A police spokesman said: 'The sculpture this man was famous for was on other people's faces.'

1979   CONCRETE CAVES

At Glasgow High Court, nine members of the Ulster Volunteer Force received sentences ranging from twelve to eighteen years for bomb attacks on two Glasgow pubs, the Old Burnt Barns in Calton and the Clelland bar in the Gorbals. During the trial nearly half the charges against the accused men were dropped, including the charge that they were involved in the bombing of Derry Treanor's pub in Cathcart Road in 1977.

The security net as the men were sentenced was the tightest ever seen in a Scottish court, with frogmen being brought in to search underground sewers. The jury heard that the fingerprints of one of the accused men, Angus McKenna (24) from Bridgeton, had been found on a glass amid the wreckage of the Clelland bar in Hospital Street. Bar staff had noticed McKenna because he had asked for sherry, a drink seldom in demand in Gorbals pubs. Shortly after McKenna left the pub, it was ripped apart by a bomb. Bar owner John Rawley told the court: 'There was an orange flame. I was knocked off my feet. Then we just started getting customers out and into the street.'

After being alarmed by the second explosion at the Strathclyde distillery in two years, residents of the neighbouring Riverside flats voiced their opposition to 'noise, pollution and the risk to life and limb'. A distillery spokesman claimed that the plant had managed to eliminate 90 per cent of the smell from the distilling process. The Riverside Action Group vowed to campaign until the last 10 per cent had been removed. P. J. King, monumental masons of Cumberland Street, invited punters to send for their 'Jewish headstone catalogue'. The stately classical facade of the Citizens' theatre was taken down and the crowning statues by James Mossman – Burns, Shakespeare and the Four Muses – went into storage in preparation for a £500,000 renovation scheme funded by Glasgow District Council.

The Gorbals, 'completely dissected by busy dangerous roads', was reported to be 'paying the high price for calm, city centre pedestrian precincts'. City councillors were informed that even a £2 million investment in heating, ventilation and insulation wouldn't necessarily make the seven-year-old Hutchesontown Area E flats – nicknamed 'concrete caves' – habitable. Police arrested two teenage youths after eighty-year-old twice-widowed Charlotte Anderson was brutally beaten and left bound and gagged in her Crown Street flat. Her attackers made off with fifty pence. A detective said: 'This is one of the worst beatings I have ever come across. It was sadistic and senseless.'

William Donald was sent to a young offenders' institution for six years for attacking an Orangeman in Ballater Street with an old-fashioned cut-throat razor. Police launched a hunt for three mini-thugs – boys 'as young as twelve' – after cashier Sally Gallagher (18) was mugged in Queen Elizabeth Square and robbed of £6,000. In spite of redevelopment, the Guild of Aid, run by Miss Marald Dingwall Grant with the help of a distinguished group of directors led by Viscount Weir, was still going strong, with five hundred members and its own savings bank.

1980 GORBALS CHAMPION

At the High Court in Glasgow, jail sentences totalling seventy-two years were imposed on seven members of the Scottish Republican Socialist League, dubbed 'tartan terrorists' by the media. In their struggle to 'liberate' Scotland, League members had made an armed raid on Oxford Street post office in the Gorbals and, after hijacking a post office van in the same district, had escaped with £100,000. Though successful, the raid on the van had its farcical side; the masked and armed bandits locked themselves in the back of the vehicle and had to untie the driver to release them. Sentencing the men, Lord McDonald said he refused to regard them as 'bungling amateurs'. The highest sentences fell on commander-in-chief Peter Wardlaw (a television mechanic) and his second-in-command Alex Ramsay (a taxi driver). Wardlaw was sent down for sixteen years while Ramsay was jailed for fifteen years.

Jimmy Boyle (35), Scotland's best-known prison inmate, married psychiatrist Dr Sarah Trevelyan in a register office in the Stirlingshire village of Balfron. Margaret Kinnear, Boyle's common law ex-wife, said: 'I hope she has a better life with Jimmy than I ever had.' A derelict pub in Maryhill was used as a set for Scottish Television's controversial big budget film based on Boyle's autobiography. Since the Gorbals tenements of the former debt collector's criminal heyday no longer existed, the film crew had to go to Springburn in the north of Glasgow for location shots.

Queen's Park Terrace in Eglinton Street (1860), a structurally sound building designed by world-famous architect Alexander Thomson, was demolished in one of the greatest acts of vandalism in Glasgow's history. Councillor John Lavelle of Laurieston-Gorbals described the demolition of the unique category 'A' listed building as 'an important success'. Adelphi Terrace secondary school in Commercial Road, opened in 1967, faced closure because of a falling school roll. Designed for 900 pupils, the school had only 390.

Pensioner Willie Roxburn of Norfolk Court was voted the Scottish Consumer Council's champion for his work as leader of the campaign to win rates rebates for the inhabitants of the appalling Hutchesontown Area E development, where the houses were so badly affected by damp that water ran down walls, furniture went mouldy and carpets bred maggots. Mr Roxburn (69) said: 'I'm delighted with the award. It is for everyone who helped fight for better conditions in the Gorbals and not just for me.' After a long struggle, including a prolonged rent strike, Glasgow District Council agreed to rehouse all the remaining tenants in the blocks. As part of the Gorbals Fair, there was a rock day in the Playbarn youth club in Cumberland Street. The disc jockey failed to turn up, but six bands – including Sammy and the Badgers – did manage to get their acts together. The Coliseum cinema, the first Glasgow movie house to show a feature-length talkie, closed with Jack Nicholson in *The Shining*.

The death was announced of Dan Flynn (96), who became a leading Glasgow bookmaker and racehorse owner after a glorious sporting career. A fitness fanatic, Flynn was not only the Empire cycling champion six times but was also heavyweight boxing champion of Scotland. During his time in the ring he fought Hollywood great Victor McLaglen, who would later star with John Wayne in the classic movie *The Quiet Man*, and the two became lifelong friends. He opened his first, credit-only betting shop in Queen Street, Glasgow in 1912 and then expanded throughout Scotland.

1981   GHOST TOWN

MP Harry Ewing – a former minister in charge of Scotland's prisons – claimed that Gorbals-born murderer Jimmy Boyle, who had been moved to Edinburgh and slotted into the government's Training for Freedom scheme, had been in control of the Special Unit at Barlinnie. Mr Ewing said: 'Boyle was running the place. He imposed his personality on the unit.'

The ITV network screened *A Sense of Freedom*, a £500,000 film based on Boyle's less than candid autobiography. Arnot McWhinnie, a top Scottish crime reporter, slammed the film, hyped as 'the most powerful piece of television ever to come out of Scotland', for glossing over the former loan-shark enforcer's atrocious crimes: 'It doesn't show how he ran down a street in the Gorbals slashing innocent people. It doesn't show how Boyle's murder victim was literally hacked to death. It doesn't show Boyle's links with the Kray brothers who led a vicious gang which terrorised London. It doesn't show that Boyle had appeared in court twice on murder charges before he was finally convicted.' As the controversial film was released, it was reported that loan sharks were once again preying on vulnerable people in Glasgow's most deprived communities, charging 50 per cent interest *per week* on transactions ranging from £1 to £100.

The Hutchesontown Area E development was described as, 'The most modern and expensive ghost town on record.' A council spokesman said: 'We haven't even begun to work out what it would cost to attempt to remedy the dampness. Even to knock the houses down would probably run into millions.' Mrs Margaret McManus of Pine Place told a reporter that for nine years she had suffered a 'pure hell' of creeping green and black mould: 'The only solution, from what I can see, is to knock the whole lot down and start again.'

Sociologists at Glasgow University compiled a report highlighting heroin addiction in the Gorbals and other deprived areas of the city. Dr Jason Ditton, a sociology lecturer, said: 'The figure of a thousand addicts is a relatively conservative estimate.' Some of the junkies were as young as fourteen. Gorbals heroin addict Frank Smith warned teenagers against drugs and said: 'In some ways I am lucky; I am alive. A close friend of mine, aged nineteen, died recently through heroin addiction.'

Scotland's first custom-built mosque near the old Gorbals Cross lay half-finished because the city's twelve-thousand-strong Muslim community was £1.5 million short of the total needed to complete the building. Inflation had added many thousands of pounds to the bill. Glasgow Muslims had raised £400,000 on their own and another £600,000 had come from Saudi Arabia and other sources.

1982 PANTS TO THE PROVOST

Feisty Gorbals pensioner Mrs Catherine McColl of Caledonia Road hung out her undies on a washing line outside Glasgow city chambers in protest against the council's closure of Fauldhouse Street steamie, which for many years had served the Gorbals and Oatlands districts. Strathclyde Region councillor James Wray called for convicted drug pushers to be evicted from council houses. Mr Wray, who represented the Gorbals, said: 'We are determined to stamp out this evil.' A council spokesman said: 'Drug pushing would make anyone an anti-social tenant and there is provision for taking action against anti-social tenants.'

The ruling Labour group on Glasgow District Council ran into trouble with the city's Labour Party over a plan to sell off the notorious Hutchesontown Area E, a two-square-mile area of mainly empty deck-access houses. Builders Barratt offered to pay £1,000 for each of the 759 damp-riddled dwellings. Only a handful of families were left in the failed development, where staircases were littered with discarded beer cans and wine bottles. Down-and-outs dossed in the empty flats and heroin junkies and solvent abusers used them as a convenient haven. Mrs Margaret Orr and her family of Sandiefield Road had somehow come to terms with the appalling living conditions. She said: 'We got used to it. Of course it gets bad in the winter but we still love it here.'

At Jimmy Boyle's press conference, held to mark his release on licence from Saughton prison, a reporter noted that 'there were no expressions of sorrow for his victims'. Boyle, who had been the chief heavy for a gang of loan sharks, said: 'After all, most of my victims were people involved in crime and that's part of my life I just want to forget.'

Four girls, returning from Edinburgh where they had gone to see the Pope, were taken to the Victoria Infirmary after thugs pelted their bus with bricks near the Bedford bingo hall in Eglinton Street. A police spokesman said: 'No one was apprehended. But we do not believe it was a sectarian incident.'

Almost ten years after the Queen opened the £7.2 million Hutchesontown Area E flats – the notorious 'Dampies' – the last tenant was rehoused. In a disgraceful act of official vandalism, the magnificent McNeil Street United Co-operative bakery, built in the 1880s at a cost of £131,000 to resemble a Loire château, was reduced to 'a demolisher's landscape of broken brick, firewood, splintered glass and wood'.

Guitarist Alex Harvey, a veteran of the Sixties rhythm-and-blues boom, died of a heart attack in Belgium on the eve of his forty-seventh birthday while returning from a European tour with the Sensational Alex Harvey Band, described by an aficionado as being 'heavy metal when the rest of rock was still in the Stone Age'. Reared in Thistle Street, Gorbals, he made his name in the 1950s through the Alex Harvey Big Soul Band. When he got married and moved to a single end in Crown Street, he gave free gigs to raise funds to take local pensioners on bus trips. He went on to earn an estimated £15 million from pop music helped by his top-twenty hits of the mid-1970s, 'Delilah' and 'The Boston Tea Party'.

The Asian-owned D & D wholesale cash and carry warehouse in Centre Street, Tradeston, custom-built at a cost of over £2 million, consisted of '50,000 square feet packed with the finest value in drapery, fancy goods, women's and men's wear, toys, furniture, lamps and pictures'.

1983   TOO MUCH SEX

At Glasgow High Court, a jury was told that Andrew Bell of Sandiefield Road was scalped when his lifelong buddy, James Adam of Waddell Court, 'attacked him for no reason' after a Friday-night drinking bout. Mr Bell said: 'I woke hours later and did not think I was hurt as bad as I was until the skin of my scalp fell down over my eyes.' Policewoman Janice Duffy told the court of her horror in finding part of Mr Bell's scalp lying on a coffee table in his flat. Constable Macleod affirmed: 'there was blood everywhere'. Mr Adam claimed that he had left his pal drunk and sleeping in his armchair. The jury found the charge not proven. Mr Bell, who had spent six weeks in hospital and undergone three operations, said: 'Adam was my best friend since we were five years old but I haven't spoken a word to him since.'

Footballer Edwin 'Eddie' Gray was awarded the MBE in the Queen's birthday honours' list. Born in the Gorbals in 1948, he followed a road travelled by thousands of his contemporaries when he and his family moved to a council flat in the new estate of Castlemilk in 1965. He was a child prodigy and following dazzling displays at the age of fifteen in the schoolboy home internationals no less than thirty-five clubs including Manchester United, Arsenal and Liverpool queued up to offer him a professional contract. Among them was his beloved Celtic, but Gray felt that the Bhoys did not try hard enough to capture his signature and plumped instead for humble English second-division outfit, Leeds United, after being captivated by the powerful personality of the Yorkshire club's manager, Don Revie. It was a decision that Gray would never regret as Revie guided Leeds to the highest echelons of the game. In the years that followed Gray won a host of honours including two league titles and the FA cup. He was capped twelve times for Scotland, a total that would have been much higher but for serious injury. A tantalising left-winger, Gray was a model professional and, in 561 appearances for Leeds, he was never sent off. But despite his undoubted success in England he claimed in his auto-biography that his greatest thrill in football came when son Stuart played for Celtic in an Old Firm match.

Matt Lygate (44), who stood for election in the Gorbals in 1969 as the candidate for the Workers' Party of Scotland, was released on parole from Edinburgh's Saughton prison. He had served eleven-and-a-half years of a twenty-four-year sentence, imposed when he was found guilty of being involved in three armed bank hold-ups. Mr Lygate told a reporter: 'The sentence was harsh. There were murderers given life sentences about the same time as I went to prison, and they were set free years ago. But I could not retract what I know to be true.'

In the Court of Session in Edinburgh, indefatigable campaigner Mrs Catherine McColl of Caledonia Road won her battle to stop Strathclyde Region putting fluoride in the water supply. McColl versus Strathclyde Region ran for 201 days and produced 1,434 volumes of evidence amounting to 5.3 million words. The case – the second longest in Scottish legal history – cost £1.5 million, all of which came from public funds. Slamming Glasgow District Council housing bosses for blaming dampness in the Hutchie E flats on 'too much sex, heavy breathing, big dogs, paraffin heaters and indoor washing', councillor James Wray said: 'It's bad construction pure and simple.'

The firm of Goldbergs – founded by Abraham Goldberg, who started business in the Gorbals in 1908 – celebrated its seventy-fifth anniversary by handing over a £15,000 cheque to sponsor the first bed in the as-yet-unopened Prince and Princess of Wales hospice. Returning from the post office with her £20 social security benefit, Mary Murphy, a blind woman, was knocked down, kicked and robbed in a lift in her tower block home in Queen Elizabeth Square. Mary told a reporter: 'I'll never go out on my own again.'

1984 GORBALS UNITED

Cashing in on the nationwide vogue for real ale, Gorbals publican Danny Macaulay sold his own home-brewed ale over the counter of his Pig and Whistle pub in McNeil Street. Patrons were able to down pints of Pig's Brew and Pig's Light. Mr Macaulay told a reporter: 'I decided to try and take on the big breweries with my own beer. I am now selling a pint of beer for 60p, which is pretty hard to beat.'

Adelphi Terrace secondary school, which had closed down because of a decline in its roll, was the venue for an exhibition of the history of Jewish life in the Gorbals. Ms Charlotte Hutt, a former teacher at the school, and convener of the Gorbals Fair Society, said: 'Our original plan was to cover the whole early history of the Gorbals in one show. However, there was such a wealth of interesting materials on the Jewish community alone that we decided to concentrate on it first.' In addition to featuring Jewish religious, social, political and welfare institutions, from the Great Synagogue to the Jewish Institute Players and Oxford Star FC, there was put on show a remarkable collection of photographs recalling a vanished commercial Gorbals of Jewish shops and businesses. To coincide with the exhibition, Gorbals Fair Society published *A Scottish Shtetl* by Charlotte Hutt and Harold Kaplan.

Joe Ridge (45) smashed his way to safety from a blazing flat on the twentieth floor of a multi-storey block in Old Rutherglen Road, then went back to rescue twenty-seven-year-old Winnie Reeves and her two-year-old son Stephen. A fire service spokesman said: 'The incident could have been much worse had it not been for the quick-thinking of Mr Ridge and the safety structure of the doors of the flats.'

Dr James Gilchrist, who started in private practice in the Gorbals in 1928, retired aged seventy-nine. At one time almost 50 per cent of his 4,000 patients were of the Jewish faith. The Glasgow Central Mosque and Islamic centre, described by its architects as a 'fusion between Scottish tradition, forms of Islamic building and the simple logic and economics of modern constructions', was opened in the Gorbals on the site of the Adelphi distillery. Part of the £2.5 million cost was met by donations from prominent Muslims, including the prince of Mecca and the mayor of Jeddah. The world-famous Citizens' theatre in Gorbals Street was promised a £140,000 facelift as part of a major urban and environmental package to transform 'the bleak surrounding area'. A sceptical William Taylor, chairman of the Citizens' board of directors, said that the grant would do little to address the problems of the historic venue: 'For the past few winters we have had to indulge in a process of patching to keep our clients comfortable.'

At the opening of the Gorbals Fair, Lorraine Gray (11) of Blackfriars primary school was crowned Queen. From small beginnings in 1971, the Fair had blossomed into a four-week carnival with talent shows, football competitions, discos and fancy-dress parades. Twomax Fashions Ltd of Old Rutherglen Road was described as 'Glasgow's largest and finest selection of factory shops under one roof.'

The Bedford bingo club in Eglinton Street – opened in 1935 as the New Bedford picture house – applied for permission to serve drinks on Saturday afternoons. A lawyer for the Mecca social club, owners of the Bedford, pleaded: 'More men than ever are joining their wives to play bingo.' Glasgow's licensing board, unmoved, turned down the application. Gorbals United – which ran four football teams catering for sixty young people – played host to Rangers and Celtic stars at a social evening in the association's new sports and leisure facility, the James Elliot Centre in Braehead Street, Oatlands.

Families living in a high-rise block in Queen Elizabeth Square were reported to be only feet away from potentially dangerous asbestos tiles in cupboards used to store prams, bicycles and children's toys. When the tenants got the brush-off from Glasgow District Council, they commissioned a survey of their own, carried out by experts from the city's college of technology. A college spokesman said: 'There is always the chance of tiles being damaged where you have kids playing about.'

A 'teenage firebug' was sent to a young offenders' institution for six years after being found guilty of an arson attack on a warehouse owned by N & E Importers (Glasgow) Ltd of Kingston Street. Witnesses described a youth running from the warehouse, his face badly scorched and 'smoke coming out of his hair'. Donald Findlay, the accused youth's advocate, told the jury that his client had been paid £2,000 to start the fire and had been 'used by evil and unscrupulous men for their own gain'. The court heard that company boss Nawab Din had fainted when he heard the explosion from his other warehouse, D & D Cash and Carry in Centre Street.

Millionaires Yaqub Ali and Dajali Ali announced that their giant new cash and carry warehouse on the Dixon's Blazes industrial estate would be 'a complete centre for the small retailer'. Yaqub, who came to Scotland in 1952 as a young man of nineteen and started selling knitwear door-to-door, said: 'I'm confident it will succeed. Otherwise we would not have invested £13 million.' He added: 'This place is going to be for the small independent shopkeepers. They have a problem in that they cannot buy in sufficient quantities from the manufacturers to compete with the supermarkets. We will bring in stock by the container load and take a very small margin on each item. That means the shopkeepers can buy a whole range of goods that will allow them to charge prices very close to those in the superstores.'

1985 DURGA PUJA

To mark the fiftieth anniversary of Benny Lynch winning his world flyweight title, boxing fans brought his former wife from Canada for the unveiling of a gravestone in St Kentigern's RC cemetery at Lambhill. The former Mrs Anne Lynch (72) was met by Lord Provost Bob Gray and taken in the city's Rolls-Royce to the cemetery. Boxing greats Peter Keenan, Walter McGowan and Jim Watt were invited to the unveiling ceremony. The black granite gravestone bore the legend, 'Always a Fighter'.

George Davis (44) of Mosspark announced that he was trying to trace his wee Gorbals pal. In 1948, the two scruffy urchins had been photographed in Warwick Street by Bert Hardy, one of Britain's top photographers, who'd been commissioned to illustrate a *Picture Post* magazine feature on the infamous Gorbals. George said: 'The other boy is Leslie Mason and I'd love to hear from him again.' It turned out that Leslie (45) was living in the Knightswood area of Glasgow, and the two smartly-dressed middle-aged men were able to get together and pose for a photograph – in the heart of the Gorbals.

Glasgow District Council emerged from a five-hour marathon meeting to announce that the grim Hutchesontown Area E deck-access flats would be replaced by a mixture of public and private housing. Housing bosses and local people were delighted at the prospect of the desolate complex of 759 flats – dubbed a concrete *Marie Celeste* – being redeveloped. A spokesman said: 'It's a significant blight on the Gorbals. A real indictment of a whole generation of prefabricated building.' A Franciscan brother, Damian, who helped run a centre for young drug abusers, said: 'We know that the flats are being used by youngsters to take drugs.' Doctors at the Gorbals health centre complained that it was difficult to treat patients for depression because the rotting derelict blocks were right on the centre's doorstep. 'We counsel them and try to show them there is hope. The problem is when they leave and walk home they pass by one of the causes of their problems – Hutchie E.'

Though catastrophic planning decisions had wiped out the Gorbals as a shopping centre, Strathclyde Regional Council refused to allow potential developers to include plans for a large shopping precinct in Hutchesontown, claiming that shops would undermine prospects for retail development in the city centre. The coveted contract to rebuild Hutchie E was awarded to a consortium led by a local builder, ex-brickie Frank Lafferty. Three popular Gorbals watering holes – the Blarney Stone, Tucker's bar and the Corner bar – were still standing in the shadow of the doomed housing estate. Tucker's owner, Derry Treanor, said: 'My pub is worth at least £150,000, more if there was a complete redevelopment of the area.' Elsewhere in the brave new Gorbals, residents of the media-acclaimed Sir Basil Spence slab blocks in Queen Elizabeth Square won a seven-year battle to have their homes made wind-and-water-tight. John Hewitt said: 'The water comes in through the roof and cuts off the electricity supply every time we get a lot of rain.'

Durga Puja, Glasgow's fifth annual Hindu religious and cultural festival, was centred on the former Adelphi Terrace secondary school in Commercial Road. Glasgow District Council refused to allow Franciscan fathers to demolish their historic friary, attached to St Francis's RC church in Cumberland Street. Father Connelly said: 'The heating bills for the friary at the moment are colossal.' A council spokesman said that the demolition of the friary, a listed building dating from 1870, would result 'in the loss of a particularly fine piece of architecture which also assumes local importance in an area lacking such examples of building'.

The Citizens' theatre won praise for being 'no longer a no-man's-land for the ordinary punter'. Mary Lewis, the venue's publicity officer, said: 'Last year attendances were up 23 per cent on the year before and so far this season, we are doing even better.' In partnership with Wasam Khan from Saudi Arabia, Ashraf Anjum, an economics graduate who had studied at Strathclyde University, opened a massive new wholesale cash and carry warehouse in Wallace Street. Secretary of state for Scotland George Younger ruled that the Glasgow Nautical College in Thistle Street, Gorbals should be the only merchant-navy training-centre in the country.

1986 HOMES NOT JAILS

Economist and psychologist Ralph Glasser published the first volume of his autobiography, *Growing Up in the Gorbals*. The distinguished academic, who had left school at fourteen and worked as a presser in a rag-trade sweat shop before winning a scholarship to Oxford, told a reporter: 'In my childhood life was hard, but I have a lot to thank the Gorbals for. If you boil it down, growing up in the Gorbals meant that maturity was forced on you much earlier. There was little opportunity to indulge the usual childhood fantasies.' He added: 'Of course you can argue that the old community spirit grew out of the very harshness of the life that the people endured and shared and that those who manage to escape tend to view the past through rose-coloured spectacles.' In his book, Glasser evoked a Gorbals of 'one water tap for six families or more, lavatories overflowing yellow and brown down shattered stone steps, rats in full possession, and people skimping and scraping to be allowed to live in such places'.

Jimmy Boyle used a Rolls-Royce to visit prisoners in jails around Scotland. Boyle, who had served a fifteen-year sentence for a particularly horrific murder and had also taken part in a riot in which a prison officer lost an eye, told a reporter: 'It's good for the prison officers to see me in a nice Rolls-Royce. It gets right up their noses and it gives me a great kick.'

At the Islamic Centre in Ballater Street, Jamil Moghul (8) was presented with a Turban of Excellence, having memorised all 77,934 words of the Koran. Two thugs, one of them wearing a mask, burst into the Gorbals home of Ismail Veigas, a seventy-five-year-old Pakistani, gave him a terrible beating, and ransacked his home. Police investigations revealed that, on the night of the attack, Hugh McIntyre, Mr Veigas's next-door-neighbour, had said to a man in a local pub: 'I don't like Pakistanis. One stays next to me and I'm going to do him. He's loaded.' At the High Court in Glasgow, McIntyre, who had sixty-nine previous convictions, pleaded guilty to acting with another person unknown and assaulting Mr Veigas in his home. He was sent down for four years.

The Coliseum cinema in Eglinton Street and the Citizens' theatre in Gorbals Street, among the few old buildings to survive draconian redevelopment, were accorded listed building status. The Coliseum (1905) was given a B-category listing for its heritage value as 'a large Flemish-style music hall'.

The Queen opened the new £27 million Glasgow and Strath-kelvin Sheriff Court in Carlton Place, Laurieston. Hyped as combining 'the style of Charles Rennie Mackintosh with modern requirements', the fortress-like building was fancifully described as having 'the air of an exclusive yachting clubhouse, nestling behind new lawns, freshly planted trees and imaginative land-scaping by the banks of the river Clyde'. As she arrived for the opening ceremony, the monarch was greeted by locals waving banners emblazoned with the slogan 'homes not jails'.

Objecting to a yuppie property developer's proposal to move the burnt-out shell of Alexander 'Greek' Thomson's world-famous Caledonia Road church 'stone by stone' to Buchanan Street, Martin Cox of Cumberland Street pointed out that the A-listed building was one of the few remaining landmarks in a Gorbals 'now pockmarked with gap-sites more redolent of the moon's surface than a once thriving community'.

The saga of Hutchie E took a new twist when the consortium behind redevelopment withdrew their planning application for a massive shopping centre which regional councillors considered 'too big for the area'. Crossroads Youth and Community Association in the Gorbals, a voluntary organisation that had worked in the area for twenty years, described its Regional Council grant as painfully inadequate. After the irrepressible Gorbals-born Pat Lally became leader of the Glasgow Labour Group, the *Glasgow Herald* described his success as 'the greatest comeback since Lazarus'.

1987   GORBALS ECSTASY

A Gorbals grannie, Mrs Ellen McAllister – born in Rose Street before it was renamed Florence Street – authored a lively wee book called *Shadows on a Gorbals Wall.* She told a reporter: 'It was a poor childhood. But, you see, we didn't know we were poor. Children were very protected, as their mums didn't work, not with families of seven, eight, nine, and ten to look after. They played out on the streets as soon as they could toddle, their mothers standing at the close mouth, wrapped in their shawls, often breast-feeding their younger babies as they gossiped.' Mrs McAllister recalled playtime in the Gorbals of the 1920s – peever, rounders, chuckies – and rat-catching in the middens. Still fiercely proud of her Gorbals heritage, she said: 'The Gorbals folk are clannish, but they're good folk when you get to know them.'

In a two-page letter to the BBC from his cell in a top security psychiatric hospital, convicted murderer Ian Brady, who had lived in the Gorbals for the first seventeen years of his life, confessed to five other murders and claimed that two of his victims had been Scots. After Brady and his accomplice Myra Hindley agreed to help police find the bodies of some of their victims, the remains of sixteen-year-old Pauline Reade were recovered from bleak Saddleworth moor near Manchester. Glasgow's councillors were warned that dangerous levels of airborne brown asbestos made the derelict blocks of the Hutchesontown E complex 'a lethal playground for children'. Blackfriars primary school was only yards away from the mouldering concrete hulks, hyped in their brief heyday as 'a mini-garden city'. The bulldozers couldn't move in because the developing consortium was in dispute with Strathclyde Regional Council, which had refused planning permission for a 200,000-square-feet retail-development on a site which the council had designated as suitable for 20,000 feet of retail.

Mary Darby, who lived in a multi in Sandiefield Road, said: 'Bus loads of people pull up in the street to look at the Hutchie E flats.' Like some bizarre time-capsule, the abandoned development was littered with detritus of 1970s vintage, including pop posters on bedroom walls.

With more than 676,000 people in Strathclyde living on or below the official poverty line of Supplementary Benefit, illegal money-lenders were reported to be bleeding the poor in the deprived districts of Glasgow, including the Gorbals. The tallymen employed callous enforcers in the Jimmy Boyle mould and their victims were said to be 'too frightened to talk'.

In the run-up to Mayfest, Glasgow's cosmopolitan arts festival, staff at the Citizens' theatre reported a huge demand for tickets for a new production of Robert McLeish's play *The Gorbals Story*. Heroin dealer George McCann of Queen Elizabeth Court was jailed for six years. As policemen approached McCann, he threw a bag of the drug – worth £4,150 – from a car window. When searched, he had £350 in his underpants.

The posthumous Victoria Cross awarded to Gorbals war hero James Stokes in 1945 was sold at Christie's in London for £16,000.

Its current whereabouts are unknown. The recreational drug ecstasy was reported to have 'spread to the Gorbals'. Local traders opposed millionaire Yaqub Ali's plan for a £1.5 million expansion of his Castle cash and carry business in Crown Street, which employed 320 people, drawn from the Gorbals and surrounding areas.

Families in the Gorbals cheered when Burnthills Demolition of Johnstone moved into Hutchie E to demolish the 759 asbestos-ridden deck-access flats, a monument to the inhuman 'brutalist' architecture of the 1970s. Connie Andrew (19) of Norfolk Court said: 'We are so pleased to see it going at last. We lived with its ugliness for all these years. Getting rid of it will help the Gorbals.'

1988   GORBALS YUPPIE

James 'Jamer' Boyle (22), the son of convicted murderer Jimmy Boyle, was jailed for three years for holding up a local fish-and-chip shop in Queen Elizabeth Square and attacking the Pakistani owner with a crowbar before escaping with £600. His defence counsel said: 'He has had added pressure in his life because he is the son of a man with a past reputation and he has had to live in the shadows of that in the Gorbals.'

Ralph Glasser published volume two of his autobiography, *Gorbals Boy at Oxford*. In the book he described his reception at the august seat of learning in 1938 as a genuine proletarian. For his fellow undergraduates, Glasser wrote, the Gorbals was 'as distant, as unknowable, as the Kalahari desert.'

A 'Gorbals-born yuppie' residing in the pleasant southern suburb of King's Park, was sent to jail for a year for a string of mortgage frauds involving more than £315,000. The court heard that he gave false names and references to building societies. The money then went to buy properties which he let out to tenants.

Members of Glasgow District Council opposed Strathclyde Region's multi-million pound plan to extend Glasgow's motorway network, claiming that it would 'create a spaghetti junction in the Gorbals'. Mrs Nancy Harvey of Gorbals 88, a group set up to oppose the plan, said: 'What we need in the Gorbals is good housing so that the community can be built up again; we don't need more families dispersed so that motorists can save ten minutes on their journeys.' The Frank Lafferty-led consortium, which had made a successful bid for the Hutchie E site, announced that they were pulling out of the redevelopment project. Shortly afterwards, local tycoon Lafferty's building empire collapsed with debts of £5 million. Steven Hamilton, Glasgow's town clerk, said: 'Glasgow District Council is now free to deal with the site as its own.'

After his son died of a heroin overdose on a stairway in Waddell Court, a high-rise block in Hutchesontown, David Cameron said: 'We both knew it was inevitable the drugs would kill him.' The Citizens' theatre presented *No Mean City*, a play based on the controversial McArthur-Long novel about life in the pre-war Gorbals slums. The tenants of a Norfolk Court tower block adjacent to the new Sheriff Court complained that their car park was being monopolised by well-heeled lawyers and court officials in Porsches, Jaguars and Mercedes. Raymond Neil said: 'It's driving us all up the wall. The flashy cars start arriving around seven a.m. and they jam up our car park until about six p.m.'

The Gorbals Fair history group reported that their survey of the Southern Necropolis was yielding excellent results. Ms Charlotte Hutt said: 'We have found early Chartists and socialists, agents of banks long ago collapsed, people involved in the India trade. There's a heroine of the Mexican fight for freedom from the Spanish Empire. There are poets, artists, street musicians, actors, cotton workers, engineers, soldiers, miners and industrialists.' She added: 'It's not as spooky as it sounds – though there is rumoured to be a White Lady floating around.'

1989 HERITAGE TRAIL

Angry locals called for immediate action to clean up 'the Hutchie Horror', the huge wasteland in the heart of the Gorbals where the Area E housing estate had been located. James Connolly (67) said: 'It looks like a film scene from *All Quiet on the Western Front.*' Residents of Sir Basil Spence's Queen Elizabeth Square slab blocks were evacuated to the John Mains community centre after being flooded out. A council official said: 'There has been trouble because of flooding in the past and recently the whole building was re-roofed.'

A former fire station in Centre Street, Tradeston was turned into the Hamish Allan centre, emergency accommodation for homeless people. The unit, which provided accommodation for up to forty-eight hours, consisted of seventeen single-bedrooms and eighteen fully-furnished family flats. Bill Hood, Glasgow's chief housing officer, said: 'One of the major problems we still have is of people's perception of homelessness. Some people still think of it as being a man with a wine bottle. That is totally wrong. At least 99 per cent of our people are not like that.' Actress Caroline Paterson, who had a starring role in *Winners and Losers,* a boxing-themed Scottish Television series, said: 'I'm a lassie out the Gorbals, you know. I have worked very hard and want to do well. I spent too many years on the dole thinking I was not good enough.'

Gorbals-born poet Kenneth White (53), a professor at the Paris Sorbonne, paid a nostalgic visit to Portugal Street before returning to his home in Brittany. Professor White, whose father was a railway signalman, had come to Scotland to read extracts from two recently published books. After Strathclyde Regional Council scrapped plans to put a motorway through the Gorbals, freeing over sixty acres of land for redevelopment, councillor Charles Gordon said: 'This is the start of a renaissance in the Gorbals.'

Carlton Place, the jewel in the crown of Regency Laurieston, was promised a £3 million facelift. The campaign to restore the two riverfront terraces had been led by William Cuthbert, chairman of Clyde Shipping, a firm that had been based in Carlton Place for more than a century. Strathclyde Region councillor Charles Gordon, arguing that the Gorbals should never be allowed to become 'a haven for yuppies', said: 'The yuppies don't tend to have families and don't assimilate into the local community. We need more families in the Gorbals, not pricey flats.' Councillor Jimmy Mutter backed up his colleague and said: 'Although we welcome private houses on the Hutchie E site, we don't want yuppie-style flats. We want this to be a family area where people who moved away years ago will come back.'

More than four hundred Muslims from all over Scotland met in the Central Mosque near Gorbals Cross to call for a ban on Salman Rushdie's award-winning novel *Satanic Verses.* The Prince and Princess of Wales hospice in Carlton Place, Laurieston, opened its first in-patient unit for eight terminally ill cancer patients. Dr Anne Gilmore, founder and medical director of the hospice said: 'We haven't had huge amounts of money from big business. Much of the funding has come from the generosity of the people of Glasgow.'

The Citizen's theatre – opened in 1878 as Her Majesty's theatre and opera house – was tarted up with a new brick facade. The Muses of tragedy, comedy, music and dance, which had adorned the original classical facade, were repositioned in the refurbished theatre, which also contained relics from the demolished Palace theatre. The Scottish Development Agency and Glasgow District Council unveiled a £3.2 million plan 'to breathe new life' into the Gorbals. A population plunge to under 11,000 in ten years had left the area 'demoralised and under-serviced' according to the compilers of the Gorbals local plan. Fewer than thirty people in the greater Gorbals area owned their homes while 99 per cent lived in social-housing developments.

The proposed demolition of four popular local howffs – the Blarney Stone, the Corner bar, the Govanhill bar and Treanor's bar – aroused strong sentiments. John Devine of Caledonia Road, whose local was the Blarney Stone, lamented: 'These four pubs are known throughout the world. Americans, Europeans and the Irish have all visited.' Ex-boxer Derry Treanor, a licensee in the Gorbals for over twenty years, complained that the Scottish Development Agency's proposals would 'take away another bit of Glasgow's character'. A Gorbals Heritage Trail started at Victoria Bridge and took in Florence Street, the old Gorbals burial ground, the Southern Necropolis and the site of Dixon's Blazes.

1990 GORBALS MAGIC

Police investigated a possible drugs link after a man was kidnapped in broad daylight in Hutchesontown. The thirty-seven-year-old victim, who was pursued through the Gorbals by a gang of men on foot and two men on a motorcycle, was later admitted to hospital with serious injuries. The Pig and Whistle pub in McNeil Street was described as 'the HQ of a nationwide sexy phone-in operation'. Owner Danny Macauley operated over fifty lines, with his female employees taking calls on a shift basis. Barmaid Donna told a reporter: 'I'm not allowed to have dates with customers. It's against the company rules.'

Gorbals residents were reported to be 'hardened to the fact that the shopping arcade in Cumberland Street is a regular haunt of drug dealers, and the pasty-faced young men and women who buy from them'. After police swooped on the Arcade café, Patrick Feeney was jailed for five years for possessing packets of heroin 'with intent to supply'. Police patrolling in Gorbals Street, near the new Sheriff Court, found Gary McGuire (19) lying dying in a pool of blood. He had twenty-one stab wounds.

A Gorbals task force was formed to 'turn the area round and end its infamous image forever'. Included in the task force were local councillors and Sir Robert Grieve, an eminent academic who had written a major report into Glasgow housing.

The site of the nightmare Hutchie E estate was renamed Crown Street after one of the best-known streets in the old Gorbals. A spokesman for the Crown Street regeneration project said: 'The idea is to retain the community spirit while building a fresh, new future for the Gorbals.' Receivers took failed building tycoon Frank Lafferty to court where he was obliged to cough up £130,000, trousered from his company's work on a putative Hutchie E redevelopment project. Old Gorbalite Eddie Perrett, a pensioner, was so incensed by the area's bad reputation that he published, at his own expense, a book called *The Magic of the Gorbals*. Mr Perrett refused to concede that the Gorbals had deserved its worldwide notoriety: 'The real truth is that compared to modern standards of behaviour, the Gorbals must have been peopled by a race of angels.'

The tenants of the media-acclaimed Queen Elizabeth Square tower blocks were told that their homes would be demolished. Councillor Pat Lally described the blocks, designed by Sir Basil Spence, as 'a monumental monstrosity', while his colleague Jimmy Mutter said that he would fight to have the residents rehoused in the Gorbals. Eddie Brown (74), who had lived in the flats for twenty-five years, said: 'They're in a bit of a state but I like living here.' Glasgow Muslims contributed to the City of Culture celebrations with a series of exhibitions and guided tours at the Central Mosque in the Gorbals. Franco Fraioli took over the Granite City Inn, Cathcart Road, a popular howff which dated back to 1879. The College of Nautical Studies in Thistle Street offered tours of the Gorbals at £15 a head, including morning coffee, lunch and after-noon tea. The tour organiser, Fiona Cherry, said: 'The Gorbals has a tremendous history and heritage.'

Building workers upgrading Riverside View, a Hutchesontown high-rise block known for its high proportion of heroin addicts, found the site littered with syringes. Wimpey worker Rab Heron said: 'I've volunteered to pick up all the dirty needles and syringes. I'm single while most of my work-mates are married with kids.' Local residents were angry when they found out about plans for a Gorbals addiction service, to be based at the Adelphi centre in Commercial Road. A Regional Council spokesman said: 'It is always difficult to get the location right for this type of drugs project. But there is a crying need for such a project in the Gorbals and we hope we can work it out with the community.' The receivers sought a buyer for the nationwide Goldberg store empire, built up from scratch in the Gorbals by Jewish immigrant Abraham Goldberg.

1991   FINANCIAL PSYCHOPATH

At the High Court in Glasgow, Anthony Lennox and Gary Seymour were found guilty of murdering Gary McGuire in Gorbals Street and sentenced to life imprisonment. The court heard that, after Mr McGuire was stabbed to death, his assailants walked into the Hacienda club in Carlton Place and asked the cloakroom attendant to look after their knives. The attendant, fearful for his own safety, hid the weapons in the disc-jockey's turntable.

After the city fathers turned down a suggestion for a plaque in memory of Alexander McArthur, co-author of *No Mean City*, which sold more than five hundred thousand copies worldwide, public relations man John Struthers said: 'I think *No Mean City* is bad news. I spent six years trying to get rid of that image.' Gorbals residents had mixed feelings about the plaque idea. Bridie Drysdale was in favour: 'I think the book was brilliant and it was really true to life. Times were violent then, you must face facts.' Nancy Livingstone disagreed: 'I think people get the wrong impression from reading this book. McArthur never showed the good side of the place like the clean homes and the decent people. We'll never get rid of the bad name he gave the Gorbals.'

In an armed siege that lasted seven-and-a-half hours, police wearing bulletproof vests arrested Noel Ruddle (36), a paranoid schizophrenic who had run amok with a Kalashnikov assault rifle in a high-rise block in Queen Elizabeth Square, shooting one man dead and firing at several other people, including two policemen. One of the shots went through a car windscreen, narrowly missing the driver. Police questioned Glasgow prostitutes in connection with the murder of one of their colleagues: twenty-three-year-old Diane McInally, from the Gorbals. Ms McInally was last seen by a colleague getting into a car in the city's red-light district. Some six and a half hours later, her battered body was found in a wood behind the Burrell gallery in Pollok park. Two men were charged with her murder but were later released due to lack of evidence.

Old Gorbals boy Jack Caplan (75) saw the publication of his book *Memories of the Gorbals.* His mother and father – from Vilna and Kovno in Lithuania – reared seven children in South Portland Street, which in the 1920s was a 'good' address by Gorbals standards. Like many Gorbals Jews, Caplan's father Morris was a tailor by trade. His verdict on the old Gorbals was that it was 'as good a place to live in as any working-class area in the whole of Britain', mainly because it was 'cosmopolitan'.

It was announced that footballer Frank McLintock – capped nine times by Scotland – had decided to auction off his personal memorabilia, including an FA Cup winner's medal. Born in the Gorbals, McLintock was a keen Celtic fan and the Parkhead club was eager to sign him. But he felt that he would not get the chance of first-team football at Celtic and signed instead for Leicester City in 1956. An outstanding centre back, he was later transferred to Arsenal and had a distinguished career at Highbury, captaining the Gunners as they achieved the double of league and FA Cup in 1971. He was honoured with the player-of-the-year award in England, and later became an MBE. After spells in club management McLintock moved into television punditry and is now a regular fixture on the popular *Soccer Saturday* programme on Sky Sports.

The site of the infamous Hutchie E blocks was sold to the Scottish Development Agency, paving the way for the £80 million Crown Street regeneration project. Project director Mike Galloway promised that the new Hutchesontown wouldn't become 'another yuppie development'. Mr Galloway said: 'The vast majority of houses in the Gorbals will be affordable family homes.' He added: 'The only similar scheme on this scale was carried out in Berlin.'

Within the space of seven months, two successful raids were made on the Bank of Scotland in Bridge Street, near Carlton Place. In the first raid, masked men in boiler suits held up security guards at gunpoint and forced them to hand over £350,000 before making their getaway in a powerful sports car. In the second, more amateurish raid, two young men in baseball caps and bomber jackets threatened staff, stole cash and made off across the nearby suspension bridge towards the city centre.

Gorbals Initiative, funded by the taxpayers and the European Union, was set up to encourage inward investment and help people to create their own employment in the area. With the media-acclaimed high-rise blocks in Queen Elizabeth Square scheduled for demolition, tenants were told that if they refused to be rehoused outwith the Gorbals they would be evicted. A council spokesman said: 'We cannot guarantee to rehouse everyone there.' The Alexander Thomson Society was launched to campaign on behalf of the world-famous architect's threatened city buildings, including Caledonia Road church, gutted by fire in 1965.

Tycoon Sir Isaac Wolfson, born in a tenement in Hospital Street, Hutchesontown died in Israel aged ninety-three. He was born into an orthodox Jewish family and his father Solomon was president of the Chevrah Kadisha synagogue in Buchan Street. In 1920 Wolfson left the city and set up his own importing business in London. He joined Great Universal Stores in 1931, became managing director in 1935 and built the company into the largest mail-order concern in Europe, with 20 per cent of the British population as customers. Sir Isaac, who left school at fourteen, and had honorary doctorates from many universities, including Oxford, Cambridge, London, Strathclyde and Glasgow, once quipped: 'I got my education by degrees – honorary degrees.'

Wolfson was praised as 'a financial genius with an instinctive feel for consumer trends and a talent for spotting undervalued property', but in 1960 the police sought to prosecute the tycoon for frauds on his own company, in which, during the 1950s, he allegedly enriched himself at the expense of GUS shareholders by at least £857,000, the equivalent of about £13 million in today's money. A whistle-blower described Wolfson as 'a financial psychopath', but the police dropped their investigation on the advice of the director of public prosecutions, and Wolfson was knighted by Harold Macmillan in 1962.

Two families of Gorbals homeowners refused to be decanted to allow builders to proceed with redevelopment. Scottish Homes considered scrapping its scheme, but compromised by issuing the families with hard hats. It was claimed that the young people of the Gorbals found it hard to get work, 'simply because they've got the wrong address'. Memorabilia from the life of Sir Thomas Lipton, millionaire grocer, philanthropist and yachtsman – who was buried in the Southern Necropolis in the heart of the Gorbals – went under the hammer at Phillips in London.

1992 FORTRESS GORBALS

At the High Court in Glasgow, Noel Ruddle pleaded guilty to a charge of culpable homicide because of diminished responsibility, having shot James McConville (30) dead with a Kalashnikov rifle in a Gorbals high-rise block. The judge ordered him to be detained in Carstairs state hospital without limit of time. At another sitting a young Gorbals woman, who had stabbed her lover through the heart in a flat in Stirlingfauld Place, pleaded guilty to a charge of culpable homicide and was jailed for three years. The woman had told her lover in confidence that she had been sexually abused as a child. Her agent told the court: 'As the relationship deteriorated, the deceased constantly threatened to tell others about the abuse.'

Police raided a Gorbals warehouse and seized huge quantities of fake designer sportswear with top brand names such as Adidas, Reebok and Nike. Interviewed in the Adelphi Centre, a heroin addict, described as 'a slim, attractive, fair-haired girl in her early thirties, intelligent and articulate', told a reporter: 'Getting drugs in the Gorbals is like going to the shops for a pint of milk.' The *Jewish Echo*, Scotland's only Jewish newspaper, published in the Gorbals since 1928, appeared for the last time.

Plans were unveiled for the first phase of the Crown Street regeneration project, scheduled to be completed 'in time to take the Gorbals into the twenty-first century'. Project director Mike Galloway said: 'Our aim has been to recreate the Gorbals community, retaining all that was best about the district, but learning from the mistakes of the past to achieve a lasting success. Crown Street is now set to show the way towards the new Gorbals, a mixed community where people from all walks of life can live and work together.' Lord Provost Bob Innes enthused: 'We are seeing the renaissance of the Gorbals and it is marvellous.'

Gorbals-born Jeff Torrington won the Whitbread Book of the Year award for *Swing Hammer Swing!*, the bizarre adventures of novelist *manqué* Thomas Clay in a Gorbals of semi-derelict tenements, pubs, cafés and cinemas. The book was hailed as a Joycean portrait of the embattled community. Torrington said: 'People have said why be nostalgic about the Gorbals. But the book is about the spirit it produced.' When news of the award became public, the novel sold out in city bookshops and publishers Secker and Warburg had to rush out an additional twenty-five thousand copies.

Work began on a £2.2 million programme to build tenement-style affordable family homes in the Gorbals. Fraser Stewart, director of the New Gorbals housing association, said: 'We are going back to the past to build for the future.' Gorbals police set up a twenty-four-hour hotline to encourage local people to grass on drug dealers. The area had some of the highest concentrations of drug dealers and abusers in the country, and it was alleged that scores of young Gorbals women worked as prostitutes or went shoplifting to finance their addiction.

After an American Associated Press correspondent decried 'mean Gorbals slums', and referred to 'drug-crazed young people', Glasgow MP David Marshall suggested that Americans 'should look in their own backyards'. Families living in the Sir Basil Spence tower blocks in Queen Elizabeth Square dubbed their homes Fortress Gorbals after housing chiefs surrounded the blocks – scheduled for demolition – with a twelve-foot-high fence. Between 1986 and 1990, the council had tried to improve the blocks by spending £2 million on metal roofs, new lifts and a concierge system. James McCabe, one of only thirty-five tenants left in the buildings, said: 'I don't believe this has been put up to protect us. I think they are trying to force us out.'

1993 JUNKIE HOUSE

Whitbread Prize-winner Jeff Torrington paid a sentimental visit to his old neighbourhood. Born in Abbotsford Place, he was two years old when he moved with his family to Logan Street. In 1959 he married a girl from the same street and the couple set up home in

Govanhill. Like many bright working-class kids, Jeff was brought up in a home devoid of books, but he discovered Hutchesontown public library in McNeil Street at nine, and began writing at fourteen.

Gorbals-born lawyer and merchant banker Alexander Stone donated a collection of around 1,500 antiquarian books to the University of Glasgow. His parents, Jewish refugees fleeing from the Russian pogroms, landed in Scotland in 1903. Alexander, born in 1907, was educated at Hutcheson's boys' grammar school in Crown Street. On leaving school he joined the family furniture business as a salesman and auctioneer, but later decided to study law at Glasgow University, graduating in 1932. He acquired a tiny London-based merchant bank in 1956 and, by 1967, had built it up into a major concern with 125 employees and capital assets totalling £40 million. Through the Alexander Stone Foundation, the banker, knighted in 1994, endowed university chairs, scholarships and lectureships in his native city.

After two young men fell 160 feet to their deaths from a burning flat in a tower block in Caledonia Road, police revealed that the death flat was known among locals as 'the junkie house'. One of the men had clung to a ledge while an angry crowd urged the fire-fighters to get a move on. Tenants who witnessed the tragedy called for the block to be demolished. John Kenny said: 'There are teenagers jabbing themselves with drugs on the back stairs and on the landings. People who live here see it every day. Many are terrified, especially the older ones.' More than a thousand anxious callers flooded emergency switchboards after a Gorbals general practitioner was admitted to hospital suffering from AIDS.

Tragedy struck when Sir Basil Spence's slab blocks in Queen Elizabeth Square, hyped in the early 1960s as 'tower blocks with gardens like the gardens of Babylon', were 'blown down' by controlled explosions, less than thirty years after they had been opened to media acclaim. As debris from the collapsed buildings flew straight into the Hutcheson Court area where hundreds of people had gathered, Mrs Helen Tinney (61), a mother of four, was hit by a flying lump of concrete. She died from head-and-neck injuries, though she was 140 metres from the blast, which was outside the exclusion zone set by health-and-safety officials at 120 metres. Another three onlookers were injured.

Spectators claimed that they were given little or no warning that the massive explosions were about to take place. Margaret Henderson of Hutcheson Court said people ran for cover as a huge dust cloud erupted: 'I started to head towards my house when all of a sudden the dust came. Everybody ran into the close to shelter. They were running in from all over the place. The dust cloud came in and covered our clothes and everything. People were frightened.' Demolition boss David Stainer provoked fury when he claimed that the operation had been 'a great success'. The successful tender by Wreckers of Johannesburg's had been £800,000 lower than that of their nearest competitor.

Dr Ezra Golumbok, editor of the defunct *Jewish Echo* and son of its founder, donated to Glasgow's famous Mitchell Library a complete set of the publication, covering its sixty-four years of existence. Over two thousand people packed St Francis's church in Cumberland Street – a focus for Catholic community life in the Gorbals since the 1890s – for an emotional closing ceremony. The Franciscan Order – which owned the church and adjoining friary – had moved to nearby St Luke's, a modern building, because it would have cost £2 million to carry out major repairs to the historic listed buildings.

Destitute men using the Salvation Army's Laurieston Centre in South Portland Street were reported to be 'victims of sad situations: broken homes, broken marriages or unemployment'. Grace Arnott, who ran the centre along with husband Dave, was known to the regulars as 'amazing Grace'.

1994 URBAN VILLAGE

Bandleader Louis Freeman, known as Glasgow's Mr Music, died aged 101. Born in the Gorbals in 1893, he was cantor at the Chevrah Kadisha synagogue at the age of eleven. Two of Scotland's leading house-builders, Wimpey Homes and Miller Partnerships, joined forces with the Crown Street regeneration project to build the first phase of an £80 million urban village in the Gorbals.

In Norfolk Street, Laurieston, police tried to restrain Philip McFadden (18) a knife-wielding schizophrenic, who had run amok in nearby Wellcroft Place. Constable Lewis Fulton (28) of A (city centre) division – who had arrived on the scene in a patrol car to assist his Gorbals colleagues – suffered multiple stab wounds as he tried to disarm the severely disturbed teenager. He died in the Victoria Infirmary. McFadden's sister said he had received check-ups for his condition at his local health centre but had stopped taking his medication in the weeks leading up to the tragedy. PC Fulton was posthumously awarded the chief constable's very high commendation for bravery.

Heroin addict James 'Jamer' Boyle (28) was found with stab wounds in a back-court in Rosebery Street, Oatlands. Rushed to the Victoria Infirmary, he was dead on arrival. Nearly two hundred mourners, including the dead man's father – former Gorbals gangster Jimmy Boyle – attended the funeral service at St Luke's RC church in Ballater Street.

At the fatal accident inquiry into the death of Mrs Helen Tinney of Hutcheson Court, a sheriff hit out at inadequate blast-protection measures and said that the woman's death could have been avoided. The inquiry heard that the exclusion zone for the controlled explosion was twice the height of the Queen Elizabeth Square towers, which one expert said was an outdated method. More than double the specified amount of explosives were used to topple the tower blocks, and the demolishers had forgotten to bring a klaxon to warn spectators that the explosion was about to take place. A witness told the inquiry that the explosion took hundreds of spectators by surprise, after it had been cancelled twice in just over an hour. There were no prosecutions. Ladkam, one of the two companies which carried out the demolition work, had gone into receivership, and the other, Wreckers, had its headquarters in South Africa.

Pint-sized Margaret Linsay (55) was presented with the chief constable's commendation for bravery after grabbing a handgun from a masked youth who tried to hold her up in an off-sales in

Norfolk Street. A fatal accident inquiry heard that David Kelso (27), one of two men who had fallen to their deaths from a burning flat in a Caledonia Road tower block, had 9.08 milligrams of morphine per litre of blood. A scientist told the inquiry that a level of one or two milligrams was potentially fatal.

The Central Mosque in Adelphi Street, the only purpose-built mosque in Scotland, was described as 'a veritable Mecca for Glasgow's 20,000 Muslims'. Hutchesontown library in McNeil Street was refurbished for use as the Gorbals economic development centre. Lynn McNamee (25) became the five-hundredth person to find work through the Gorbals Initiative. Italian-born Franco Fraioli turned the Granite City Inn – a long-established Gorbals watering hole – into an Irish-Italian theme pub called the Brazen Head, after one of the best-known howffs in Dublin. The new pub boasted a collection of Italian football shirts and a big drum from the Donegal flute band. The first family homes to be built in the Gorbals for almost twenty years were opened in Moffat Street. In West Street, Tradeston, five people – including three Girl Guides – were killed when a double-decker bus had its top deck ripped off while passing under a railway bridge.

By court order, mother of two Marie Clark (29), a resident of a tower block in Norfolk Court, was told to get rid of her tiny cairn terrier Blue. Mrs Clark, a divorcée, said: 'I have had Blue for more than nine years and he is a great wee pet.' A spokesman for the council said: 'We know how much a pet can mean to a family but in order to reduce inconvenience to tenants the only way we can deal with dogs in multi-storey flats is to impose a blanket ban.' Grandmother Lizzie Martin moved from a flat on the twenty-second storey of a tower block in Old Rutherglen Road to a brand-new low-rise block in Waddell Street, part of a £2.4 million development by the resident-controlled New Gorbals housing association. The Prince and Princess of Wales hospice in Carlton Place appealed for funds, pointing out that the hospice had created over one hundred jobs in the Gorbals area.

At Glasgow High Court, Gary Moore (31), was cleared of murder but convicted of culpable homicide for stabbing James 'Jamer' Boyle to death after Boyle formed a relationship with Moore's girlfriend.

Moore, one of Scotland's most violent criminals, had twenty-nine previous convictions and was on weekend leave from prison at the time of the offence. He was caged for eight years. Appearing at the same court, Edward Christie, a Sandieford Road drug addict convicted of mugging elderly and disabled women in Gorbals tower blocks, was jailed for five years. The Crown Street regeneration project awarded Tay Homes the first prize in a competition to build the £5 million second phase of the £80 million Gorbals urban village.

1995   CANNABIS FACTORY

Hollywood moguls were reported to be showing interest in acquiring the film rights of a biography of the man behind the world's best known detective agency, Gorbals-born Allan Pinkerton (1819–84). A cooper by trade, he helped organise the Chartist movement in Scotland before emigrating to the USA, where he set up his detective agency in 1850 with a staff of two in a tiny office in Chicago. The expression 'private eye' originated in the eye logo on Pinkerton's Chicago headquarters. By the 1990s, Pinkerton Security Services had 250 offices in twenty countries worldwide and 50,000 employees.

Benny Lee, a Jewish boy from the Gorbals, died in London aged seventy-nine. Starting his working life as a tailor's apprentice, he went on to become an acrobat, drummer, fairground barker, actor, dance-band crooner and television comic. Police raided a 'cannabis factory' in the Gorbals and discovered dozens of plants and 'a home-made greenhouse and growing equipment, including thermal lights, yards of tin foil, and gas canisters to enhance growth'. A police spokesman said: 'We are very pleased with the find. We think it is the second biggest cannabis find in Glasgow.' As part of a project to refurbish an unsightly railway viaduct in the vicinity of the world-renowned Citizens' theatre, the Glasgow Development Agency commissioned a series of galvanised steel abstract/figurative sculptures illustrating scenes from plays by famous Scottish playwrights. The project took three years to complete.

The Cumberland arcade – a rundown mini-shopping-centre – was reported to be 'a focal point for dealers and addicts who come by foot, taxi or even mountain bike'. Brian Hallum, chairman of John Bosco's RC secondary school in the Gorbals, complained that parents were biased against his school because of its location. While John Bosco's had just 310 pupils, nearby Holyrood secondary in Crosshill was bursting at the seams with more than 2,000 pupils. Mr Hallum said: 'It is down to snobbery. The middle class people up in that area don't want to send their children down to this area.'

Housing chiefs saw red when community activist Owen Meharry hung a twenty-foot high banner supporting Scottish Militant Labour from his seventh floor flat in Waddell Court. An unrepentant Mr Meharry said: 'I spoke to all the neighbours before I put it up – the tenant upstairs allowed me to tie the banner to his veranda.'

In a showpiece private-housing-development in Crown Street, William and Patricia Armstrong's dream of a perfect home in the new Gorbals turned into a nightmare. Since moving into their £51,000 three-bedroom house, the Armstrongs had been flooded four times. The couple said that their complaints to developers Miller Partnerships had gone unheeded. Constable Lewis Fulton was posthumously awarded the Queen's commendation for bravery for attempting to disarm violent schizophrenic Philip McFadden in the Gorbals.

1996   GORBALS JEWELS

Harry Diamond, who retired as Glasgow's public relations' chief in 1991, published his memoirs, entitled *Can You Get Me Into The Papers?* Raised in Abbotsford Place from a family of Lithuanian Jewish immigrants, Mr Diamond slammed Gorbals books full of 'sentimental, nostalgic drivel'. His Gorbals had been a place of 'ignorance, stupidity . . . malice, violence, illiteracy and unbelievable cruelty to partners and children.' He accepted that lawyers, doctors and journalists now lived in luxury penthouse flats in the trendy new Gorbals, but said: 'There isn't enough money in the Royal Bank of Scotland to persuade me to live there again.' Boxing greats Jim Watt, Johnny McManus and Walter McGowan attended a commemorative service in St Kentigern's RC cemetery, held to mark the fiftieth anniversary of the death of Benny Lynch.

Old Gorbals boy Hugh Thomson (56) was promoted to the post of chief yeoman warder at the Tower of London, with responsibility for the security of the crown jewels. Hugh, a former boy soldier who had worked his way through the ranks from yeoman warder to gaoler before getting the top job, was reported to be one of London's most photographed people.

The Brazen Head, described as Glasgow's biggest Irish pub, had its Sunday afternoon licence withdrawn following complaints about the level of noise from live bands playing in the beer garden. As a result of the ban, owner Franco Fraioli had to scrap ambitious plans for St Patrick's Day. Mr Fraioli said: 'When the pub was the Granite City there were no complaints about live pop and rock music. It appears that Irish folk music threatens the public. That sounds Irish to me.' The police training centre in Oxford Street, Laurieston, a listed building, was reported to be 'totally inadequate to meet modern police training needs'.

Glasgow's most controversial politician, Gorbals-born Pat Lally, who left school at thirteen, was installed as the first Lord Provost of the newly created Glasgow City Council. He also received an honorary doctorate in law from the University of Strathclyde.

Reviewing work by murderer-turned-sculptor Jimmy Boyle, the art critic of *The Herald* newspaper was bemused: 'Someone has to say it. Jimmy Boyle's sculpture has no merit. He is not a bad artist – just no artist at all. So why does Boyle get so much attention? Whatever the reason, it has nothing to do with his work.'

Mrs Margaret Wallace, from the Gorbals, was among parents who protested outside Glasgow's city chambers over the impending closure of Abbotsford primary school in Abbotsford Place. The protest was in vain and the school, built in 1879 as Abbotsford public school, closed its doors for the last time. Former pupils included Sir Hugh Roberton, founder and conductor of the world-famous Glasgow Orpheus Choir, and Ralph Glasser, author of a critically acclaimed Gorbals trilogy.

At Mayfest, the Citizens' theatre company staged their adaptation of *Swing Hammer Swing!* at the King's theatre. As Christmas approached, the Hamish Allan centre in Tradeston was one of five Glasgow winter shelters that were opened early in response to homeless people 'seeking refuge from the Arctic weather'.

1997 DON'T DRINK AND FRY

Many people with local connections – as well as 'returning exiles' and 'total outsiders' – were buying houses in the rejuvenated Gorbals. Asian tycoon Yaqub Ali, who arrived in Glasgow in 1953 with a few pounds in his pocket and earned his living as a door-to-door peddler, closed down his twenty-four acre Castle Cash and Carry in Tradeston; at its peak it had a turnover of £100 million, and employed four hundred people. Devastating losses of more than £3 million in four years had finally prompted Mr Ali to throw in the towel. He put the blame firmly on the demise of corner shops and the dramatic growth of supermarket chains such as Tesco and Asda.

Breakfast-television presenter Lorraine Kelly – who lived in a single end in Ballater Street in the Gorbals as a child, before moving to Bridgeton and later to East Kilbride, where she got her first job in journalism on the *East Kilbride News* – commissioned an Aberdeen horticultural firm to produce two new roses in memory of the teacher and children who died in a hail of bullets at Dunblane. Ms Kelly, who covered the Dunblane tragedy at the time it happened, said: 'I will have both roses in my garden. A Dunblane rose could be given for happy occasions, but would also be a very special gift to remember someone who has died, especially a child.' When working for BBC Scotland as a researcher, she was told that she would never get in front of the camera unless she got rid of her Glasgow accent. She left the BBC for London's newly-launched TV-AM and a hugely successful career in daytime telly.

The Safe Gorbals project joined forces with Strathclyde Fire

Service to cut fire fatalities in the Gorbals. Spokesman John Hynes said: 'We have a large elderly population, and there are also problems with alcohol and drug abuse. That mixture leads to us having more than the average number of fires.' Project organisers put up posters throughout the district, advising people: 'Don't drink and fry.' City councillor Jimmy Mutter pledged that the Gorbals would remain at the forefront of Glasgow's redevelopment plans 'for the next decade'. Mr Mutter said: 'Glasgow City Council remains committed to the regeneration of the Gorbals. It's very high on the city's agenda.'

As bulldozers moved into Oatlands, the last traditional tenements in the greater Gorbals bit the dust, to the dismay of conservationists. Private-housing developers already saw Oatlands, adjoining Richmond Park, as a future extension of the smart new Gorbals of luxury duplexes and penthouses. Twelve police cars rushed to Stirlingfauld Place, where a young father was holding his two sons hostage on the twenty-third floor of a tower block. Police officers in riot gear were sent into the building as a 'precautionary measure' but weren't needed. After thirteen hours of negotiations, the man gave himself up and the children, aged one and three, were reunited with their mother. A neighbour said: 'The couple only moved into the house with their sons a few months ago. The man worked as a security guard but neighbours do not really know the family.'

The Crown Street regeneration project continued to commission artworks for the new Gorbals, and beaten-copper bird panels were a feature of a social-housing development in Errol Gardens, Cumberland Street and Pine Place.

Old Gorbals boy Ralph Slater died in a Glasgow hospital at the age of seventy-seven. Slater Menswear in Howard Street – founded by Mr Slater in the 1970s – achieved worldwide acclaim and made the *Guinness Book of Records* as the biggest men's outfitters in the world. The family empire began when Ralph's father Samuel, a Jewish immigrant from Latvia, set up a clothing factory. The Prince and Princess of Wales hospice in Carlton Place – a wedding gift from the citizens of Glasgow to the royal couple in 1983 – reported a significant rise in donations following the death of

Princess Diana in a Paris car crash. Oatlands Action Group's food co-op was reported to be 'turning over £1,000 per week from a clientele mostly dependent on state benefits'. The Lord Nelson in Nelson Street, Tradeston advertised a 'psychic evening'. In the Clyde Inn, Kingston Street customers dived for cover as two masked men shattered the gantry with gunshots.

1998   LORD OF TRADESTON

Young couples known as dinkies (double income, no kids yet) were reported to be snapping up chic apartments and town houses in the new Gorbals. With community ventures in the area starved of funds, and 18 per cent of local people numbered among the long-term unemployed, George Mackay, co-ordinator of the Unemployed and Community resource centre, said: 'There is a perceived divide between those who have lived through the regeneration process and those who have come in because of regeneration. There is extreme poverty in one street, and in the next the comparative wealth of the incomers who can afford a £40,000 new house.'

Promoting the Gorbals as a family-friendly place, Glasgow Development Agency boss Stuart Gulliver said: 'Glasgow's Merchant City appeals to single people or couples without children. We set out to create an environment which would attract families back to the Gorbals, recolonising an important part of the city which has suffered massively from population decline.'

Scottish Homes chiefs sparked fury with plans to demolish two rundown tower blocks in the Gorbals. Tenant Elizabeth Sharkey, an aficionado of high living, said: 'This is bloody disgraceful. They'll have a hard job shifting me.'

At the High Court in Glasgow, a life sentence was passed on teenager Brian Donnelly, who had picked up prostitute Margo Lafferty (27) of Oxford Street, Laurieston, as a nineteenth-birthday present for himself; then battered and strangled her after sex. Ms Lafferty was the seventh hooker to be murdered in Glasgow since

1991. Her naked body was discovered in a yard off West Regent Lane, the place she and her clients regularly used. Beside her body there were used condoms, from which forensic scientists recovered Donnelly's DNA. The jury saw closed-circuit television footage of Ms Lafferty being picked up by Donnelly on the corner of Wellington Street and Bothwell Street, the heart of the city's red-light district. A senior detective said after the trial: 'I hope the result of this case sends a clear and unmistakable message that there is not, and never has been, a serial killer of prostitutes loose in Glasgow.'

Members of the Alexander Thomson Society hit out at Glasgow for allowing one of its most famous sons to lie in an unmarked grave in the Southern Necropolis, Caledonia Road. A spokesman for the society said: 'No record exists of any tombstone or memorial, but it is highly unlikely the grave was not originally marked.' The death was reported of Sir Alexander Stone, lawyer, banker, art patron and philanthropist, born in 1907 to parents who'd settled with other Jewish immigrants in the Gorbals. For many years, numerous charities in Glasgow had benefited from Sir Alexander's provision of legal services at reduced cost or no charge at all. His benefactions included chairs at the universities of Glasgow and Strathclyde and a new building for the microbiology department at Glasgow University. Asked on one occasion what impelled him to give away large sums of money, he replied: 'When you are young you want to make money, but as you get older you realise you cannot take it with you.'

Media magnate Gus Macdonald (58) who grew up in Tradeston, started work as an apprentice in Alexander Stephens' Linthouse shipyard on the same day as comedian Billy Connolly and went on to become Scottish business and industry minister in Tony Blair's first New Labour government received another accolade. He became Lord Macdonald of Tradeston.

Gorbals-born Lord Provost Pat Lally, credited by the *Sunday Times Scotland* with 'spearheading the city's renaissance at the turn of the decade' was suspended from the Labour Party after allegations of sleaze within Glasgow City Council. Mr Lally – dubbed Lazarus on account of his ability to make miraculous political comebacks – described the charges as 'woolly, inconsequential and unsubstantiated' and refused to step down as Lord Provost. After the Court of Session in Edinburgh granted an interim interdict preventing the council from removing Lally from office, the Labour Party dropped its case against him.

At their plant on the Dixon's Blazes industrial estate, Matthew Algie (established 1864), Britain's largest producers of roasted coffee, produced 'more than twenty-five million cups of coffee every day'. The company employed a staff of 194 and supplied 64 per cent of all London hotels, including the Ritz and the Savoy. The firm's managing director, said: 'The majority of our workforce comes from the Gorbals and we have had, on occasion, two or three generations of the same family working for us.'

Sir Jimmy Saville and Bailie James Mutter opened the St Francis centre, an award-winning conversion of category A-listed St Francis's church in Cumberland Street into the area's main community facility, adult education centre and arts venue. By an ingenious arrangement, a new barrel-roofed structure containing three floors of flexible space was comfortably located within the original barrel-vaulted nave of the church. The new construction was theoretically reversible so that, in the unlikely event of a great religious revival in the Gorbals, the historic church could return to its original function. Lord Provost Pat Lally said: 'I was baptised here so it has very fond memories for me.'

Delegates arriving in Glasgow for Urban World, a regeneration conference, had the Gorbals at the top of their 'must see' tour list. A spokesman explained: 'The old gangland reputation of the Gorbals was known throughout the world and there was massive interest in the work being done to transform it.' Half the houses in Caledonia Gardens – the latest phase of the Crown Street regeneration project – found buyers, even though the buildings were only at foundation level. Many of the homes reportedly went to people with Gorbals connections, including a lady who had spent forty years in the USA.

Tommy Smith, who made a name for himself with models of old Gorbals tenements, unveiled his latest line in Gorbals memorabilia; model middens complete with graffiti. The distinguished Gorbals-born educational psychologist John McLeish died at his home in Victoria, British Columbia. The younger brother of playwright Robert McLeish, who wrote *The Gorbals Story*, he spoke seven languages and had a deep lifelong commitment to left-wing politics and to pacifism. The Phoenix bar in Old Rutherglen Road featured 'Geraldine Starr, drag artist'. American billionaire Bill Gates obtained a civil warrant to search premises in Tradeston for dodgy computer software.

1999 GORBALS SAINT

Benny Lynch, inducted in 1998, was the only British fighter to feature in the International Boxing Hall of Fame in Canastota, New York state. Frank O'Donnell, president of the Scottish ex-boxers' club, went to the USA for the ceremony and later told a reporter: 'The only world-class champion who couldn't make it was Mohammed Ali who was not well enough to travel.'

Notorious 'Kalashnikov killer' Noel Ruddle exploited a legal loophole to be released from the state psychiatric hospital at Carstairs. Ruddle, detained without limit of time for gunning down neighbour James McConville in 1992 in a Gorbals multi-storey with a rifle he bought in a pub, walked free after claiming that his personality disorder could not be treated. The loophole was closed following a public outcry. A brass-bound wooden casket containing the remains of the third century Christian martyr St Valentine was put on display in the atrium of the new Greyfriars centre at the Blessed John Duns Scotus church in the Gorbals. The Franciscan friars of the area had looked after the remains since 1868 when a Belgian friar brought them to Glasgow.

A Gorbals man who plunged 150 feet from the tenth floor of a tower block at Waddell Court, missing concrete paving by a few feet and landing on a grass lawn, was reported to be 'serious but stable' in the Victoria Infirmary. The impact left a man-size indentation in the grass. Comedian Billy Connolly starred in a new movie called *The Debt Collector*, loosely based on the violent career of Gorbals gangster Jimmy Boyle. Slamming the movie, convicted murderer

Hugh Collins – a former inmate of Barlinnie's Special Unit – wrote: 'To glamorise a moneylender exploiting ordinary working people, as this film does, is obscene. To suggest that the rehabilitation of a criminal is a happy-ever-after ending, as this film does, is an affront to the victims of murder. It is arguable whether Boyle is rehabilitated at all. Part of that process involves the admission of guilt and Boyle still insists he was innocent of murder.'

Gorbals lass Kara Dooley (10) was selected by Hollywood star Robert Duvall to play a street kid in *The Cup,* a football-themed movie. Many of the scenes were shot around Cumberland Street, with regulars of the Queen's bar in the Cumberland arcade being roped in for crowd scenes. Seventy years after Revd Cameron Peddie set up youth centres for the unemployed, members of the Gorbals youth forum were reported to be 'working flat out to give young people in the area an alternative to standing on street corners'. The Prince and Princess of Wales hospice in Carlton Place sought volunteers to join a trek in the Himalayas to raise sponsorship cash.

The Gorbals was reported to be 'awash with trendy new properties'. The final phase of an eight-year £74 million plan to turn the area into a showcase urban village got the green light from Scottish minister for enterprise Henry McLeish. As well as being the UK training centre for marine hopefuls, the Gorbals-based Glasgow College of Nautical Studies in Thistle Street offered courses in telecommunications, child care, business administration and information technology.

The man dubbed Lazarus Lally – Lord Provost Pat Lally – retired after three decades in local politics. The seventy-two-year-old, born in a Thistle Street room-and-kitchen flat, was labelled Stalinist and under his administration the Dear Green Place was dubbed Lallygrad. In Edinburgh's St Mary's Episcopalian cathedral, the controversial local politician was invested into the Order of St Lazarus of Jerusalem. Planners unveiled a £35 million scheme to create more than 550 new homes and eight new streets in an area that included the site of Sir Basil Spence's Queen Elizabeth Square slab blocks. A spokesman said: 'This is the last piece in the jigsaw in the Hutchesontown area of the Gorbals.'

Glasgow jeweller Julius Lewis Lyons, who was born in the Gorbals to Polish-Jewish immigrants, died aged ninety-three and left his valuable art collection to Kelvingrove art gallery. The bequest included fifty-two Italian Old Master drawings and twenty major pieces of antique silver. A director of McTear's auctioneers in Glasgow, who first met Mr Lyons in 1959, said: 'He was perhaps one of the most gentlemanly yet secretive people in our business. I'm not surprised to learn he had substantial amounts of silver but I don't know where he kept it. I was only in his flat once and that did not have anything out of the ordinary in it. It was very basic.'

A Glasgow newspaper traced three of the four Pied Pipers of Florence Street, the teenage boys who led an assault on the local rat population in 1956. One of the four – John Kinnaird, a Canadian refinery worker – said: 'The conditions in the Gorbals at that time were terrible. There were always rats around. I was glad to get out of the Gorbals as soon as I could.'

2000 HIGHWAY ROBBERY

The Gorbals became the first area in Glasgow to have its own website – www.gorbalslive.org.uk – created with Gorbals social-inclusion-partnership funding. A spokesperson said: 'In the future, being familiar with computers and the internet will be a must for the majority of jobs. Yet only 5 per cent of Gorbals residents have access to the net compared with nearly 50 per cent in better off areas.'

The 'new' Gorbals was reported to be home to a core of middle-class professionals. Evelyn Bowie (57), who lived in a multi-storey block in Sandiefield Road in the 'old' Gorbals, said: 'Of course, it's yuppified, but that doesn't bother us and most of the newcomers are very friendly.'

Police launched a search for a couple who forced a man to drive his Mercedes to the Gorbals before robbing him. The sixty-three-year-old driver had stopped his car at traffic lights in the busy Saltmarket when the couple jumped into the vehicle, forced him at knife-point to drive to a car park in Florence Street and made off with his cash. After years of lying derelict, Eglinton Congregational church (1866), one of the last historic buildings in the Gorbals, was reduced to rubble, just days after Glasgow ended its reign as 1999 City of Architecture and Design. A spokesman for the local authority said: 'There was outline planning and listed building consent for conversion into residential use several years ago but that was never acted on.'

The Gorbals Fair was resurrected after a hiatus of fifteen years. City bosses enlisted the help of lawyers in a bid to rid their flagship regeneration area in Crown Street of social problems blamed on a high concentration of methadone users. Frightened residents of the smart new housing complex were up in arms because local chemists supplied the heroin substitute to up to 160 addicts a day. The Princess Royal opened the new Gorbals leisure centre in Ballater Street, planned as part of an initiative to help Glasgow shake off its unenviable reputation as the unhealthiest city in Scotland. No sooner had the £10 million complex opened than 'louts of all ages' were 'inflicting misery' on the mass of people flocking to the new facility, obliging council chiefs to hire bouncers. One attendant said: 'I've worked in several of the city's sports centres and have seen more incidents in one week here than I have in several years in all of the others put together.'

Pat Lally published his autobiography, entitled *Lazarus Only Done it Once, The Story of My Lives.* Lally, whose father and mother came from County Mayo in the north-west of Ireland, recounted his formative years in the Gorbals. His father, Patrick – who worked as a gravedigger and casual labourer – died when Pat junior was ten, leaving his widow Sarah to bring two boys up on eighteen shillings a week with the help of donations of clothes from the parish. Pat Lally left school at fourteen and found work as an apprentice cutter with a tailoring firm. After wartime service with the RAF, he returned to his native city and became active in local politics. A large part of the book dealt with how New Labour tried to oust him from local politics. The septuagenarian told a reporter that he would like to be Glasgow's first elected mayor: 'It would be a very interesting job. If there was a demand from the people for me to stand as mayor I would have to accept it.' Despite receiving a huge advance from his publishers, sales of the book were derisory.

Locals were incensed when a leaked document revealed that the city fathers were considering demolishing the remaining tower blocks in the Gorbals, with only 700 of the 2,000 tenants likely to be rehoused in the area. Sean Clerkin said: 'It will be the same pattern as Ruchill and Drumchapel, locals being kicked out to make way for middle-class settlers.'

There were plans afoot to make Alexander Thomson's Caledonia Road church, built in 1856/7 – and last used for religious services in 1962 – 'the jewel in the crown of the Gorbals regeneration'. The director of the Crown Street project, Tom Macartney, said: 'This church is a centrepiece, an amazing gateway to Glasgow. The regeneration of the area has been the catalyst for giving it new life.'

Barman Christopher Cawley (35), known as Big Chris, died in a pool of blood after being stabbed through the heart in the Laurieston bar in Bridge Street. The fatal attack took place as Mr Cawley tried to escort two drunks from the pub. Louis McDonald and Gary Sanders were charged with the murder and went on trial in the city's High Court. Sanders was acquitted and the case against McDonald was found not proven. Mr Cawley's family claimed that the Crown had bungled the trial.

Strathclyde Police got the green light for a new training centre after complaints that the existing centre in Oxford Street, Laurieston, a historic B-listed building, was 'bursting at the seams'. At the High Court in Glasgow, Philip McFadden, who stabbed PC Lewis Fulton to death in Norfolk Street in 1994, was acquitted of the policeman's murder after his lawyers lodged a special plea of insanity. McFadden was sent to the state psychiatric hospital at Carstairs without limit of time. Hard drugs claimed yet another victim in Glasgow when the body of a thirty-three-year-old man was found in a flat in a high-rise block in Sandiefield Road. A 5.18 metre replica statue of Michelangelo's David, cast in bronze in Milan, was unveiled at Cosmo Ceramics on the Dixon's Blazes industrial estate. The £80,000 statue, weighing more than a ton, was the company's contribution to the Gorbals regeneration project.

As Mrs Elizabeth Currie (67) and her husband James, of Waddell Court, climbed a set of stairs leading from the Clyde walkway to Gorbals Street, a teenage boy tried to grab Mrs Currie's shoulder bag. When she bravely held onto the bag, he stabbed her in the head. She died in the Southern General hospital. Gary McGowan (15) of Hutcheson Court, who had been high on valium, vodka and Buckfast wine when he committed the crime, was later sentenced to be detained without limit of time. Following an appeal, the sentence was reduced to twelve years.

The first unit at the new Riverside business park, sponsored by Gorbals Initiative, was let to city sandwich-purveyors Banana Brothers. The £5.5 million, 114-room Days Inn in Ballater Street – the first hotel to open in the Gorbals in living memory – boasted a Benny Lynch room. Days Inn was America's biggest hotel chain, and franchise holders, Premier Hotels PLC, expected the new caravanserai to be 'popular with Scots whose families fled the poverty of the old Gorbals for a new life across the Atlantic'. A month before opening, the hotel had already taken two thousand advance bookings. One of the first guests, a man who lived in a nearby tower block, walked in and told the receptionist: 'I never thought I'd ever see a hotel in the Gorbals; give me a room for the night.'

The Blessed John Duns Scotus friary sought 'men who are interested in learning about the Franciscan vocation'. The Gorbals arts project offered instruction in the 'authentic Argentinian tango'. Hutchesontown bowling club, over 135 years old, was reported to be 'on the brink of closure'. Dilapidated railway arches in the Gorbals were transformed into the St Luke business estate. Unveiling 100 new homes-for-rent, Bill Sharkey, chairman of the award-winning New Gorbals housing association said: 'These are built on the site of the notorious Hutchie E, known as "the Dampies", which was probably the worst housing scheme ever built in Glasgow; I should know, I lived there.' The Prince and Princess of Wales hospice launched a lottery to raise £250,000 a year towards its £1.9 million running costs. Other fundraising events included a charity ball and a sponsored abseil down the giant Finnieston crane.

Franco Fraoili – owner of the Brazen Head in Cathcart Road, a shrine to Celtic FC – was told by planners that his pub would probably be flattened when plans went ahead for a gateway to Glasgow centred on Alexander Thomson's Caledonia Road church. After hearing that Robert Carlyle had ambitions to play Gorbals boxing legend Benny Lynch in a movie, Benny's only surviving son Robert – living in Canada near to his mother Anne – said: 'She's terrified about what this guy will put in the film, given the track record of the films he has been involved with.'

2001 UP-AND-COMING PLACE

The Gorbals was described as the fastest growing part of the city, with 'incoming professionals, career singles, couples and families bringing new values to the area'. But while prestigious building projects had transformed the physical appearance of the Gorbals, 49 per cent of people of working age in the area were still living on state benefits.

Smart new homes in Cathcart Road, opposite Alexander Thomson's Caledonia Road church, were embellished with twelve female figures cast in aluminium, the work of the design partnership Heisenberg (Dan Dubowitz and Matt Baker). The sculptures, called *The Attendants*, reputedly symbolised the spirit of regeneration in the Gorbals. A spokesperson for the Gorbals Arts Project promised bemused locals that 'artists will not be parachuting into the Gorbals with ideas that are not wanted by people in the area'.

Heroin addict Jake Wardlaw (30), found dead in his Gorbals high-rise flat, was revealed to have been a victim of necrotising fasciitis, the so-called flesh-eating bug which had already killed eighteen drug addicts in and around Glasgow. His sister Louise said: 'At Christmas he sold the *Big Issue* until well after midnight, making sure he had money to buy his daughter presents.'

The Safe Gorbals Initiative announced plans to honour Gorbals hero Joseph Hughes, who died in Hong Kong in 1946, by putting up a plaque near his birthplace in Pollokshaws Road. Hughes's cousin Irene Finn said she was overjoyed at the move. She added: 'Sadly, while Joseph is still well known today by the people of Hong Kong, he is largely forgotten about in Glasgow.'

Convicted murderer Jimmy Boyle – once the most violent thug in Scotland – posed for photographs in the garden of his villa in Cap d'Antibes, an exclusive enclave on the French Riviera. An enraptured hackette gushed: 'Gardeners manicure his exotic grounds, chamber music has been ordered, and floral arrangements take shape before our eyes.'

Scotland's oldest woman, Gorbals-born Isabella Cross, died aged 107. As a young woman, Isabella had worked in a munitions factory. Until she became totally infirm at the age of 103, she was marooned on the fourteenth floor of a Gorbals tower block. It took fire crews twelve days to extinguish a spectacular blaze at Sher Brothers' cash and carry warehouse in Kilbirnie Street, Tradeston. The fire brought back memories of the tragic blaze in 1972, when seven fire-fighters died trying to control a fire in a Sher Brothers' warehouse in the same street. Strathclyde Police left their historic training school in Oxford Street for a new state-of-the-art training centre near East Kilbride. A gang raided the ANC Couriers warehouse on the Dixon's Blazes industrial estate and escaped with 975,000 electricity power cards after blindfolding a security guard, dousing him with petrol and threatening to burn him alive. Police said the stolen cards, each worth £5, would probably be offered to the public at £1 a time.

As he prepared to lead his team into the first cup final of the season – the Challenge Cup – footballer Owen Coyle (34) of Airdrie United, was interviewed by the media. He told reporters that he was proud of his roots in the Gorbals and remembered with great affection delivering papers in the area's many high-rise blocks. In his career he had played for Dundee United, Bolton Wanderers and Motherwell – among others – scoring more than 250 goals, an exceptional total by any standards. Coyle has the classic Irish Catholic background of fellow Gorbalites like Pat Crerand, Charlie

Gallagher and Tommy Docherty, all of whom played for Celtic and he once said that he would have 'crawled over broken glass' to play for the Bhoys. Indeed, in 1994, when faced with the choice of turning out for Scotland, the land of his birth, or the Republic of Ireland, where his parents were born, Coyle plumped for Éire.

Researchers from the prestigious Organisation for Economic Co-operation and Development arrived in Glasgow to spend six months studying the Gorbals and other urban regeneration projects. As demolition teams tore down the Cumberland arcade, described as 'a notorious drug-ridden shopping mall', the popular Queen's bar also bit the dust.

Explaining that the new £40 million Queen Elizabeth Square development, consisting of 700 private houses and 250 properties for social renting, would close the gap between Hutchesontown and Crown Street, Tom Macartney, director of the Crown Street regeneration project, said: 'Since the first phase in Crown Street five years ago, people have recognised the Gorbals as an up-and-coming place to be. Many have bought properties in what is, again, fast becoming a popular area of town.'

Timothy Dalton played Gorbals-born pioneer detective Allan Pinkerton in a movie called *American Outlaws.* Glasgow City Council unveiled plans to turn the rundown Tradeston area – stretching from Bridge Street to the Kingston Bridge – into an integral part of the vibrant new Gorbals. Council leader Charles Gordon admitted that historic Tradeston was 'shabby' but said it had immense potential. In Tradeston's Hamish Allan centre for the homeless, police mounted twenty-four-hour patrols after violent attacks on staff. Some powerful Gorbals images by photographers of the calibre of Bert Hardy and Joseph McKenzie went on show at the Scottish National Portrait gallery in Edinburgh.

Buyers were reported to be queuing up to purchase the £5.5 million Days Inn in Ballater Street. It had been launched in a fanfare of publicity as 'the first hotel to open in the Gorbals in more than 100 years' but the founding company, Premier Hotels, had gone into liquidation. BBC Scotland screened a documentary about rock star Alex Harvey, chronicling his life from his childhood in the Gorbals, through his early career (he won a newspaper talent competition to find Scotland's answer to chart topper Tommy Steele) to his death in 1982 at the early age of forty-seven.

2002   MIRACLE IN THE GORBALS

The first hanging sculpture in Britain, suspended thirty-five feet on an anchor chain, was unveiled in the Gorbals. Known as *The Gatekeeper*, the twice-life-sized bronze female-figure weighed a ton-and-a-half and linked two modern apartment-blocks. Heisenberg designer Matt Baker explained the idea behind the sculpture: 'The Gorbals has always been a gateway for immigrant communities coming to Glasgow. It has seen Irish, Jewish and Asian people coming in and bringing new ideas to the city.' Welcoming the new artwork, Tony Devlin, a graphic designer who was born in Cumberland Street and who had recently bought a flat in the new Gorbals, said: 'I travel with my work and I would often hear the clichés about the gangs and stabbings. Now when I say I live in the Gorbals, people say, "It's all changing there, isn't it?" and this kind of work helps get that across.'

It was reported that 75 per cent of housing in the new Gorbals was privately owned. In 1984, only 1.2 per cent of Gorbals housing was in private ownership. Phylis Markham (88) was admitted to the Victoria Infirmary after being robbed and severely beaten in her sheltered flat in Cavendish Place. A police spokesman said: 'This was a particularly nasty and cowardly attack on a frail and vulnerable woman in her own home.' In a bid to enable privileged youngsters to appreciate the hardships endured by the less fortunate, Fettes College in Edinburgh, Prime Minister Tony Blair's old school, sent pupils to the Gorbals to participate in various community projects.

An online store was launched to sell a range of Gorbals memorabilia, including paintings, prints, videos, and wee hand-crafted models of slum tenements. Project manager Nicola Rossiter, who set up the charitable organisation which ran the

Gorbals Live website, said she hit upon the idea because of the website's popularity. She added: 'We receive around 70,000 hits on the website each month from people who used to live in the Gorbals, as well as their descendants. Many reminisce about the old days and have used the site to link up with former neighbours and friends.' The website had proved popular with people from as far afield as Australia, Hong Kong and the USA.

Glasgow launched its first-ever Festival of Love in a tribute to St Valentine, whose partial remains were a treasured Gorbals relic. Alexander Thomson's severely vandalised Caledonia Road church (1857) was among the first city landmarks to be floodlit as part of a £2.6 million campaign to highlight some of Glasgow's finest architectural assets. The great architect's unmarked grave in the Southern Necropolis finally received a headstone.

Homes in The Paragon development, planned for Queen Elizabeth Square, went on sale at the Days Inn in Ballater Street – before the foundations had even been laid. Purchasers of two-storey duplexes in the development, designed by Piers Gough, the trendy architect behind the regeneration of London's Docklands, were promised 'moveable walls so that living spaces could be transformed into spaces to sleep, dine, bathe, cook and relax as the resident wishes' (former residents of the Gorbals had adroitly performed all of these functions in their one-roomed family homes).

A bizarre art project was launched to recreate the famous sounds of tenement patter by broadcasting computer-generated phrases like 'gaun yersel, wee man' across the courtyard of a showpiece Queen Elizabeth Square housing development from speakers hidden in park benches. The artist responsible for the project said: 'It will involve some suspension of belief.' Local resident Anne Fletcher (70) welcomed the idea: 'The way things are going, I think the Gorbals dialect will be extinct in the next few years. But it's good that they are not just ignoring the past.'

Old Gorbals boy Vic Herman, who won fame as 'the Jewish bagpiping flyweight', died in London. In 1949, at the height of his boxing career, Herman – who always piped himself into the arena – knocked Peter Keenan out of the ring, but lost the fight on points. At the High Court, Joseph Cowan – a door steward hired for the night at the Brazen Head, charged with the murder of thirty-six-year-old Gorbals man Stephen Byrne – was sent down for two-and-a-half years after being found guilty on a lesser charge of stabbing Byrne to his severe injury. Byrne died outside the pub, not far from his home in Stirlingfauld Place. The court heard the attack occurred when an argument in the pub's Durtie Nellie's late-night disco spilled out into Cumberland Street. Detectives complained that they had encountered a wall of silence while investigating the murder.

Jimmy Boyle – who, in his role of violent debt collector for loan sharks had bled the poor dry during his reign of terror – was the subject of a French documentary film. It portrayed him as a hard-done-by Scottish rebel. Council bosses won their fight to prevent a leisure company from including a lap-dancing area in a new club in Carlton Place. A spokesman said: 'Such clubs are seen to provide well-paid opportunities for young women. The reality is different, with many women reporting physical, sexual and verbal abuse.' During the national fire-fighters' strike, a military Green Goddess team rescued invalid Emily Findlay from her twenty-first floor Gorbals flat. Just days after Emily was rescued, a man died in a neighbouring tower block when fire ripped through his twenty-second floor home. The Days Inn, opened in 2000, was acquired by Dutch-based Golden Tulip UK and underwent a £300,000 upgrading, emerging as the Tulip Inn. Calling for a crackdown on 'sectarian' pubs, MSP Sandra White named two local pubs – the Brazen Head and Bingham's – as prime examples. The former had a green-and-white exterior and sold a compact disc featuring songs by IRA hunger striker Bobby Sands, while the latter displayed a portrait of UVF icon John Bingham, killed by the IRA in 1986.

The distinguished psychologist and economist Ralph Glasser, born in 1916 to poor Jewish immigrant parents, died aged eighty-five. Glasser, famous in Scotland for his acclaimed Gorbals trilogy, started his working life as a soap boy in a barber's shop. In Tradeston, 'New York-style loft apartments' in a converted mill were available at prices ranging from £128,500 to £189,000. The massive bronze *Gatekeeper* sculpture in Crown Terrace, referred to locally as the Angel, was reported to be 'dripping blood from its hand'. Father Brian of the nearby church of Blessed John Duns Scotus was cautious about the alleged miracle and said: 'A lot of things have to be discounted first. I'd get the liquid scientifically analysed for a start.'

2003   DUSTY MEMORIES

Having done a £2.3 million film deal with American media conglomerate Disney, Jimmy Boyle bought a luxury home in Marrakesh. Boyle's old Gorbals gang – the Cumbie – gravitated to cyberspace, with a website that listed the names of young nutters followed by descriptions such as Number One Headcase. John Carr, an authority on the misuse of the internet said: 'When I was a youngster in Glasgow, the slogans were on walls; now it's the internet.'

The London-based Richard Rogers Partnership won a design competition to build a crescent-shaped pedestrian and cycle bridge linking the rundown Tradeston district with the new international financial services district around the Broomielaw area. The turnover of family firm Cosmo Ceramics, founded by Rudolfo Benacci, was reported to have grown steadily from £5.7 million in 2000 to £6.7 million in 2002. Mr Benacci said that when he first planned to transfer his business from Port Glasgow to the Dixon's Blazes industrial estate in the Gorbals, he was warned about moving to what was once one of Glasgow's least desirable areas. He had paid no attention to the Jeremiahs, and his tile showroom was now the largest in Britain.

Irate residents of a prestigious housing development in the Gorbals, built by Redrow Homes, gatecrashed the homes of directors of the company to complain about incomplete gardens, faulty heating systems and leaky pipes. The Citizens' theatre celebrated its diamond anniversary. After thirty-three years, Giles Havergal retired from the post of artistic director of the Citz. His successor

Jeremy Raison emphasised his commitment to keeping all three performance spaces open in the world-famous Gorbals drama multiplex. Mr Raison said: 'A Citz show shouldn't be cosy. But at the same time we shouldn't alienate audiences.'

Under threat of litigation, the London-based McKenzie Group, owners of the £3 million, 2,500-capacity Glasgow Academy rock music venue in Eglinton Street – originally the New Bedford picture house – agreed to change the name of the venue to the Carling Academy to distinguish it from the 150-year-old independent school.

Prince Charles formally opened the Jamiat community centre at the Central Mosque in the Gorbals. Used for social events and fund-raising dinners, the facility could comfortably seat one thousand people. The Prince said he had wanted to see the mosque ever since he had been told it was the biggest and one of the finest in Europe. At the Gorbals Fair, Amir Merrouche (11) and Jodie McKenna (10) were crowned as the prince and princess. As part of the Fair celebrations, the site for a community-run orchard was marked out in the Rose Garden in Old Rutherglen Road, formerly the old Gorbals burial ground. After months of hard graft, homeless and ex-homeless men harvested their first crop of organic fruit and vegetables from allotments in Oatlands. Iain Maclean, one of the men involved in the project, sponsored by the Glasgow Simon Community, said: 'Getting access to healthy food can be difficult for homeless people living in hostels, but this project helps overcome those problems in a rewarding way.'

Franco Fraioli, owner of the Brazen Head, was allowed to keep his licence, despite police complaints against him. The police cited a catalogue of violent incidents which had taken place near or inside the pub, including Celtic fans gathering to throw stones at a passing bus carrying Rangers supporters. Mr Fraioli, who had held the licence of the pub since 1980, said he had contacted the Commission for Racial Equality, claiming he was being victimised because his pub was 'an Irish haunt popular with Celtic supporters'.

Local politicians, distressed because Oatlands was tarnishing the image of the smart new Gorbals, announced a £100 million plan to 'breathe new life' into the rundown area. The *Gorbals Live* online store, based in the Adelphi centre in Commercial Road, offered for sale a replica model of a demolished Gorbals slum tenement – titled *Dusty Memories* – for £85. Also on offer was a clay model of a Gorbals Irish immigrant, complete with nine-carat gold earrings; a snip at £99.

2004   GORBALS SLAVE

At the High Court, heroin dealer Rose Broadley (38) was jailed for life. The jury heard that Broadley sold the drug to amateur prostitute Joanna Colbeck (30) and beat the young woman with a baseball bat in the months before her death in May 2002. The Crown prosecutor told the court: 'Joanna worked for Broadley and was terrified of her. She was little more than a slave.' Joanna had earlier told her accountant mum that she owed the dealer hundreds of pounds and would be killed if she didn't pay up. Closed-circuit television footage showed Broadley frogmarching Joanna into a lift in a Norfolk Court tower block in the Gorbals. Hours later, passers-by saw Ms Colbeck dangling from a window ledge then plunging 150 feet to the ground.

With wealthy gangsters in the Dear Green Place fighting for control of the lucrative trade in hard drugs, a London-based broadsheet newspaper branded Glasgow as the murder capital of western Europe and claimed that the city was in danger of reverting 'to its "No Mean City" days of ferocious gang warfare and random violence.'

After Cruden Homes announced plans for the Aurora building, a thirteen-storey residential development in Crown Street – including penthouse flats expected to fetch £300,000 – the company's sales and marketing director explained: 'The Gorbals is phenomenally successful. Even second-hand properties sell quickly. People want to live there. They want to be part of the regeneration.'

Old Gorbals girl Christina Murphy (79), who began married life in a tenement flat in McNeill Street, had sixteen children, sixty-five grandchildren and thirty great-grandchildren, all but twelve of them living within a ten-mile radius of her flat in Castlemilk. Mrs Murphy told a reporter: 'I came from a Catholic family so it was normal to have a lot of children. Living in a Gorbals room-and-kitchen was a tight squeeze. The youngest two slept in drawers and the other six slept in a double bed. But that sort of arrangement wasn't unusual. Almost every family in our close had people living on top of each other.'

International gaming giant London Clubs International obtained outline planning permission for Scotland's largest casino, to be built at Springfield Quay in the shadow of the Kingston bridge. The city already had five of Scotland's twelve casinos, with more in the pipeline as gambling laws were relaxed across Britain. In the month after the new £1 million hi-tech Gorbals library and learning centre in Crown Street opened, 12,500 books were borrowed and 5,000 computer sessions booked. A spokesman said: 'It's a library for the new millennium. It has fifty PCs, free internet access and e-mail.'

In Tradeston, nineteenth-century listed buildings faced demolition to make way for a £8.5 million block of luxury flats. During Glasgow's third Festival of Love, the city hosted 115 events over thirteen days, including a ninety-minute bus tour to romantic locations such as the Barrowland ballroom and the Blessed John Duns Scotus church in the Gorbals where the remains of St Valentine were held.

Commenting on the ubiquitous nature of a picture of her grandmother Helen Gallagher – snapped by top photographer Oscar Marzaroli while she was 'windae hinging' in Florence Street, Gorbals in the 1950s – Mrs Eileen Shephard (47) said: 'We never know where she's going to pop up next. She would be gobsmacked, especially as at the time she was not aware of the photo being taken.'

The Gorbals premises of the *Big Issue* were chosen as the world headquarters of the International Network of Street Papers, comprising fifty-four papers sold in twenty-seven countries worldwide. Producers at the Citizens' theatre announced plans for a show based on the life of the original private-eye: Allan Pinkerton, who emigrated to the USA in 1842 and became head of the US secret service during the Civil War. Commenting on rising property values in the Gorbals, a leading estate agent said: 'People who came in at the beginning and bought in the new Gorbals six or seven years ago might have paid £45,000 for a two-bedroom flat. The same flat is probably now worth double that.' The Gorbals was chosen as one of twelve United Kingdom locations for a pilot scheme 'to find jobs for people who may have given up hope of ever being in employment.'

Lorraine Kelly (44), the queen of daytime telly, was installed as rector of Dundee University after out-drinking students on a celebratory pub crawl. She started her speech by confessing: 'I'm afraid I've been drinking absinthe so this might not come out right.'

Laurieston was numbered among Scotland's twenty poorest areas in an official poverty-league-table published by the Scottish Executive. With news of a projected £150 million transformation of Laurieston, tenants in the area feared that they would lose their affordable homes in the much sought-after Gorbals. Murdo Ritchie, a tower-block resident, said: 'Make no mistake. This is a land grab. House prices in the Gorbals are already skyrocketing and the land the tower blocks are on will make ideal space for more expensive houses for sale.' Roddy Ramsay, who lived in a tower block, was all in favour of the 'nightmare' block being razed and said: 'I feel unsafe as soon as I step out of my flat. You wouldn't go down the backstairs for fear of the junkies shooting up.'

Glasgow Housing Association, the city's not-for-profit landlord, decided to demolish two 23-storey tower blocks in Stirlingfauld Place. Laurieston. Factory worker Chris Miller (19) who had lived all his life in the thirty-year-old development – dubbed Glasgow's Bronx – said: It's twenty times worse than it used to be. It's a dive and should come down.'

Local schoolgirl Emma Porter produced a winning design for a memorial to the unsung war heroes of the Gorbals. Erected in the rose garden in Old Rutherglen Road, the memorial took the form of a twelve-foot-high bronze rose embedded in a marble plinth in the shape of the Victoria Cross.